THE CELESTIAL FORTUNE COOKIE

The 48 *Laws of Power*
with Robert Greene

The Secret Language of Birthdays
with Gary Goldschneider

The Secret Language of Relationships
with Gary Goldschneider

Play with Your Food
with Saxton Freymann

THE CELESTIAL FORTUNE COOKIE

An Astrological Book of Days with

Quotations for Every Sign

Andrea Valeria

A Joost Elffers Book

VIKING STUDIO

VIKING STUDIO
Published by the Penguin Group
Penguin Putnam Inc., 375 Hudson Street,
New York, New York 10014, U.S.A.
Penguin Books Ltd, 27 Wrights Lane,
London W8 5TZ, England
Penguin Books Australia Ltd, Ringwood,
Victoria, Australia
Penguin Books Canada Ltd, 10 Alcorn Avenue,
Toronto, Ontario, Canada M4V 3B2
Penguin Books (N.Z.) Ltd, 182-190 Wairau Road,
Auckland 10, New Zealand

Penguin Books Ltd, Registered Offices:
Harmondsworth, Middlesex, England

First published in 2000 by Viking Studio,
a member of Penguin Putnam Inc.

1 3 5 7 9 10 8 6 4 2

Produced by Joost Elffers Books

Grateful acknowledgment is made for permission to reprint a selection from
Selected Poetry of Rainer Maria Rilke, translated by Stephen Mitchell. Copyright
© 1982 by Stephen Mitchell. Reprinted by permission of Random House, Inc.

Perpetual Calendar source: Smithsonian Physical Time Tables, ninth edition, rev. 1956.

LIBRARY OF CONGRESS CATALOGING IN PUBLICATION DATA
The celestial fortune cookie : an astrological book of days with quotations for every sign
[compiled by] Andrea Valeria
p. cm.
"A Joost Elffers book."
ISBN 0-670-89378-1
1. Quotations, English. 2. Astrology. I. Valeria, Andrea.
PN6081 .C45 2000
133.5—dc21   00-032509

This book is printed on acid-free paper. ∞
Printed in the United States of America

Acknowledgments

The Celestial Fortune Cookie now has a life of its own. Most of the acknowledgments carry their own weight in words all by themselves for they are the authors of all the quotations plus those I did not or could not use either for lack of cosmic placing or days in the year. Then there are those whose spirit and encouragement, wise words plus intelligent manner, fine ways as well as simple "good old advice" need to be written on this page so that in a couple of hundred years they will be thought of as celestial, fortunate, or just plain cookies, if not all of the three words together. To Leon Garcia Soler with everlasting love. To Andreas Landshoff just because and to Joost Elffers for his amazing spirit. Certainly to Anne Edelstein for her wonderful ways. Caroline Leavitt because she understands and bears with my words and Lindy Judge who is so exquisitely clever. Radha Pancham and her absolute grace as well as the breeze of a thought to Paul Ravi, to whom she soon will be reading. Laura Klein who placed the "celestial" in the cookie, Marie Timell who dropped the astro-kalendarium in my lap, and last but not least any reader who happens to come across this book and find that it is useful, special, and worth a smile or a thought a day. I am sincerely grateful to you all.

Contents

v   Acknowledgments

ix   Introduction

xi   Some Words for Every Sign

xiii   Signs in the Sun

1   January
The die for the year's events has not yet been cast . . .

37   February
Many of us find our true heart's delight is ourselves . . .

71   March
Amazing and contradictory things happen now . . .

107   April
All Fool's Day lofts our spirits to greater heights . . .

143   May
The signs of the Zodiac are actually pictures of character . . .

179   June
All of us smile in complicity with ourselves . . .

215   July
Your own personal midsummer's night dream . . .

251   August
The summer sun makes things grow and this means you too . . .

287   September
We'll be able to tell the difference between a rule and what the rule applies to . . .

323   October
A month to think about what you stand for and why . . .

359   November
A month of great creative force . . .

395   December
Do some thinking as the year unfolds and the new one begins . . .

432   Perpetual Calendar

Introduction

To have another language is to possess a second soul.
Charlemagne

The Nobel Prize–winning novelist José Saramago chose one at his acceptance reading in Stockholm. The *New York Times* has one every day. Fortune cookies entice us with them. For centuries, people have relied on quotations as a source of solace, amusement, advice, or inspiration, and few people are without a favorite saying or wise word from a grandparent or person they admire.

There are more than six billion people on the Earth. This works out to be about 500 million for each astrological sign—Aries, Taurus, Gemini, Cancer, Leo, Virgo, Libra, Scorpio, Sagittarius, Capricorn, Aquarius, or Pisces. While no two human beings can be exactly like each other, just as there are no two identical snowflakes, members of each of the twelve signs of the Zodiac may find solace in certain words or share feelings that resonate deep within because of their sign.

The Earth spins around the sky, the seasons appear again and again. Day follows night, night follows day, millenniums come and go, and everybody has a birth date, a birthright—an astrological moment—and thus each of us requires our own particular brand of advice depending on our astrological origins.

With this in mind, I bring you *The Celestial Fortune Cookie*, a book of nearly 4,400 quotations, each reflecting the mysterious order and synchronicity of life's celestiality.

I have loved, studied, and practiced astrology for more than thirty years now—but, please, don't think of this as merely a book that advocates astrology. You don't have to even believe in astrology to enjoy what this book has to offer, and you don't have to know anything about astrology other than your birth sign to use it. It's not about predictions, but, rather, about intelligence. Yours. Mine. And that of the wise voices contained in these thousands of quotes! Think of astrology as I do, as a second language, pure and beautiful, stirring the soul, inspiring, consoling. Astoundingly accurate or poetically to the point. I mean this book to be a gift to anyone with an astrological sign who loves and is moved by the written word. And like a fortune cookie, I think you'll find it delicious, surprising, and forever imparting tiny bits of wisdom.

Designed as a book of days, it's my hope that *The Celestial Fortune Cookie* will bring wisdom and inspiration to the Capricorn in January, the Libra in March, and the Cancer in springtime. I've pored over more than three hundred books of quotations, searching for just the right quote for each sign for every day of the year, including words from Aristotle, Mae West, Stephen Hawking, and Woody Allen. I've provided a general statement of the tone or core energy of every day, which is reflected in the twelve quotes for the day. And along with the daily wisdom, you'll also find astrological snapshots of each month, and keywords to use as a personal reference, a hint or an overall byline for that month.

I like to see this collection as a responsibility rather than an intention. This is a book that doesn't give you an answer, but after a while, its wisdom will speak for itself, making a philosopher out of each of us.

And what could be better than that? Each day has a quote. What is remarkable here is that the meaning of each quote may shift according to what you bring to it—and when. "Anything is going to happen, you just don't know when" can come to pass each and every day! Feel that a quote is warning you of a bad day ahead? Don't be so quick to hide under the covers! For some, a bad day is a breakup with a loved one, but for others a bad day can mean nothing more than a broken heel on your shoe. You supply the meanings, you interpret the quotes. The quotes don't interpret you.

Sometimes a quote is a riddle for which you must find the answer. Sometimes it's a question for yourself, or an answer, a thought, or an idea. But your celestial cognitive self will grasp the answer before you do. Just as "flowers are pledges of fruit," these words find their place. Sometimes you'll find quotes blending across two days, one after another. They can be used as the same idea, or taken as a new idea, much like the same lyrics with a different melody. Some quotes are for you alone, some are for you to peruse with someone dear to you, and some are for you to gain insight into others around you. Some quotes are just bait for each sign, having to do with the inner workings of each sign's personal myths. Some are meant for you to just hang in there. Or spur you on to do your best. There will be times when you will ask yourself why a quote has been used, repeated, or how it slipped its way into your sign. Never fear. If you don't get it one year, you will the next.

Some Words for Every Sign

The complete Zodiac is embedded in all our souls. Each of us has aspects of all twelve signs in our personal constitution (like the building blocks that construct edifications), making each of us a complete human being. The quotations deal with one's sun sign, and are thus tailor-made for you, but please remember that each quotation is a pearl of wisdom and truth in its own right. Here, now, a few brief words about the sun signs, a short map for your everlasting journey.

ARIES
At the spring equinox the Earth stirs and the celestial energy lights our fire, bringing us power, ability, and newness once again. Was Aries chosen to be the first astrological sign by chance, or because Aries sets us on the path of fate, fills our heads with ideas, and provokes our self-assertion? Or is Aries the first sign in our eternal journey because "anything is going to happen, one just doesn't know when," and Aries will always teach us to cope?

TAURUS
Taurus energy gives everyone what they need to endure and to take more time for whatever, be it to count numbers, heartbeats, or situations. The Taurus part of everyone's astrological fortune has to do with "contact." When Taurus is involved, things seem to last, since someone always does better, tries harder, and perseveres.

GEMINI
Jan Kott once said that "fate is nonawareness." Gemini has a direct and intricate understanding of the mind, awareness, and words—in short, whatever it takes to put things right on track. Perhaps those of us of all the other signs should get a Gemini on our side to help us understand our own fate and how to deal with it.

CANCER
"Whatever you choose today will be with you forever." This ancient Iranian saying surely lingers in the Cancer soul. Collector of dreams, wishes, and possibilities, Cancers have an energy that develops and finds its own cause as each day passes. Cancer people usually help others to develop emotionally. Surely, we can all relate to Cancer since its everlasting mentor, the Moon, has been part of us forever.

LEO
Intense pleasure is Leo's strength. Everyone needs to be in touch with Leo at least once a day, since Leo finds ways to show anyone how to make the best out of any situation. Leo can turn things inside out to make any dream pleasurable. Leo, bound to creation and creativity, is about how to find one's own.

VIRGO
Something had to be done and everyone was certain that someone would do it. Anyone could have done it but nobody did. It was everybody's job and

everyone thought that somebody else was about to start. This story goes on and on, but the only one who could really get started, keep on going, and finish to perfection was a Virgo. We must thank them all—lovingly.

LIBRA
According to Jonathan Lear, the active and imaginative mind creates its own experience of its so-called reality. However, Libra's reality is usually a reflection of what goes on around them. Their reality is created in the minds of others. Librans are the alter ego's of all the other signs, but they don't know it because they are constantly searching for true meanings. It seems that not even the speed of light can be completely defined or given a true meaning, so Libras need "others" (that can be words or people) to understand.

SCORPIO
To be a Scorpio is a valuable commodity. Scorpio can transform, sum up, and turn one simple word into a magic potion. Powerful enough to transform a nanosecond into eternity, Scorpio is the sign that makes his own luck. Scorpio believes in "deeds, not words" as John Fletcher once said, but is also able to change words into deeds at the flick of a page.

SAGITTARIUS
One can always rely on a Sagittarian. Their profound exploratory capabilities allow them to bond and relate to others appropriately. Anything that puzzles you about the new millennium can be answered by a Sagittarian. It is their nature to understand that life is a paradox and to know how to come to terms with any reversal. We need to be able to count on at least one Sagittarius in our lives.

CAPRICORN
"Try harder." Capricorn usually says it at just the right moment. Whether to themselves or to others, when a Capricorn gives advice, it usually is for the good of our highest self. Capricorns also know instinctively that "patience is the best cure for any tribulation" (Plautus). Capricorns not only know why, but they usually understand how—even if they don't always tell.

AQUARIUS
"I am he that inspired to know" (Robert Browning). Aquarians are filled to the brim with a deepseated need to explore and inspiration that comes in flashes. The consciousness of the collective is their homestead, their heimat, their abode. Within the unity and the diversity of our celestial cosmos, human beings are enlightened by Aquarians, who as a general rule know no boundaries.

PISCES
"I would help others out of a fellow feeling" (Robert Burton). Perpetuity is the celestial key word with a Pisces at our side. Just as Earth's orbit takes us around and around the Sun, so is Pisces ever comforting to his fellow human beings. Memory is a living process to Pisces, who deals with it as a translator deals with language. This depth of experience means that Pisces points the way for the rest of us so we can start over.

Signs in the Sun

ARIES   March 21 – April 20

TAURUS   April 21 – May 21

GEMINI   May 22 – June 21

CANCER   June 22 – July 23

LEO   July 24 – August 23

VIRGO   August 24 – September 23

LIBRA   September 24 – October 23

SCORPIO   October 24 – November 22

SAGITTARIUS   November 23 – December 21

CAPRICORN   December 22 – January 20

AQUARIUS   January 21 – February 19

PISCES   February 20 – March 20

JANUARY

JANUARY

A billion stars go spinning through the night, blazing high above your head.
But in you is the presence that will be, when all the stars are dead.
Rainer Maria Rilke

The Thief left it behind:
the moon
at my window.

As this lovely Ryokan haiku—written over two hundred years ago—shows, something from the previous year is always left behind to help us in the next. Oh yes, January is a promise. We are here because we were here once before, and will be here again. Time flies. Abracadabra and here we are. January is the start of our calendar—the word *calendar* coming from the Latin *calare*, "to call," and that is just what Aries, Taurus, Gemini, Cancer, Leo, Virgo, Libra, Scorpio, Sagittarius, Capricorn, Aquarius, and Pisces all do in their own way on the first day of the new year. They call out to you, offering a little bit of help from our celestial forefathers to map out a way to make things work. Well, the die for the year's events is not cast. You can do a lot about your fate. So say I, and so say all the myriad voices that populate this book. Just start to read, start to listen, and you'll see.

ARIES

During the first twenty-one days of the month, edify or improve something at least once a day. As you feel useful, helpful, or of service you will be not only sowing but reaping the best your celestial harvest has to offer. This universe is your home and these times are yours within the gamut of your orbit. For as the world turns, the stars shine gloriously on your sign.

Keyword: Enlightenment

TAURUS

You are infused with the primary energy of the Universe, which is another way of saying that in January, nothing is better for you, Taurus, than you! This month, more than any other, you know where the greenest pastures are, when to graze, and when to charge ahead. So rely on your own instincts, reflect, and if you choose, you might even let your earthy sign be a little more airy by dabbling in the esoteric, such as Buddhism or meditation.

Keyword: Awakening

GEMINI

This bright new millennium and its emphasis on the number two, Gemini, creates sparks in your firmament. So put to good use all the millions of electrical impulses charging about you (they outnumber the infinite number of stars in the sky) and figure out how to win that award, get that mate, or put the rabbit in the bag. Just try to take your time and use clear thinking.

Keywords: Clever-minded

CANCER

All you romantic Moonchildren can turn your favorite dreams into reality right now. This is a month during which you can maneuver in such a way that you could turn most feelings into meaningful emotional intelligence. The trick, however, to getting all that you desire, is to try to relax a bit more, and let time slip loosely by.

Keywords: Wishful thinking

LEO

"I will help myself first, because my name is Leo," said Phaedrus, a contemporary of Socrates. And so should, you, Leo! This is the month to claim your throne. But just because you can be lord of any jungle you choose doesn't mean you shouldn't pay careful attention to your subjects. So tread softly yet firmly. Play devil's advocate so as to see the other side a bit more. Take heed of your time and of your money. If you do all this, you'll find yourself slipping in and out of the situations life presents you with your usual feline flair.

Keyword: Interrelating

VIRGO

January is a perfect month for a little mix mastery, Virgo. Question, demand, investigate, consolidate, and merge with whatever you believe to be good for you. Dare to do all this and January could be a stellar month. But take care: the more you freeze your personal assets (meaning your psychological ones) with rigid thinking, the less you will be able to reinforce your celestial strengths, which are more numerous than you probably think. Now is the time to uncover them!

Keyword: Constructing

LIBRA

Generally, your best passwords to success are compromise, cooperation, and clear-thinking. The exception to this rule occurs in January, particularly during the first three weeks. While this does not mean that you can't turn things to your advantage, it does mean that while the Sun is in Capricorn, be sure to get—and take—good advice. Instead of thinking that you should sing every song solo, harmonize with others and the music you make will be that much more beautiful!

Keyword: Harmonize

SCORPIO

The weather outside might be wintry, but your personal forecast is really heating up. Help it along. Warm up to those around you, open and extend yourself so people have a chance to know and understand the real you. Find out, speak out, and nurture. Do not confuse or get confused. Once in a while give in. Keep your word. Once a day you should try to do all the above, and then you will see how even the coldest January can be a day at the beach for you.

Keywords: To thine own self be true!

SAGITTARIUS

You Sagittarians never need to be stimulated. You are born invigorated and this month you can put that vigor to good use. Make your own personal wish list; map out the physical, mental, and economical ways and means to get just what you want, and then, go for it—watch as it comes to you; you can spend the rest of the year doing everything else that comes to your oh-so-active mind.

Keyword: Manifestation

CAPRICORN

Lao-Tzu said it better than anyone else ever could: "Project the difficult part, starting from where it is easiest. Everything great had a small start. The journey toward eternity begins at your feet." So, Capricorn, no matter how high the mountain seems before you, or how jagged the rocks below, know you can traverse any path you chose. All you have to do is start.

Keywords: Setting in motion

AQUARIUS

If you could fit more than 60 minutes into each hour of the day during January, you wouldn't have to worry at all about the other 485,960 minutes of the rest of the year. Time flies while you're having more than your share of fun this month, but try to take a couple of those minutes every day to do nothing more than relax, so you will not overextend yourself, but rather fully accomplish what you set out to do.

Keyword: Clear-mindedness

PISCES

Now's the time to enjoy some of the fabulous fruits from your family tree, Pisces. Use what you have inherited, be it skills or personality traits, in your own personal way, and in such a way that people around you might even end up saying to you later on, "It's just like that nice thing you did for me last January." You'll find things working out in exceptional ways. Keep in mind your own deeply rooted knowledge. As Delacroix said, "We work not only to produce but to give value to time." This will prod you on in the right direction, with lasting results.

Keyword: Go!

1

JANUARY

ARIES
The genius of love and the genius of hunger, those twin brothers, are the two moving forces behind all living things.
Turgenev

TAURUS
Man is God's astrolabe.
Jelal al-Din Rumi

GEMINI
We need more understanding of human nature, because the only real danger that exists is man himself.
Carl Jung

CANCER
Life is ten percent as we make it and ninety percent as we take it.
Irving Berlin

LEO
Will is wish, and liberty is power.
Voltaire

VIRGO
The language of truth is unadorned and always simple.
Marcellinus Ammianus

LIBRA
The only thing to know is how to use your neurosis.
Arthur Adamov

SCORPIO
For producing everything out of nothing one principle is enough.
Leibniz

SAGITTARIUS
Rich or poor, what one needs is enough money.
Welsh Quote

CAPRICORN
The basic fact of today is the tremendous pace of change in human life.
Jawaharlal Nehru

AQUARIUS
Wonders are many, and none is more wonderful than man.
Sophocles

PISCES
A word at the right time can work wonders for you and save the situation. With words you can build a system.
Goethe

Recover, renew, improve.

ARIES
He who kisses the Joy as it flies, Lives in Eternity's sunrise.
William Blake

TAURUS
I am not afraid of tomorrow, for I have seen yesterday and I love today.
William Allen White

GEMINI
All words are pegs to hang ideas on.
Henry Ward Beecher

CANCER
The supposition that the future resembles the past is not founded on arguments of any kind, but is derived entirely from habit.
Anonymous

LEO
Kindness with words creates confidence. Kindness with thoughts creates profoundness. Kindness with giving creates love.
Lao-Tzu

VIRGO
The stars are setting and the Caravan starts for the Dawn of Nothing. Oh make haste!
Omar Khayyam

LIBRA
Take what you can use, and let the rest go by.
Ken Kesey

SCORPIO
The certainties of one age are the problems of the next.
R. H. Tawney

SAGITTARIUS
Error is not to believe, and guilt, to believe it all.
Fernando de Rojas

CAPRICORN
Clearly, the city is not a concrete jungle, it is a human zoo.
Desmond Morris

AQUARIUS
The world belongs to the daring.
Anonymous

PISCES
Dreams are the touchstones of our character.
Henry David Thoreau

3

JANUARY

ARIES
Behind time, time comes.
José Saramago

TAURUS
Taste is the literary conscience of the soul.
Joseph Joubert

GEMINI
The only liberation is to forget.
E. M. Cioran

CANCER
To forgive is the key of action and liberty.
Hannah Arendt

LEO
Knowledge without a conscience ruins the soul.
François Rabelais

VIRGO
Life is neither a spectacle nor a feast: it is a dilemma.
Santayana

LIBRA
I would rather worry without need than live without heed.
Beaumarchais

SCORPIO
Success is a journey, not a destination.
Ben Sweetland

SAGITTARIUS
Science is what you know, philosophy is what you don't know.
Bertrand Russell

CAPRICORN
The reputation of power is power.
Thomas Hobbes

AQUARIUS
The biggest liar in the world is: "They say."
D. Malloch

PISCES
The cause of what is caused is because of what has been caused.
Roman Law

Use your consciousness as an adventure.

ARIES
Men have become tools of their tools.
Henry David Thoreau

TAURUS
Where id was, there shall ego be.
Sigmund Freud

GEMINI
There are some who look inside their own imagination to find facts.
Anonymous

CANCER
Idealism grows in exact proportion to the distance one has from the problem.
John Galsworthy

LEO
Let us train our minds to wish for what the situations demands.
Seneca

VIRGO
Mature man needs to be needed.
Erik H. Erikson

LIBRA
We all carry fault within.
Hannah Arendt

SCORPIO
Every age confutes old errors and begets new.
Thomas Fuller

SAGITTARIUS
A zoo is an excellent place to study the habits of human beings.
Evan Esar

CAPRICORN
The true spirit of delight is to be found in mathematics.
Bertrand Russell

AQUARIUS
Who desires to see, desires also to be seen.
Puerto Rican Quote

PISCES
Those who serve a greater cause may make the cause serve them.
T. S. Eliot

5

JANUARY

ARIES
Art flourishes when there is a sense of adventure.
Alfred North Whitehead

TAURUS
The modern rule is that every woman must be her own chaperon.
Amy Vanderbilt

GEMINI
Equality is the result of human organization. We are not born equal.
Hannah Arendt

CANCER
A discussion is an exchange of knowledge; an argument is an exchange of ignorance.
Robert Quillen

LEO
The conceptual mind and the conceived object are mutually interdependent.
The Dalai Lama

VIRGO
They intoxicate themselves with work so as not to see what they really are like.
Aldous Huxley

LIBRA
The less I understand life, the more I live it!
Jules Renard

SCORPIO
There are people who don't say a thing and sound magnificent!
Huneker

SAGITTARIUS
By perseverance the snail reached the ark.
Charles H. Spurgeon

CAPRICORN
Mathematics may be defined as the subject in which we never know what we are talking about.
Bertrand Russell

AQUARIUS
One generation cannot tie down another.
Thomas Jefferson

PISCES
Good luck is what happens when preparation meets opportunity.
Anonymous

ARIES
I believe that a sign of maturity is accepting deferred gratification.
Peggy Cahn

TAURUS
I leave before being left. I decide.
Brigitte Bardot

GEMINI
A child without an education is a lost child.
John F. Kennedy

CANCER
He is a great man, the one who keeps a hold on his childhood's heart.
Meng-Tse

LEO
The memory of every man is his own private literature.
Aldous Huxley

VIRGO
If you don't shut up, how can I answer your questions!
Lucero Isaac

LIBRA
If I knew why I worried so much, I wouldn't worry.
Mignon McLaughlin

SCORPIO
Happiness is the space between unhappiness.
Don Marquis

SAGITTARIUS
Talent is culture with insolence.
Aristotle

CAPRICORN
To exist is a positive propriety.
René Descartes

AQUARIUS
True generosity towards the future consists in giving everything to the present.
Albert Camus

PISCES
There are no typical situations, only determined meanings.
Vogelman

7
JANUARY

Seven is a number with magical significance; it alludes to going on and on. Continue.

ARIES
Within today, tomorrow is already walking.
Samuel Taylor Coleridge

TAURUS
The wit we wish we had spoils the wit we have.
Jean-Baptiste Gresset

GEMINI
Be equal to your talent, not your age. At times let the gap between them be embarrassing.
Yevgeny Yevtushenko

CANCER
You lose your immorality when you lose your memory.
Vladimir Nabokov

LEO
I would love to live like a poor person, with a lot of money.
Pablo Picasso

VIRGO
It is not necessary to hope in order to undertake, nor to succeed in order to persevere.
Charles the Bold

LIBRA
I like a man who likes to see a fine barn as well as a good tragedy.
Ralph Waldo Emerson

SCORPIO
For the mighty, even to give way is grace.
Aeschylus

SAGITTARIUS
Music was invented to confirm human loneliness.
Lawrence Durrell

CAPRICORN
Common places are the tramways of intellectual transportation.
José Ortega y Gasset

AQUARIUS
He who can properly define and divide is to be considered a god.
Plato

PISCES
Great minds discuss ideas, medium minds discuss events, and little minds discuss people.
Hindu Quote

ARIES
Time is born in the eyes, everybody knows this.
Julio Cortazar

TAURUS
Take warning by the mischance of others, that others may not take warning by thine.
Sa' Di

GEMINI
Friendship is the finest balm for the pangs of despised love.
(not to worry, Gemini, this is for you to help someone else)
Jane Austen

CANCER
He is not wise that is not wise for himself.
English Quote

LEO
Money is a terrible boss but an excellent servant.
P. T. Barnum

VIRGO
Immature artists imitate. Mature artists steal.
Lionel Trilling

LIBRA
Hope to be remembered as someone who has embellished this world.
Mexican Quote

SCORPIO
Give me where to stand, and I will move the earth!
Archimides

SAGITTARIUS
Music quickens time, she quickens us to the finest enjoyment of time.
Thomas Mann

CAPRICORN
The numeric system was invented to help man to put order in the chaos of the world.
John Maynard Keynes

AQUARIUS
Vision is the art of seeing things invisible.
Jonathan Swift

PISCES
An equation is something eternal.
Albert Einstein

9

JANUARY

ARIES

Doubts can only exist if there is a question; and to a question there must be an answer.
Ludwig Wittgenstein

TAURUS

Facts and facts do not always create a spirit of reality, because reality is a spirit.
G. K. Chesterton

GEMINI

The family that comes before you is not as important as the family you will have.
Ring Lardner

CANCER

You need to become a connoisseur of your fears.
Graffiti

LEO

Be obscure clearly.
E. B. White

VIRGO

So tomorrow perfections today.
Umberto Eco

LIBRA

A painting of a rice cake does not take away hunger.
Zen Quote

SCORPIO

First I'll play it, and then I'll tell you what it is.
Miles Davis

SAGITTARIUS

Whereas each man claims his freedom as a matter of right, the freedom he accords to other men is a matter of toleration.
Walter Lippmann

CAPRICORN

The people who don't think are rarely at a loss for words.
Huber A. Newton

AQUARIUS

One should be able to reflect on one's selections.
Michael John Carlyle

PISCES

There is a craft and a power in listening.
Glenn Gould

ARIES
Though I am always in haste, I am never in a hurry.
John Wesley

TAURUS
The teeth are smiling, but is the heart?
Congolese Quote

GEMINI
All animals are equal, but some animals are more equal than others.
George Orwell

CANCER
Judge a tree by its fruit, not by its leaves.
Euripides

LEO
The best marksman may miss the mark.
Anonymous

VIRGO
Perhaps writing and the spirit are one and the same thing, but life moves on and writing stays in a place.
Anonymous

LIBRA
Implicitly, there should be something mysterious in every day.
D. T. Suzuki

SCORPIO
Every calling is great when greatly pursued.
Oliver Wendell Holmes

SAGITTARIUS
The present is an item that gets slightened.
Anonymous

CAPRICORN
Time wounds all heels.
Jane Ace

AQUARIUS
The word reality frightens me.
Arthur S. Eddington

PISCES
An error is not a mistake until you refuse to fix it.
Anonymous

11
JANUARY

To swim in the waters of human compassion you must dive in head first.

ARIES
It is much easier to begin than to end.
Plautus

TAURUS
The test of good education is seeing how it behaves in a fight.
George Bernard Shaw

GEMINI
Reading without reflection is like eating without digesting.
Edmund Burke

CANCER
Each child should be more intelligent than his parents.
Clarence Darrow

LEO
Lives based on having are less free than lives based either on doing or on being.
William James

VIRGO
He that hath ears to hear, let him hear.
Matthew 11:15

LIBRA
To sleep well one also needs concentration.
Zen Quote

SCORPIO
You've got to keep fighting—you've got to risk your life every six months to stay alive.
Elia Kazan

SAGITTARIUS
People in the west are always getting ready to live.
Chinese Quote

CAPRICORN
Be intent upon the perfection of the present day. Or,
The man who has no inner life is the slave of his surroundings.
Henri Frederic Amiel

AQUARIUS
I love criticism, as long as it's good.
Noël Coward

PISCES
The future is as irrevocable as an inflexible yesterday.
Jorge Luis Borges

---

*Prudence and patience work better
than pride and prejudice.*

12

JANUARY

ARIES
Thought is the seed of action.
Ralph Waldo Emerson

TAURUS
Genius is power, talent is applicability.
Ralph Waldo Emerson

GEMINI
Except during the nine months before he draws his first breath, no man
manages his affairs as well as a tree does.
George Bernard Shaw

CANCER
Examine the contents, not the bottle.
The Talmud

LEO
Time goes by: reputation increases, ability declines.
Dag Hammarskjöld

VIRGO
Put your cards on the table.
Anonymous

LIBRA
There is a lot of dignity in having the ability to confront the inconsequence of
reality.
Martin Esslin

SCORPIO
There can be no real freedom without the freedom to fail.
Eric Hoffer

SAGITTARIUS
A good vacation is had with people whose measure of time is vaguer than
yours.
John Boyton Priestley

CAPRICORN
He or she who knows everything has a lot to learn!
Anonymous

AQUARIUS
You should not wish for the wished to be prevented, rather hope that the
unwished could be wished for.
Turkish Quote

PISCES
You only live once—but if you work it out right, once is enough.
Joe E. Lewis

It all depends on the quality of your will.

ARIES
Men understand the worth of blessings only when they have lost them.
Plautus

TAURUS
The art of being wise is the art of knowing what to overlook.
William James

GEMINI
Our strength is often composed of the weakness that we're damned if we are going to show.
Mignon McLaughlin

CANCER
Your treasure is deep within you: that is what holds all you need.
Hui-Hai

LEO
What is originality? Undetected plagiarism.
Dean William R. Inge

VIRGO
The only question with wealth is what you do with it.
John D. Rockefeller, Jr.

LIBRA
Love is not what makes the world go round, love is what makes it worth while to go around.
F. P. Jones

SCORPIO
The earth belongs to the living, not to the dead.
Thomas Jefferson

SAGITTARIUS
The truth is more important than the facts.
Frank Lloyd Wright

CAPRICORN
If opportunity has shut one door, Resolve can open thrice a hundred more.
Arthur Guiterman

AQUARIUS
Life runs by so that your spirit can stay calmly in one spot.
Anonymous

PISCES
The most important thing a father can do for his children is to love their mother.
Theodore Hesburg

Reciprocity is a matter of give and take—
and one of enormous trust.

ARIES
Never go to bed angry. Keep awake and fight it out.
Anonymous

TAURUS
One has to choose in life, to either make money or spend it.
E. Bourdet

GEMINI
One good thing about egotists: they don't talk about other people.
L. Harper

CANCER
At this instant a moment of time is passing. We must transform ourselves into that moment.
Paul Cézanne

LEO
Modesty is the kind concession that courage grants inferiority.
Princess Diana

VIRGO
It is gratifying to give advice; difficult to ask for it and normal to ignore it!
Anonymous

LIBRA
To love is to admire with the heart; to admire is to love with the mind.
Gautier

SCORPIO
A neurotic is the man who builds a castle in the air. A psychotic lives in it. A psychiatrist collects the rent.
Anonymous

SAGITTARIUS
When we deliberate it is about means and not ends.
Aristotle

CAPRICORN
To see a hill, a mountain, a sea, a river, then everything has been seen.
Socrates

AQUARIUS
Once what you have learned finds its emotional place, it is never forgotten.
F. Tirenzi

PISCES
History repeats itself, but not as much as the movie does.
Graffiti

Study an object as a physicist studies a particle.

ARIES
Nothing is as good as it seems at the beginning.
T. S. Eliot

TAURUS
One must care about a world one will not see.
Bertrand Russell

GEMINI
A person who never makes mistakes, usually never does anything.
Archbishop W. C. Magee

CANCER
Freedom is what you do with what's been done to you.
Jean-Paul Sartre

LEO
Failure also goes to ones head.
Wilson Minzer

VIRGO
Experience makes you better or makes you bitter.
Anonymous

LIBRA
No woman has fallen in love without having a better opinion of him than he deserves.
Ed Howe

SCORPIO
It is just as important to know what is not solemn as it is to know what is.
John Kenneth Galbraith

SAGITTARIUS
Equipped only with his feelings, man explores the universe and calls it science.
Croatian Quote

CAPRICORN
A man is really never poor if he still can laugh.
Irish Quote

AQUARIUS
Physics has cosmic tones.
Timothy Leary

PISCES
Laughter is the music of the soul.
Anonymous

Anxiety can be transformed into creative ambition.

16
JANUARY

ARIES
You must lose a fly to catch a trout.
George Herbert

TAURUS
Seeing's believing, but feeling's the truth.
Thomas Fuller

GEMINI
The greatest right in the world is the right to be wrong.
(Dedicated to all Cancers, from all Geminis!)
Harry Weinberger

CANCER
I want to know if I can live with what I know, and with only that.
Albert Camus

LEO
One of the greatest necessities in America is to discover creative solitude.
Carl Sandburg

VIRGO
Our five senses would be incomplete without the sixth; sense of humor.
Anonymous

LIBRA
Hate the sin and love the sinner.
Mahatma Gandhi

SCORPIO
A nose that can see is worth two that sniff.
Eugene Ionesco

SAGITTARIUS
Every individual has his own measure of time.
Stephen Hawking

CAPRICORN
We earn our living with what we do, but we make a life with what we give.
Chinese Quote

AQUARIUS
Tranquility thou better name/Than all the family of Fame.
Samuel Taylor Coleridge

PISCES
I think we need more liberty of expression than is worth listening to.
Jerry Seinfeld

17

JANUARY

Nature does have a spirit; play with it.

ARIES
You need nothing on the outside if you carry enough inside.
José Martí

TAURUS
The wealth of the soul is the only true wealth.
Lucian

GEMINI
Certain signs precede certain events.
Cicero

CANCER
Laughter is a tranquilizer without after-effects.
Arnold Glasgow

LEO
The best eloquence is the one that get things done.
David Lloyd George

VIRGO
The best way to be right or wrong is to do it in all humility.
Anonymous

LIBRA
Let me tell you that the true revolutionary is guided by a great sense of love.
Che Guevara

SCORPIO
There's nothing I'm afraid of like scared people.
Robert Frost

SAGITTARIUS
God, do not lose your equilibrium.
Rainer Maria Rilke

CAPRICORN
Pessimism from reason and optimism from will.
Antonio Gramsci

AQUARIUS
Orgasm is a paroxysm; despair, too. One lasts an instant; the other a lifetime.
E. M. Cioran

PISCES
Things don't change as much as feelings.
Michel de Montaigne

A doubt is a portal to another realm
of questioning. Reinvestigate.

ARIES
Float like a butterfly, Sting like a bee!
Muhammad Ali

TAURUS
Teach me, like you, to drink creation whole, And casting out my self, become a soul.
Richard Wilbur

GEMINI
Two things fill my mind with ever-increasing wonder and awe: the starry heavens above me and the moral law within me.
Immanuel Kant

CANCER
These days, if you are not confused, you are not thinking clearly.
Mrs. Irene Peters

LEO
Each human being is like a primary number, divisible only by himself.
Jean Guitton

VIRGO
Good ideas need, besides wings, good landing gear.
Anonymous

LIBRA
Never use another as an instrument.
C. M. Martini

SCORPIO
Forty years are the old years of youth; fifty are the young years of old age.
Victor Hugo

SAGITTARIUS
Those who ignore history condemn themselves to repetition.
Nicholas Campion

CAPRICORN
Plan with meaning. Prepare with devotion. Proceed positively. Pursue with persistence.
Anonymous

AQUARIUS
Anxiety is no more than a spider's web.
Chinese Quote

PISCES
Nobody gets bored when they dream.
Fernando Savater

19
JANUARY

There can be a hidden meaning in anything.
Read deeply.

ARIES
There is glory in a great mistake.
Nathalia Crane

TAURUS
Fame is a bee. It has a song, It has a sting. Ah, too, it has a wing.
Emily Dickinson

GEMINI
I know that you believe you understand what you think I said, but I am not sure you realize that what you heard is not what I mean.
Berry & Homer Inc. (public relations firm)

CANCER
If you can't convince them, confuse them!
Harry S. Truman

LEO
Be not afraid of greatness: some are born great, some achieve greatness and some have greatness thrust upon 'em.
William Shakespeare

VIRGO
Remorse without repentance.
Chester Himes

LIBRA
Teach us delight in simple things and mirth that has no bitter springs.
Rudyard Kipling

SCORPIO
One chops wood, the other does the grunting.
Yiddish Quote

SAGITTARIUS
The new quantic combinations give time a space with no boundaries.
Stephen Hawking

CAPRICORN
The best things in life are free, plus taxes.
Will Rogers

AQUARIUS
What is the worth of anything, But for the happiness 'twill bring?
Richard Owen Cambridge

PISCES
Everything is easier than one thinks.
Goethe

New responsibilities should always give you
more opportunity to interact with others.

20
JANUARY

ARIES
Believing something possible is to make it come true.
Friedrich Hebbel

TAURUS
The heart has reasons that reason does not understand.
Blaise Pascal

GEMINI
There are no eternal things, just as there are no absolute truths.
Nietzsche

CANCER
Man's liberation should manifest itself in both sexes.
Saint Augustine

LEO
Men are but children of a larger growth.
John Dryden

VIRGO
One anecdote of man is worth a volume of biography.
William Ellery Channing

LIBRA
The spirit remains young. It's the same spirit I remember living with during my childhood.
Stanley Kunitz [on being 90]

SCORPIO
Opinions cannot survive if they cannot be defended.
Thomas Mann

SAGITTARIUS
It is the mind that maketh good or ill, that maketh wretch or happy, rich or poor.
Edmund Spenser

CAPRICORN
If opportunity has shut one door, Resolve can open thrice a hundred more.
Arthur Guiterman

AQUARIUS
I sound my barbaric yawp over the roofs of the world.
Walt Whitman

PISCES
Hope makes an aim of "an aim."
C. M. Martini

21
JANUARY

Stick to your guns and nourish yourself.

ARIES
Man is something between two lips that tries to attach but cannot.
Friedrich Hebbel

TAURUS
The bird of paradise alights only upon the hand that does not grasp.
John Berry

GEMINI
Man prefers to believe that what he believes is true.
Francis Bacon

CANCER
If the shoe fits, you're not allowing for growth.
Robert N. Coons

LEO
To be without some of the things you want is an indispensable part of happiness.
Bertrand Russell

VIRGO
They also serve who only stand and wait.
Milton

LIBRA
Besides man, no other being questions of himself: who am I?
Arthur Schopenhauer

SCORPIO
Sooner or later, false thinking brings wrong conduct.
Julian Huxley

SAGITTARIUS
Familiar acts are beautiful through love.
Percy Bysshe Shelley

CAPRICORN
The earth could be the lunatic asylum of our solar system.
S. P. Cadman

AQUARIUS
Heaven means to be one with God.
Confucius

PISCES
The unnameable is the eternally real.
Lao-Tzu

Wonder at the usual.

ARIES
I feel bad that I don't feel worse.
Michael Frayn

TAURUS
In Chinese, the word for crisis is wei ji, the character wei means danger, and ji, means opportunity.
Jan Wong

GEMINI
If one is forever cautious, can one remain a human being?
Aleksandr Solzhenitsyn

CANCER
I am he, As you are me, And we are all together.
John Lennon and Paul McCartney

LEO
To be somebody you must last.
Ruth Gordon

VIRGO
Just as courage imperils life, fear protects it.
Leonardo da Vinci

LIBRA
There are some people that if they don't know, you can't tell 'em.
Louis Armstrong

SCORPIO
The genius of Einstein leads to Hiroshima.
Pablo Picasso

SAGITTARIUS
With high hope for the future, no prediction is ventured.
Abraham Lincoln

CAPRICORN
The future is not a gift, it is an achievement.
Harry Lauder

AQUARIUS
The greater love is a mother's; then comes a dog's; then a sweetheart's.
Polish Quote

PISCES
Respect is love in plain clothes.
Frankie Byrne

23
JANUARY

Keep steady, but get out there and make waves.

ARIES
My favorite words, "tremendous" and "marvelous" come rolling out wonderfully.
Archbishop Desmond Tutu

TAURUS
Love your neighbor as if he were yourself, but choose your neighborhood.
Louise Beal

GEMINI
It is much easier to forgive your enemy if you already got even.
Oskar von Miller

CANCER
Everything I know I learned after I was 30!
George Clemenceau

LEO
Not believing shortens down horizons.
Hans Holzer

VIRGO
Logic is the art of making a mistake with assurance.
Joseph Wood Krutch

LIBRA
A woman is a woman until she dies, but a man is, only while he can be.
Moms Mabley

SCORPIO
When one paints, one doesn't think.
Raphael

SAGITTARIUS
The truth about everything, the entire wild beautiful utterly useless truth.
Edward Abbey

CAPRICORN
I would rather die of pure love than let God escape from me in dark wisdom.
Mechthild of Magdeburg

AQUARIUS
Philosophy is composed of many more questions than answers.
Fernando Savater

PISCES
No one knows how what changes, changes. One half of the planet is grass,
The other half is grazing.
Rumi

Put action into beliefs that can work for you.

ARIES
I respect faith, but doubts are what get you educated.
Wilson Mizner

TAURUS
Perfection comes when you use your mind as a mirror.
Chuag-Tse

GEMINI
Living is doubting, and faith without a doubt is no more than death.
Miguel de Unamuno

CANCER
I try to take one day at a time, but sometimes several days attack me at once.
Ashleigh Brilliant

LEO
We look like angels until our passion dies.
Thomas Dekker

VIRGO
I would not exchange my spare time for all the gold in the world.
Victor de Mirabeau

LIBRA
A man is only rich in proportion to what he can let go of.
Henry David Thoreau

SCORPIO
Mistakes are tolerable when reason has the freedom to confront them.
Thomas Jefferson

SAGITTARIUS
The greatest peacefulness should come as you breathe.
Tantric Literature

CAPRICORN
A little of what you fancy does you good.
Marie Lloyd

AQUARIUS
Voluptuosity is peacefulness of the spirit and bodily health.
B. Argens

PISCES
Either do not attempt at all, or go through with it.
Ovid

25

JANUARY

ARIES
A pound of pluck is worth a ton of luck.
James A. Garfield

TAURUS
I close my eyes, the better to see.
Paul Gauguin

GEMINI
You are free, and that is why you are lost.
Franz Kafka

CANCER
Few women and fewer men have enough character to be idle.
E. V. Lucas

LEO
We are tomorrow's past.
Mary Webb

VIRGO
The mass of men lead lives of quiet desperation.
Henry David Thoreau

LIBRA
There is the same difference between us and one, as between us and any other.
Michel de Montaigne

SCORPIO
Most of the stars in the universe cannot even be seen.
J. Audouze

SAGITTARIUS
When an artist rationalizes, it is because he doesn't understand a thing anymore.
André Derain

CAPRICORN
Strengths, merits and talents, make men, in principle, unequal.
John Locke

AQUARIUS
A book is like a garden that one carries in one's pocket.
Arabian Quote

PISCES
Work is good, provided you do not forget to live.
Central African Quote

ARIES
I prefer future dreams to history of the past.
Thomas Jefferson

TAURUS
Silence is not always tact, and it is tact that is golden, not silence.
Samuel Butler

GEMINI
Talent is something you possess; genius is something that possesses you.
Malcolm Cowley

CANCER
One learns to keep silent and make one's own confusions.
C. Otis Skinner

LEO
The future influences our present as much as the past.
Nietzsche

VIRGO
Sentimentality is a failure of feelings.
Wallace Stevens

LIBRA
Curiosity is a lust of the mind.
Thomas Hobbes

SCORPIO
If there be hell on earth, it is to be found in a melancholy man's heart.
Robert Burton

SAGITTARIUS
A man does not have to be an angel in order to be a saint.
Albert Schweitzer

CAPRICORN
God does not play dice.
Albert Einstein

AQUARIUS
There's never time enough.
Anonymous

PISCES
Departure should be sudden.
Benjamin Disraeli

27
JANUARY

Hiranyagarbha in Sanskrit is the cosmic egg from which a new universe is born. Be an idealist.

ARIES
Only the past is immortal.
Delmore Schwartz

TAURUS
Any style that does not bore you is good style.
Voltaire

GEMINI
God is not a cosmic messenger.
Harry Emerson Fosdick

CANCER
Only when you have pity for every living soul are you really noble.
Buddha

LEO
The past at least is secure.
Daniel Webster

VIRGO
Ideas are strange things, they only work if you function.
Santayana

LIBRA
Read between the lines.
Dutch Quote

SCORPIO
Money is something you got to make in case you don't die.
Max Asnas

SAGITTARIUS
God is a fire, and we are all little flames.
Anne Rice

CAPRICORN
Fall seven times, get up eight.
Japanese Quote

AQUARIUS
Man should not strive to eliminate his complexes, but to get in accord with them; they are legitimately what directs his contact in the world.
Sigmund Freud

PISCES
The chess-board is the world; the pieces are the phenomena of the universe; the rules of the game are what we call the Laws of Nature.
T. H. Huxley

ARIES
The measure of man is what he does with power.
Pittacus

TAURUS
In solitude, be a multitude to thyself.
Tibullus

GEMINI
There is no cure for birth and death, save to enjoy the interval.
Santayana

CANCER
Life can only be understood backwards, but must be lived forwards.
Søren Kierkegaard

LEO
Ignorance is less remote from truth than prejudice.
Denis Diderot

VIRGO
It is not enough to be alive, one must know when to have a life!
Mexican Quote

LIBRA
The brain is as strong as its weakest think.
Eleanor Doan

SCORPIO
Being a philosopher, I have a problem for every solution.
Robert Zend

SAGITTARIUS
Life is the childhood of our immortality.
Goethe

CAPRICORN
Weight and mass are not the same thing. Weight is strength, mass is resistence to acceleration.
Stephen Hawking

AQUARIUS
Everyone plays with their own Apocalyptic ghost.
Umberto Eco

PISCES
We must admit that there is a lot to be said for the huge importance of chance.
Carl Jung

29
JANUARY

Equality gives an inner sense of fair play.

ARIES
Learning makes a person fit company for themselves.
Thomas Fuller

TAURUS
Probe the earth and see where your main roots run.
Henry David Thoreau

GEMINI
Those who speak most of progress measure it by quantity and not by quality.
Santayana

CANCER
Immature love says "I love you because I need you."
Erich Fromm

LEO
We are citizens of the world; and the tragedy of our times is that we do not know this.
Woodrow Wilson

VIRGO
The common man does not think himself so.
German Quote

LIBRA
The most you can expect, is that the others pretend to have a good character.
Fran Lebowitz

SCORPIO
The surest protection against temptation is cowardice.
Mark Twain

SAGITTARIUS
Emotion has taught mankind to reason.
Marquis de Vauvenargues

CAPRICORN
It is better to be criticized than to be ignored.
Romanian Quote

AQUARIUS
You can give without loving, but you can't love without giving.
Romanian Quote

PISCES
You get more knowledge from failing than you do from success.
Japanese Quote

Create a choice. Yours or someone elses.

30
JANUARY

ARIES
The message from the moon is that no problem need any longer be considered insoluble.
Norman Cousins

TAURUS
The thing that hath been, it is that which shall be.
Ecclesiastes 1:9

GEMINI
Be thine own palace, or the world's thy jail.
John Donne

CANCER
Mature love says "I need you because I love you."
Erich Fromm

LEO
Now is the accepted time.
2 Corinthians 6:2

VIRGO
The more you know, the more you know what you should know.
Alfred North Whitehead

LIBRA
True friendship comes when silence between two people is comfortable.
Dave Tyson Gentry

SCORPIO
Happiness does not depend on what you are or have; it only depends on what you think.
Dale Carnegie

SAGITTARIUS
God created natural numbers, everything else is man made!
Leopold Kronecker

CAPRICORN
With one, it's enough.
Babe Ruth

AQUARIUS
Love is a little word, people make it a big one!
Romanian Quote

PISCES
You can only predict things after they happen.
Eugene Ionesco

31
JANUARY

*Perhaps time belongs to God
and we only live through it.*

ARIES
Hope is an echo, hope ties itself yonder, yonder.
Carl Sandburg

TAURUS
Man's many desires are like the small metal coins he carries about in his pocket. The more he has, the more they weigh him down.
Satya Sai Baba

GEMINI
I am an idealist. I don't know where I am going, but I am on my way.
Carl Sandburg

CANCER
All that we do is done with an eye to something else.
Aristotle

LEO
The Way of the sage is to act but not to compete.
Lao-Tzu

VIRGO
It does not depend on efficiency: getting something achieved depends on your karma.
Nomadic Tibetan Quote

LIBRA
A philosopher is a person who never feels bad after being ridiculous.
Bertrand Russell

SCORPIO
To err is human, but to really foul things up requires a computer.
Anonymous

SAGITTARIUS
No one can make you feel inferior without your consent.
Eleanor Roosevelt

CAPRICORN
A little credulity helps one through life very smoothly.
Mrs. Elizabeth Gaskell

AQUARIUS
Man is the measure of all things.
Pythagoras

PISCES
Hope is a dream for the awakened.
Aristotle

FEBRUARY

FEBRUARY

Though February is always the shortest month, even with the addition of one more day every four years, it can be filled with rapid changes, sudden insights, eccentricities, unique opportunities, individual autonomy, and, for those who enjoy breaking established rules, ways to interact more positively. This may sound like a lot of heavy stuff for a month that never has more than 696 hours, but consider that most of the time, February is ruled by the planet Uranus, first of the "outer planets," and historically connected to nonconformity!

In February, we tend to collect, buy, put away, and choose our Valentine's Day cards. Even so, this month could be called the "singleness time." Dwelling on the why and how of our own particular fates, many of us may find our true heart's delight is ourselves.

ARIES

Aries, the first sun sign, won't be bothered again by troublesome Saturn until the year 2026! Use the upcoming Februaries (yes, all of them) to put things into place as calmly as you can and to gain surer footing. There will be two interesting eclipses in February 2008 that will make for a really joyful noise—but until then, the joy might be a bit more muted. On Saturday, February 14, 2026, Saturn can make you worry again, but just bear in mind, daring, dash-ahead Aries, that a little contemplative worrying can actually make you wiser and counting on yourself this month is the best thing to do of all!

Keyword: Detect

TAURUS

This month, you jam-packed Bulls may suddenly find your skin a little thinner. You'll pick up on and be affected by all the lost vibrations emanating from other signs. Although this may seem a little disruptive, think of it as Uranus's way of shaking up your sometimes bullheaded love of the status quo, making you more aware of your own self and vibrations. Let go. Fall in love with people and things. Just remember that you are at your best when helping other people count their blessings.

Keywords: The knack and how to get it

GEMINI

You Geminis, the Twins, have a real knack for finding the right circumstances to double your pleasure, and February should offer so much opportunity for joy that it's a real shame there are only twenty-eight days to the month. You'll sail through any waters as long as you remember to be a little more compassionate to other people (which isn't your forte). Gazing at someone else's reflection as well as your own could make life twice as nice.

Keywords: Deeper meanings

CANCER

February is no time to hide in your shell. You're now on notice: Get in touch with those who have fallen from your grace, made you uncomfortable, or just disappeared from view. The Sun now is at a funny angle to your sign and Mercury is passing at a quick silvery pace, making it the perfect time for you to feel good about forgiving and forgetting.

Keywords: Better yourself

LEO

For Leos, February means choices, letting go, and reminding yourself that it's all right to make mistakes. How to find the right "drive" (in your life, in your car, or on your computer) is the foremost question Leos will be pawing over this month. Let things happen to you instead of insisting on being the King of the Jungle all the time. Your roar could become a purr. Bravo!

Keywords: Give in

VIRGO

You should be reminded more than once this month that if you want to do your own thing in your own neat and precise manner, you need to let others do theirs in whatever way they choose as well. Though this may simply seem reminiscent of what Virgo is about generally and it may seem unlikely that this is only advice for February, even so, find your own resources and, please, let others find theirs, too!

Keywords: Loosen up

LIBRA

The first three weeks in February could be as good as it gets for most of you Librans. Although you may not see it, there is a larger scope to matters for you right now, and you can count on your lucky stars to eventually tip the scales in your favor. Try to keep things harmonious while letting life make you feel and experience more, which is always a good thing.

Keywords: Harmonious ways

SCORPIO

This month is rather like a flash-flood watch for many of you Scorpios. You'll need a tough shell, otherwise you may start to blame things on the Sun's storms, even if it isn't their usual eleven-year cycle. You need to translate your experiences into a language more personal to you. Who's right? What's right? It will be hard to know until the tide turns, (which can't be predicted). Until then, keen observation and the occasional experiment gives overwhelming relief.

Keywords: Nothing murky, please

SAGITTARIUS

Everyone should have an optimistic, generous Sagittarian as a best friend (I know I do!). People naturally gravitate toward you, and this month you score even higher if you share even more than usual. So give advice, point the way, help others find solace, and play matchmaker—for yourself as well as for others. The good things in your celestial field are fruitful and multiplying.
Keywords: Roll the dice

CAPRICORN

This month, as long as the Earth keeps moving around the Sun, Capricorns could discover some unexpected truths. What you get out of it depends on whether or not you discover how to ease up on your need for careful planning and give chance a chance. Remember, you goats love to climb every mountain, no matter how steep, and now is the time to keep your chin up, have your eyes wide open, and allow for surprises along the way.
Keywords: Astound yourself

AQUARIUS

Aquarians, it's your time to soar! Leave any discontent for a rainy astrological day (like maybe in November). Dream, but try to focus and find out why you have been avoiding certain things. Reason—or chance—are on your side and could help you find your answers. Share with others and celebrate yourself.
Keywords: Use the wind beneath your own wings

PISCES

Leaning on other people may make any Pisces feel like a fish out of water, but letting yourself rely on others is the best thing that could happen to you during most of February! Just assure yourself that whoever it is you're counting on is the right person—trust, or you might get lost. Treat yourself to something special once a day early in the month and twice a day later in the month when the Sun is back in your sign and things are going swimmingly again.
Keywords: Worthy perspectives

Not every story changes your life, but many a story can.

FEBRUARY

ARIES
A consistent man believes in destiny, a capricious man in chance.
Benjamin Disraeli

TAURUS
When it is dark enough, one can always see the stars.
Ralph Waldo Emerson

GEMINI
The world is for those who were born to conquer it; not for those who dream that it can be conquered, even if they are right.
Fernando Pessoa

CANCER
Awareness requires a rupture with the world we take for granted.
Shoshana Zuboff

LEO
There is no end. There is no beginning. There is only the infinite passion of life.
Federico Fellini

VIRGO
One must always be aware, to notice even though the cost of noticing is to become responsible.
Thylias Moss

LIBRA
To love without criticism is to be betrayed.
Djuna Barnes

SCORPIO
A man must swallow more beliefs than he can digest.
Havelock Ellis

SAGITTARIUS
Nothing is more original, more oneself, than to be nourished by others: only one must be able to digest them.
Paul Valéry

CAPRICORN
Chance does nothing that has not been prepared beforehand.
Alexis de Tocqueville

AQUARIUS
The unexamined life is not worth living.
Socrates

PISCES
Greet the unseen with a cheer.
Robert Browning

Character is not a fixed thing, it is a process.

2
FEBRUARY

ARIES
As soon as we are born, we begin to die, and the end depends upon the beginning.
Manilus

TAURUS
When a feeling of spiritual contraction comes over you, o traveler, it is for your own good.
Rumi

GEMINI
A moment's insight is sometimes worth a life's experience.
Oliver Wendell Holmes

CANCER
We need a reason for speaking, we need none for keeping silent.
Pierre Nicole

LEO
Happiness is good health and a bad memory.
Ingrid Bergman

VIRGO
You are lost the instant you know what the result will be.
Juan Gris

LIBRA
A proverb is no proverb to you till life illustrates it.
John Keats

SCORPIO
Experience is the name everyone gives to his mistakes.
Oscar Wilde

SAGITTARIUS
To live according to nature is to live as the gods have chosen.
Pythagoras

CAPRICORN
Why stay on earth unless to grow?
Anonymous

AQUARIUS
Thinking should speed up time.
Ivan Doig

PISCES
We know what we are, but we do not know what we can be.
William Shakespeare

3

FEBRUARY

Every person generates energy.
Use yours to create warmth.

ARIES
It is not how much what, you see, as how you look at it.
William Hazlitt

TAURUS
He measures others by himself.
French Proverb

GEMINI
Instinct is intelligence incapable of self-consciousness.
John Sterling

CANCER
If you can laugh at it, you can live with it.
American Proverb

LEO
We have a choice: to plow new ground or let the weeds grow.
Jonathan Westover

VIRGO
Perhaps God, when he said his first word, thought that he was saying his last word.
José Saramago

LIBRA
I have lived for I have felt.
Casanova

SCORPIO
Nothing is so good as it seems beforehand.
George Eliot

SAGITTARIUS
A wise man will make more opportunities than he finds.
Sir Francis Bacon

CAPRICORN
Protest long enough that you are right and you will be wrong.
Yiddish Proverb

AQUARIUS
Love owns one universal claim. To Love, it only needs to Be.
Calderón de la Barca

PISCES
One must judge men, not by their opinions, but what their opinions have made of them.
Lichtenberg

ARIES
I am what I do.
Samuel Beckett

TAURUS
I was so cold that I almost got married.
Shelley Winters

GEMINI
Love—erotic art, filled with beauty and grace.
Arabian Quote

CANCER
Every day is filled with new opportunities, one just has to be there.
Anonymous

LEO
It is easier to forgive an enemy than a friend.
William Blake

VIRGO
It is not the struggle that makes us become artists, rather art that obliges us to struggle.
Albert Camus

LIBRA
One may say foolish things, but important foolish things.
Nora Astorga

SCORPIO
The strongest iron, hardened in the fire, most often ends in scraps and shatterings.
Sophocles

SAGITTARIUS
We look all over for the absolute, and we always only find the concrete.
Novalis

CAPRICORN
Our convictions will be our absolute passport to success.
Elizabeth Taylor

AQUARIUS
The cage, without a bird, is worthless.
Persian Quote

PISCES
There is no past, nor is there any future. Only the present forever.
Anonymous

5
FEBRUARY

ARIES
You do what you are, you do a fraction of what you are.
Samuel Beckett

TAURUS
After us, the deluge.
Madame Pompadour

GEMINI
I know . . . can only have its meaning in connection with the other evidence of my "knowing."
Ludwig Wittgenstein

CANCER
Sometimes a scream is better than a thesis.
Ralph Waldo Emerson

LEO
The bigger a man's head, the worse his headache.
Persian Proverb

VIRGO
There is, indeed, no such thing in life as absolute darkness.
Gelett Burgess

LIBRA
The many can err grossly as the few.
John Dryden

SCORPIO
A half truth is a complete lie.
Yiddish Proverb

SAGITTARIUS
Only our true friends tell us when we have a dirty face.
Sicilian Quote

CAPRICORN
My "daimon" always tells me, "do it and don't worry about anything."
Anonymous

AQUARIUS
If something is attained, it was already there from the beginning of time.
Ryokan

PISCES
Writers as well as words can change the dreams of others.
A. Sarabia

Keep your cool. Take a closer look.

6
FEBRUARY

ARIES
You suffer a dreary ooze of your being into doing.
Samuel Beckett

TAURUS
Pride is the virtue of bad fortune.
Chateaubriand

GEMINI
It is a fine thing to command, even if it be only a herd of cattle.
Cervantes

CANCER
God gives the milk, but not the pail.
English Proverb

LEO
A generous confession disarms slander.
Thomas Fuller

VIRGO
"Around the Day in 80 Worlds."
Title by Julio Cortazar

LIBRA
A rising tide will lift all boats.
Anonymous

SCORPIO
There are times when you have to protest.
The Mighty Sparrow

SAGITTARIUS
Who desires more will live longer.
Kahlil Gibran

CAPRICORN
A painted cake is also a cake.
Dogen

AQUARIUS
If we loose something, it is hidden somewhere near us.
Ryokan

PISCES
All I ask is a tall ship and a star to steer her by.
John Masefield

7

FEBRUARY

Promises should only be made to be kept.
Believe that they will be.

ARIES
Sometimes, simply by sitting, the soul collects wisdom.
Zen Proverb

TAURUS
Doubt is not below wisdom, but a step above it.
Anonymous

GEMINI
Sex soothes tension. Love causes it.
Democritus

CANCER
It is very possible that God is much more interested in our inside grace than in our outside space.
Anonymous

LEO
The inscrutability of the world.
Paul Wright paraphrasing Moby-Dick

VIRGO
It is better to occupy yourself with importunate things, than doing nothing.
Baltasar Gracián

LIBRA
Power is pleasurable, and pleasurable things soothes pain.
William Hazlitt

SCORPIO
Negligence of discipline is the most harmful thing.
George Washington

SAGITTARIUS
Who has a lot is not rich, he is rich who gives a lot.
Erich Fromm

CAPRICORN
Inside absolute emptiness, anything can happen.
John Cage

AQUARIUS
For an Aquarian, more can happen in any given time.
Anonymous

PISCES
I promise
Memory of any day.
Zen Proverb

Be courageous and master your craft.

8
FEBRUARY

ARIES
A chicken is the way an egg reproduces itself.
W. Heisenberg

TAURUS
Never economize on luxury.
Mae West

GEMINI
Two people should love about one another, the good that in the future they can build on.
Attributed to Tolstoy

CANCER
Comfort yourselves. God does have his hands on the universe's driving wheel.
Graffiti

LEO
A man who never changes his mind is like stagnant water, and it breeds mental reptiles.
Ambrose Bierce

VIRGO
While the sane man thinks things out, the mad man does whatever.
Anonymous

LIBRA
What makes a man be a good Christian, makes them good citizens.
Daniel Webster

SCORPIO
Aloneness makes the most noise. This is true for men as well as for dogs.
Eric Hoffer

SAGITTARIUS
It might be yes as it might be no.
Nahuatl Quote

CAPRICORN
Confronting what you like with what you do not like is a mental illness.
Seng-T'San

AQUARIUS
The sword conquered for a while, but the spirit conquers for ever!
Sholem Asch

PISCES
It is not enough to lift the weak, one must hold him up afterwards.
William Shakespeare

9

The message depends on the peace in your heart.

FEBRUARY

ARIES
Welcome tomorrow with good humor.
Robert Browning

TAURUS
Nothing is enough for the man for whom enough is too little.
Epicurus

GEMINI
Is bigger better, or is faster better?
Anonymous

CANCER
There are those who search for happiness and there are those who distribute it.
Anonymous

LEO
Anyway, nothing human is worth being taken seriously; yet.
Plato

VIRGO
The child behaves as has been taught.
Somali Proverb

LIBRA
A true friend is the best possession.
Benjamin Franklin

SCORPIO
The first draft of anything is shitty.
Ernest Hemingway

SAGITTARIUS
In its essence, the all encompassing ALL, is incognizable.
El Kybalion

CAPRICORN
What destroys one man preserves another.
Corneille

AQUARIUS
Accomplishments remain with oneself.
Anonymous

PISCES
Whoever has known how to mix the useful with the agreeable has accomplished his objective.
Horace

Every breath of air carries its own divine perk.

10

FEBRUARY

ARIES
A black hole, (with all due respect), could be a kind of Mandela of the XXI century, a place of reunion.
Timothy Ferris

TAURUS
Kind words can be short and easy; their echo, infinite.
Mother Teresa

GEMINI
To fall in love is to create a religion with a fallible God.
Jose Luis Borges

CANCER
Do not do that which you would not have known.
Benjamin Franklin

LEO
You can't walk and look at the stars if you have a stone in your shoe.
Old American Quote

VIRGO
If it can be negotiated, it can be mended.
Somali Quote

LIBRA
Teach me, like you, to drink creation whole. And casting out my self, become a soul.
Richard Wilbur

SCORPIO
Don't get angry, occupy yourself!
Jean-Louis Bourgois

SAGITTARIUS
Never believe that what is apparent is the truth.
William Safire

CAPRICORN
The world does not require so much to be informed as to be reminded.
Anonymous

AQUARIUS
Our cup is the full Moon: the wine, the Sun.
Ibn al-Farid

PISCES
Years teach many things that days ignore.
Benito Pérez Galdós

11
FEBRUARY

As they say, "toodle-fucking-loo," or, you are strong enough to manage anything.

ARIES
Today, all or nothing at all even if only of something.
Admiral Collingwood

TAURUS
Tolerance is one of the first things that should be taught.
Jean-Jacques Rousseau

GEMINI
Love is many things. But above all things it is an alteration in the digestive system.
Gabriel García Márquez

CANCER
The important thing is how you eat, not what you eat.
Epicteto

LEO
He that complies against his will, Is of his own opinion still.
Samuel Butler

VIRGO
If we cannot now end our differences, at least we can help make the world safe for diversity.
John F. Kennedy

LIBRA
I glorify myself in conflicts, so as to rejoice afterwards in victory.
Frederick Douglass

SCORPIO
Time goes forward into the unknown.
Anonymous

SAGITTARIUS
Often, the best way to win, is not to keep scores.
Marianne Espinosa

CAPRICORN
Our heart is a treasury; if you spend all its wealth at once you are ruined.
Le Pére Goriot

AQUARIUS
Whoever made an angel, also made the devil.
Blaise Pascal

PISCES
Believe whoever has already done it!
Virgil

ARIES
Tyranny begins where the law ends.
William Pitt the Elder

TAURUS
I know people of every sort. They don't measure up to their fates.
Guillame Apollinaire

GEMINI
Whoever loves the most is in an inferior position and will suffer.
Thomas Mann

CANCER
You can't unscramble scrambled eggs.
American Proverb

LEO
Simple pleasures are the last refuge of the complex.
Oscar Wilde

VIRGO
Truth never is a sin, it just is uncomfortable.
Mexican Quote

LIBRA
Thousands of fantasies have attested my memory.
John Milton

SCORPIO
Every soul should know the morning sun, the sweet fresh earth and the Great Silence, on its own.
Ohiyesha

SAGITTARIUS
When nothing is sure, everything is possible.
Margaret Drabble

CAPRICORN
If only I could love the greatest zaddik as much as God loves the worst ne'er-do-well!
Martin Buber

AQUARIUS
We love God with his own love; to know it is a challenge.
Meister Eckhart

PISCES
There is no one following the last one in line.
Anonymous

13
FEBRUARY

There is a Mayan sky god (Oxlagyn Ti Ku) who
watches over this day. Who will watch over you?

ARIES
There are three things that everybody tries to avoid at least once: cars, taxes
and responsibilities.
English Proverb

TAURUS
The absurd is an essential notion and a prime truth.
Albert Camus

GEMINI
An idealist is one who, on noticing that a rose smells better than a cabbage,
concludes that it will also make a better soup.
H. L. Mencken

CANCER
It is said that a wise man who stands firm is a statesman, and a foolish man
who stands firm is a catastrophe.
Adlai Stevenson

LEO
Modern society is bound to shining and decorating the cage within which
man is a prisoner.
Swami Nirmalananda

VIRGO
What is unnatural, is also natural.
Goethe

LIBRA
Who has never made a fool of himself in love, will never be wise in love.
Theodor Reik

SCORPIO
Worship me through meditating in the sanctuary of your heart.
Srimad Bhagavatam

SAGITTARIUS
Let us read and dance, and so we will not hurt the rest of the world!
Voltaire

CAPRICORN
You feel the cold according to the coat you wear.
Anonymous

AQUARIUS
Whoever puts his confidence in acts of piety is more culpable than he who
sins.
Bayazid al-Bistami

PISCES
Nothing really sets human nature free but self-control.
Paul Bottome

If as the ancients say, astrology is the algebra
of life, pick a logarithm, solve it, and enjoy.

ARIES
Love is a condition of the mind that happens at a moment during which the mind is out of condition.
Dame Emilie Rose Macauley

TAURUS
Hell is, madame, not to love anymore.
George Bernanos

GEMINI
We can't all be heroes because someone has to sit on the curb and clap as they go by.
Will Rogers

CANCER
Deceive not thy physician, confessor, nor lawyer.
George Herbert

LEO
Happiness rejuvenates and sadness ages.
Latin Quote

VIRGO
Civility costs nothing and buys everything.
Lady Mary Wortley Montagu

LIBRA
One eyewitness is better than a dozen hearsays.
Anonymous

SCORPIO
Love: That's self love á deux.
Madame de Staël

SAGITTARIUS
Patience, time and money overcome everything.
Fred Allen

CAPRICORN
Passion is a cosmic force, like gravity.
Amado Nervo

AQUARIUS
Always put the saddle on the right horse.
Anonymous

PISCES
Who loves a lot, forgives a lot.
Amado Nervo

15
FEBRUARY

The unifying theme is energy.
Consider your own inertia.

ARIES
Better to remain silent and to be thought a fool than to speak out and remove all doubt.
Abraham Lincoln

TAURUS
Chaste is she whom no one has asked.
Ovid

GEMINI
Love. That is the only good thing there is in life.
Virgil

CANCER
When one is loved, one doubts nothing. When one loves, one doubts everything.
Colette

LEO
The measurement of a person is found in the heart.
Latin Proverb

VIRGO
Any man is only as good as what he loves.
Saul Bellow

LIBRA
The movement of life has its rest in its own music.
Rabindranath Tagore

SCORPIO
Bigamy is having one husband too many. Monogamy is the same thing.
Erica Jong

SAGITTARIUS
God will provide if only God would provide until he provides.
Yiddish Proverb

CAPRICORN
No one lives in vain, the history of the world is the biography of all human beings.
Thomas Carlyle

AQUARIUS
Action springs not from thought, but from a readiness for responsibility.
Dietrich Bonhoeffer

PISCES
The best of what is good is done in a hurry.
Hidm al-Lajmi

Inspiration should come from the world around you. Watch people. Listen to what they say.

ARIES
If you don't have what you like, you must like what you have.
Anonymous

TAURUS
Diligence is the mother of good fortune.
Cervantes

GEMINI
Love is a word that covers a great variety of feelings. Every day it changes its meaning.
Madame de Staël

CANCER
I hope there's no one else like me.
Jane Fonda

LEO
The first duty of love is to listen.
Mexican Quote

VIRGO
If way to the Better there be, it exacts a full look at the Worst.
Thomas Hardy

LIBRA
The natural rhythm of human life is routine punctuated by orgies.
Aldous Huxley

SCORPIO
Dirty laundry should be washed in private, at home.
Mexican Proverb

SAGITTARIUS
The furniture of a man's mind chiefly consists of his recollections and the bonds which unite them.
Francis Galton

CAPRICORN
One must learn by doing the thing; though you think you know it, you have no certainty until you try.
Sophocles

AQUARIUS
The present time has one advantage over every other; it is our own.
Charles Caleb Colton

PISCES
Let us not be weary in well doing.
Galatians

17

FEBRUARY

Reserve loyalty for someone like yourself.

ARIES
All human wisdom is summed up in two words: wait and hope.
Alexandre Dumas, Père

TAURUS
The only worthwhile courage is the one that takes you from one minute to the next.
Mignon McLaughlin

GEMINI
A great deal of learning can be packed into an empty head.
Karl Kraus

CANCER
There are three kinds of men: those who think they are don Juans, those who think they have been, and those who think they could have been.
José Ortega y Gasset

LEO
No idea has been discovered and perfected at the same time.
Bulgarian Quote

VIRGO
There is an exquisite subtlety, and that in itself is unjust.
Ecclesiastes

LIBRA
Character is long-standing habit.
Plutarch

SCORPIO
Abundance, like want, ruins many.
Anonymous

SAGITTARIUS
Every moment presents, momentaneously, what happens.
John Cage

CAPRICORN
Sleep, riches, and health, to be truly enjoyed, must be interrupted.
Jean Paul Richter

AQUARIUS
If you are willing to admit you're all wrong when you are, you are all right.
Anonymous

PISCES
All's well that ends well.
William Shakespeare

There is always something similar
happening somewhere simultaneously.

ARIES
Actions always are more effective than words.
Anonymous

TAURUS
Many flowers are born to blush unseen.
Rumi

GEMINI
I'm going to add it up in a few words. "One never knows."
Fred Allen

CANCER
A woman without a man is like a fish without a bicycle.
Gloria Steinem

LEO
A horse can tell by his bridle what his rider is like.
Turkish Quote

VIRGO
Life is a handful of short stories, pretending to be a novel.
Anonymous

LIBRA
Character is that which can do without success.
Ralph Waldo Emerson

SCORPIO
Jealousy is no more than feeling alone against smiling enemies.
Elizabeth Bowen

SAGITTARIUS
The alarming reality of things is my everyday discovery.
Fernando Pessoa

CAPRICORN
Liberty is letting you do as you please, but with controls over the other fellow.
Anonymous

AQUARIUS
A creator needs only one enthusiast to justify him.
Man Ray

PISCES
A man never feels the want of what it never occurs to him to ask for.
Arthur Schopenhauer

19
FEBRUARY

You can be creating the world you envision.

ARIES
Deeds are much more effective than words, but they are much less frequent.
Alphonese Karr

TAURUS
Prayer is a powerful act that surrenders celestial forces at man's disposition.
Jean-Baptiste Lacordaire

GEMINI
Nothing rules love, and love rules all things.
Anonymous

CANCER
Imprudence seems to precede every calamity.
Alexander of Alexandria

LEO
Every extreme attitude is a flight from the self.
Eric Hoffer

VIRGO
There are some days when it is hard to catch up with the losers!
Robert Orpen

LIBRA
In analyzing (history) do not be too profound, for often the causes are quite superficial.
Ralph Waldo Emerson

SCORPIO
In order to act wisely it is not enough to be wise.
Dostoyevsky

SAGITTARIUS
Light dazzles whomever lives in darkness.
Saint Paul

CAPRICORN
Every luxury must be paid for, and everything is a luxury, starting with being in the world.
Cesare Pavese

AQUARIUS
The only universal truth is to see clearly that all great teachings are equal.
Ryokan

PISCES
The active life is a service, the contemplative life a liberty.
Saint Gregory the Great

ARIES
One's real life is often the life one does not lead.
Oscar Wilde

TAURUS
Where is your Self to be found? Always in the deepest enchantment that you have experienced.
Hofmannsthal

GEMINI
God gives to everyone what the self believes to deserve.
Roland Giguere

CANCER
Neurosis seems to be a human privilege.
Sigmund Freud

LEO
Living well is the best revenge.
George Herbert

VIRGO
Infinity transforms what is possible into the unavoidable.
N. Consines

LIBRA
He who does not know truth at sight is not worthy of her notice.
William Blake

SCORPIO
Error of opinion may be tolerated where reason is left free to combat it.
Thomas Jefferson

SAGITTARIUS
If you are not confused, you don't know what is happening.
London Underground

CAPRICORN
Even an ant can hurt an elephant.
Zulu Proverb

AQUARIUS
Striving to better, oft we mar what's well.
William Shakespeare

PISCES
Although the tree-trunk stays ten years under water, it will never become a crocodile.
Congolese Quote

21
FEBRUARY

What can you do to help?
Answer: Anything you can.

ARIES
Watch your step, because everybody else is!
Oscar Wilde

TAURUS
Every one will sleep as he makes his bed.
American Proverb

GEMINI
It is so sad to love everything, without knowing what one loves!
Publilius Syrus

CANCER
Greatness happens to common people, sometimes to people who are like me.
Tina Allen

LEO
A conclusion is the place you got to when you tired of thinking.
Anonymous

VIRGO
If you cleave the heart of one drop of water
There will issue from it a hundred oceans.
Shabistari

LIBRA
Water can either float or sink a ship.
Chinese Quote

SCORPIO
No matter how much this may shock mankind, the duty of philosophy is to say everything.
Marquis de Sade

SAGITTARIUS
This is not a just image, it is just an image.
Jean-Luc Godard

CAPRICORN
Everything that has been is eternal: the sea will wash it up again.
Nietzsche

AQUARIUS
Circles, though small, are yet complete.
American Quote

PISCES
All creation is a beginning of the conflict of one way of being against an imitation.
André Malraux

ARIES
The sage learns no learning, but reviews what others have passed through.
Tao Te Ching

TAURUS
Rest belongs to work as the eyelids to the eyes.
Rabindranath Tagore

GEMINI
The limits of your soul you could not discover, though traversing every path.
Heraclitus

CANCER
What you see is news; what you know is source; what you feel is opinion.
Anonymous

LEO
A man of virtuous words is not always a virtuous man.
Confucius

VIRGO
Nobody is more to me than I myself.
Max Steiner

LIBRA
I can believe anything, as long as it is unbelievable.
Oscar Wilde

SCORPIO
If your experiment needs statistics, you ought to have done better.
Ernest Rutheford

SAGITTARIUS
Positive, adj. Mistaken at the top of one's voice.
Ambrose Bierce

CAPRICORN
The burden of ones own choice is not felt.
American Proverb

AQUARIUS
Behold the turtle, he makes progress only when he sticks his neck out.
James Bryant Conant

PISCES
My mother was right, a marriage lasts with patience and determination.
Jeanne Buñuel (wife of Luis)

Absorb the vital energy of nature.

ARIES
A man or a woman shows their metal, doing what they can with what they have.
Charles Caleb Colton

TAURUS
Every man ponders his human condition with a certain air of melancholy.
Ralph Waldo Emerson

GEMINI
Love is but a tavern in the middle of life's journey.
Vauvenargues

CANCER
People who travel down the road of humility will never find gridlock.
Anonymous

LEO
An optimist is a fellow who believes what's going on will be postponed.
Kin Hubbard

VIRGO
The egg teaches the chicken how to breed.
Bantu Quote

LIBRA
New roads; new ruts.
G. K. Chesterton

SCORPIO
Even when a bird walks, one feels it has wings.
Antoine-Marin Lemierre

SAGITTARIUS
The saddest words are: "it could have been."
John G. Whittier

CAPRICORN
Many mediocre men have a lot of acquired knowledge.
Claude Bernard

AQUARIUS
Pleasure comes in ounces; pain comes in barrels.
Spanish Quote

PISCES
At a certain distance, everything looks the same.
Mexican Quote

Don't be afraid to ask for more.

ARIES
Proceed watching others' faults while you decrease yours at the same time.
John Wells

TAURUS
Every day hath its night, every weal its woe.
American Quote

GEMINI
To understand one another, it is necessary to be alike. To love each other, each one must be somewhat different.
Hannah Arendt

CANCER
One cannot both feast and become rich.
Ashanti Proverb

LEO
Pessimist—one who, when he has the choice of two evils, chooses both.
Oscar Wilde

VIRGO
What you don't begin, you cannot end.
Anonymous

LIBRA
And from the discontent of man, The world's best progress springs.
Ella Wheeler Wilcox

SCORPIO
God is alive—He just doesn't want to get involved.
Graffiti

SAGITTARIUS
The truth of a mistake appears before any kind of confusion.
Sir Francis Bacon

CAPRICORN
Once you sink that first stake, they'll never make you pull it up.
Matzuo Basho

AQUARIUS
Truth is the daughter of time, not of authority.
Sir Francis Bacon

PISCES
Everything alive is sacred, life delights in life.
William Blake

25
FEBRUARY

How could you not include yourself? Remember:
This world is special because you are in it.

ARIES
Marriage is the best way to discover your own faults.
Oscar Wilde

TAURUS
Everything should be simplified as much as it can, but no more.
Albert Einstein

GEMINI
Turn yourself into gold and then live wherever you please.
Sri Ramakrishna

CANCER
Too many people make the mistake of searching in the future for what they already have in the present.
Anonymous

LEO
Habit is a great deadener.
Samuel Beckett

VIRGO
The fingers of the same hand have different lengths.
Mexican Quote

LIBRA
Tact is changing a conversation without changing your mind.
Spanish Quote

SCORPIO
God has created the world in play.
Sri Ramakrishna

SAGITTARIUS
Conciseness is the sister of talent.
Anton Chekhov

CAPRICORN
Necessity is the mother of invention.
Anonymous

AQUARIUS
We must take people as they are, there are no others.
Konrad Adenauer

PISCES
To meditate has nothing to do with a "feeling," it has to do with what one is meditating on.
Charlotte Joko Beck

ARIES
A minimum good action is better than a maximum of good intention.
Mahatma Gandhi

TAURUS
Modification is the means by which all beings are produced.
Shi-ping-wen

GEMINI
Danger and delight grow on one stalk.
German Quote

CANCER
Human nature can not be changed, but many other things can be improved.
Anonymous

LEO
Tradition is a guide and not a jailer.
W. Somerset Maugham

VIRGO
Human beings have a part of animal within; their best part.
Nikito Nipongo

LIBRA
Everybody is the son of his own goings on.
Cervantes

SCORPIO
A hunch is creativity trying to tell you something.
Frank Capra

SAGITTARIUS
There are two ways of gliding through life: to believe in everything or to doubt everything; both save us from thinking.
Alfred Korzbski

CAPRICORN
Invention is the mother of necessity.
Anonymous

AQUARIUS
The luck of having talent is not enough, one must also have a talent for luck.
Hector Berlioz

PISCES
The future has not arrived as of yet, and the present is almost past.
Anonymous

27
FEBRUARY

Let strength make its own way.

ARIES
Yesterday's luxuries could be tomorrow's debts.
Arnold Toynbee

TAURUS
Transformation is the means by which all beings are absorbed.
Shi-ping-wen

GEMINI
The magic of our very first love is that we ignore that it ends.
Benjamin Disraeli

CANCER
Some young people who want to reach the moon, probably will!
Anonymous

LEO
How beautiful it is to do nothing, and then rest afterward.
Spanish Quote

VIRGO
Hope is the thing with feathers that perches in the soul.
Emily Dickinson

LIBRA
The main dangers in this life are the people who want to change everything or nothing.
Lady Astor

SCORPIO
From one learn to know all.
Virgil

SAGITTARIUS
When in doubt, leave it out.
Anonymous

CAPRICORN
If necessity is the mother of invention, what was father doing?
Ruth Weekly

AQUARIUS
Any act of disobedience, as any act of freedom, is the beginning of reason.
Erich Fromm

PISCES
Contentment is the smother of invention.
Cynics calendar

You must respect the sensitive side
of your nature to master it.

28
FEBRUARY

ARIES
There are no riches that can compensate for lack of character.
Publilius Syrus

TAURUS
The further you go, the less you know.
Lao-Tzu

GEMINI
Intelligent discontent is the mainspring of civilization.
Arnold Toynebee

CANCER
A child is a question we make to destiny.
Anonymous

LEO
Everybody believes, easily, that which he fears or desires.
Jean de la Fontaine

VIRGO
Real life is absent, we are not in this world.
Arthur Rimbaud

LIBRA
We are all standing around in each others data.
Daniel C. Dennett

SCORPIO
I never think about the future, anyway it comes too fast.
Albert Einstein

SAGITTARIUS
The value of a whole must not be assumed to be the same as the sum of its parts.
G. E. Moore

CAPRICORN
I am the proprietor of my destiny; the captain of my soul.
William E. Henley

AQUARIUS
Knowing too much is ageing prematurely.
Russian Quote

PISCES
Suffer to know, suffer to have.
Chinese Quote

29
FEBRUARY

"A lifetime of happiness: no man alive could bear it:
it would be hell on earth" George Bernard Shaw

ARIES
The wise man does at once what the fool does finally.
Baltasar Gracián

TAURUS
I am a citizen not of Athens or Greece, but of the world.
Socrates

GEMINI
The planets show again and again all the phenomena which god desired to be seen from earth.
Georg Joachim Rheticus

CANCER
Whosoever finds peace at home, is the happiest of all men.
Goethe

LEO
Only a person who can live with himself can enjoy the gift of leisure.
Henry Greber

VIRGO
Stay focused.
Lauren Hill

LIBRA
Surely the strange beauty of the world must somewhere rest on pure joy.
Louise Bogan

SCORPIO
Without effort he sets in motion all things by mind and thought.
Xenophanes

SAGITTARIUS
The way up and the way down are one and the same.
Heraclitus

CAPRICORN
One must be someone to do something.
Goethe

AQUARIUS
Chance is order in time.
Guillermo P. Villalta

PISCES
It is said that a wise man rules over the stars; this does not mean that he rules over the influences which come from the stars in the sky; but that he rules over the powers which exist in his own constitution.
Johannes Kepler

MARCH

MARCH

One day makes way for another.

Horace

What makes up March: the Ides of March, the March hare, or march ahead? Perhaps all three, as madness, mayhem, and movement sweep through the month. In March the Zodiac ends with Pisces and begins a brand-new astrological year once again, with Aries. Like the linking of atoms, the Zodiac glyphs here become an everlasting ouroboros, the medieval dragon that eats its own tail, symbolic of material and spiritual unity. Amazing and contradictory things happen now. "How much better is a word in season" goes the saying, so if things don't work out in March the way you had planned, try again, with different timing, in a different month. This is the best of times to say tomorrow is another day, even if your name is not Scarlett.

ARIES

March (and April!) are both months during which you should weigh each of your words as if they were pieces of gold. This month, focus in on what is going on around you; face reality yet feel protected. You are. Your mind should be "teaming with schemes," and as the month unfolds, things get better and better.

Keyword: Quality

TAURUS

"The moment one gives close attention to anything, even a blade of grass, it becomes mysterious, awesome, an indescribably, magnificent world in itself." This Henry Miller quote gives the clearest recommendation of what Taurus should, could, and can do in March, at any time of the night or day, or even (because of your clout) in-between! Use all your senses—and take leave of them, too, a little—if it means you'll experience life to the fullest this month.

Keyword: Experience

GEMINI

Your energy should be on double-time just now, Gemini. So plug in, recharge, and try to use your power in the best of all possible ways—even if this is not the best of all possible worlds this month. You can do so much more for yourself by following your own directions. The Earth hurling through space at 30,000 kilometers per second, reaches Aries during the last week of the month, which means your personal weather forecast calls for sunnier days ahead.

Keywords: Distract yourself

CANCER

Now is the time to plan where you are going, with whom, and why. Whether you travel in a plane, over water, upon the hardy Earth, or in your dreams, Cancer, use your imagination to the hilt. You need to build as well as climb a personal staircase but don't lose your footing. Once the Sun is in Aries, even moments after leaving Pisces, it is likely to light up your lucky stars, and you will find that things can be even better than you think. It is all a matter of perspective.

Keywords: Moving on

LEO

You don't have to be present to make your presence felt this month, Leo. You'll shine being there, or not being there. During the thirty or so days that the Sun passes through the sign of Pisces in February and March, you can replay, replenish, or retake possession of whatever you set your mind to. Go as wild as you like in order to make things happen—just remember to "look through your heart without closing your eyes."

Keyword: Mingle

VIRGO

All you have to do this month, Virgo, for things to turn out right is to listen to Cicero, who once wrote that, "no thinker has ever said that a change of mind was inconsistency." So go ahead. Change your mind and your focus! You can make your mark during the wonderful March-ahead days, as long as you keep the above in mind and do not get overwhelmed by anything!

Keywords: Setting trends

LIBRA

Some tottering in your usually balanced stance or a bit of stormy weather generally does you some good. It shakes things up so that you can get down to the business of taking better care of yourself, Libra. Forget "what's out there" and find what's within yourself, instead. "Health is better than wealth" goes an old saying, but an even wiser one states, "I've been rich and poor, and rich is better." So try to watch your body so the mind can keep up with it and help you get all the goodies you deserve.

Keywords: Cut a little slack

SCORPIO

You Scorpios are masters at inventing things—and situations—so now is the time to invent your own dreamed-for reality, because you can make anyone believe in you and you can make anything work out! So take a moment. Figure out your very own, very special effects to make it all happen, and then show the world what it is you have to give—on your own terms. Just keep your fingers crossed so lady luck is always at your side. And really, where else would she be?

Keyword: Interplay

SAGITTARIUS

Aristophanes once said that "you cannot make a crab walk straight," but you can try. And with this in mind, Sagittarius, try to check your independent ways this month. You have to learn, maybe the hard way, to relate, to share concepts and yourself. All things considered, this is a perfect time to teach yourself how to respond and react to life's little imponderables.
Keyword: Congeniality

CAPRICORN

To be "as sharp as you can," you should use to your own personal advantage any wise, witty, or popular knowledge. A quote, a proverb, or a saying that contains humor, love, fatalism, or faith. You are not one to usually depend on the fun factor but this month give it a try while you listen and learn from others.
Keywords: Be as sharp as you can

AQUARIUS

In March, Aquarians are able to deal with authority and get things done in their own way. You might have to tighten up your act with a little self-discipline. But if you let go of your inborn stubbornness, at least during this part of the year, instead of losing, you will gain. You could actually win what you thought you were losing, and then start counting your blessings.
Keyword: Mediate

PISCES

Henry Miller once said that if peace does exist among men, it will be because of being, not of having, and Pisces is perfectly cut out to show all the other signs how to go about doing just this, especially in March. You can be our household philosopher or saint. During your birthday month you seem to hold the rest of us up, with feet planted firmly on the ground (Pisces seems to rule that part of the body in general). You see, once you've made peace with yourself, you can help people find "their way."
Keyword: Revelations

1
MARCH

To look into space is to look back in time;
do it and renew a thought.

ARIES
The great use of a life is to spend it for something that outlasts it.
William James

TAURUS
Every age, like every human body, has its own distemper.
Ralph Waldo Emerson

GEMINI
Here today and gone tomorrow!
Ovid

CANCER
Eternity is written in the skies.
Edward Young

LEO
Time does not become sacred to us until we have lived it.
William Burroughs

VIRGO
I will lend you the wings of the future, for I have them.
Ralph Waldo Emerson

LIBRA
I believe the future is only the past again, entered through another gate.
Pinero

SCORPIO
The quick of all time is the instant.
D. H. Lawrence

SAGITTARIUS
In the presence of eternity, the mountains are as transient as the clouds.
Ingersoll

CAPRICORN
The comic is the perception of the opposite; humor is the feeling of it.
Umberto Eco

AQUARIUS
That which comes after ever conforms to that which has gone before.
Marcus Aurelius

PISCES
Life is a play! 'Tis not its length, but its performance that counts.
Seneca

Hold on to the present—you'll be amazed
at what you can get away with.

ARIES
It is much wiser to watch where you are going than to look at where you have already been.
Paul Harvey

TAURUS
The world has much more to offer than only to increase our speed.
Mahatma Gandhi

GEMINI
Curiosity is one of the permanent characteristics of a true and vigorous intellect.
Samuel Johnson

CANCER
Plan your work and then work out your plan.
Anonymous

LEO
Let me have my own way exactly in everything, and a sunnier and pleasanter creature does not exist.
Thomas Carlyle

VIRGO
The entity is everything that knows.
Aristotle

LIBRA
How can we be certain that we are not impostors?
Jacques Lacan

SCORPIO
Things we do not expect, happen more frequently than we wish.
Plautus

SAGITTARIUS
What is for us, today, a paradox, will be a provable truth in posterity.
Denis Diderot

CAPRICORN
Humor is to laugh about something that you don't have when you should have it.
Langston Hughes

AQUARIUS
As you try to understand everything, you will understand nothing.
Shunryu Suzuki

PISCES
Motion being eternal, the first mover, if there is but one, will be eternal also.
Aristotle

3

You are the composer of your own scale in time.

MARCH

ARIES
All is well, and all will be well, and all things will come to pass well.
Julian of Norwich

TAURUS
There are some gusts that interfere with men's humors.
T. S. Eliot

GEMINI
Being busy is one of the basic necessities to be content.
Leigh Hunt

CANCER
What is the universe like? Expansive and autoreproductive.
Stephen Hawking

LEO
If I am worth anything, it is because of the confidence that I have been given by other men.
Emiliano Zapata

VIRGO
Does God know beforehand how we act?
Boecio

LIBRA
Man plans his journey by his own wit.
Anonymous

SCORPIO
The dreamer may pass, but the dream never will.
Dana Burnet

SAGITTARIUS
We are two chasms, a well looking steadily towards the sky.
Fernando Pessoa

CAPRICORN
It is great to watch the rain while one is dry!
Mexican Proverb

AQUARIUS
The best thing is to understand yourself, and then you will understand everything.
Shunryu Suzuki

PISCES
The magic of the tongue is the most dangerous of all spells.
Bulwer-Lytton

Yes, you are a part of the great matter-transforming motor that is our Galaxy. Keep it burning.

ARIES
You do not need to anticipate the future, just to let it happen.
Antoine de Saint-Exupéry

TAURUS
Venus, your eternal vibration makes all men obey and do.
Euripides

GEMINI
Talent is to real intelligence what vinegar is to a strong wine.
Jules Renard

CANCER
The best theories are poetic creations.
Stephen Hawking

LEO
The aim of life is to live, and to live means to be aware, joyously, drunkenly, serenely, divinely aware.
Henry Miller

VIRGO
Life is a long lesson in humility.
Sir James M. Barrie

LIBRA
Man's roots are much more important than their foliage.
Rumi

SCORPIO
Future men will fight for an unknown number of liberties that we do not need yet.
Max Steiner

SAGITTARIUS
A normal person takes adversity better than prosperity.
Anonymous

CAPRICORN
If you give quickly you give doubly.
Anonymous

AQUARIUS
Good fortune is like crystal: it shines but it is fragile.
Latin Quote

PISCES
We must conceive of this whole universe as one commonwealth of which both gods and men are members.
Cicero

5
MARCH

ARIES
Words should be as clothes, carefully custom-made to fit the thought.
Jules Renard

TAURUS
I am authentic. I will make no mistake. I will not say I am sorry. I will not give in an inch, and I will make myself heard.
William Lloyd Garrison

GEMINI
May my outer head not spoil my inner head.
Yoruban Proverb

CANCER
Impossible is a word only to be found in the dictionary of fools.
Napoleon Bonaparte

LEO
The most important thing is to be honest to oneself.
Universal Quote

VIRGO
Everything great that man has done has been done by neurotics. They alone founded our religions and created our works of art.
Marcel Proust

LIBRA
A little leaven leaveneth the whole lump.
Galatians 5:9

SCORPIO
There is nothing more dangerous than a stubborn person with a good memory.
Carlos Monsivais

SAGITTARIUS
Education is an ornament in property and a refuge in adversity.
Anonymous

CAPRICORN
Who learns to live with hope, dies a happy man.
Chinese Quote

AQUARIUS
All combinations originate from the same original and simple source.
Marsilio Ficino

PISCES
We are all inside a profound hell, within which every moment is a miracle.
E. M. Cioran

Be especially aware that someone is always
ready to look for you. You are needed.

6
MARCH

ARIES
Remember: it is good for you to bear those who are around you, because they also bear you.
Samuel Johnson

TAURUS
You begin saving the world by saving one person at a time . . .
Charles Bukowski

GEMINI
Everything happens twice, and sometimes three times.
Isak Dinesen

CANCER
Our bodies are our autobiography.
Greek Quote

LEO
Honesty gives strength but it does not give much popularity.
Kin Hubbard

VIRGO
Before I realized that the best part of my life had arrived, it was gone.
Ashleigh Brilliant

LIBRA
Organize the unorganized.
John L. Lewis

SCORPIO
Man does not live by words alone, despite the fact that sometimes he has to eat them.
Adlai Stevenson

SAGITTARIUS
Since all life is futility, then the decision to exist must be the most irrational of all.
E. M. Cioran

CAPRICORN
The free mind must have one policeman, Irony.
Elbert Hubbard

AQUARIUS
Rejoice in hope, be patient in affliction, and have faith.
Saint Peter

PISCES
The soul is in each body, in all of it and in each of its parts.
Saint Augustine

7
MARCH

The best time of the day to read a quote
is when you feel ready to.

ARIES
As a general rule, prosperity is what puts us into debt.
Ethel Watts Mumford

TAURUS
Men voluntarily believe in what they desire.
Julius Ceasar

GEMINI
There is false modesty, but there is no false pride.
Jules Renard

CANCER
Men believe in the impossible, but never in the improbable.
Oscar Wilde

LEO
Very few can do better having themselves as an example.
Ogden Nash

VIRGO
We all emulate and borrow; life is theater and literature is an aphorism.
Ralph Waldo Emerson

LIBRA
I had a lover's quarrel with the world.
Robert Frost

SCORPIO
Magic has the power to experience and fathom things that are inaccessible to human reason.
Paracelsus

SAGITTARIUS
Law never made men a whit more just.
Henry David Thoreau

CAPRICORN
Put a twinkle in your eye.
Anonymous

AQUARIUS
If your heart is quite set upon a crown, make and put on one of roses.
Epictetus

PISCES
When your soul has found its remedy, you will be free from all evils.
Hindu Proverb

Find your own inherent capacity to turn lost time
into the catching of a falling star.

8
MARCH

ARIES
When one doesn't want to, two cannot have a fight.
Chinese Quote

TAURUS
In war, resolution; in defeat, challenge; in victory, magnanimity; in peace, good will.
Winston Churchill

GEMINI
With thee conversing I forget all times, all seasons and their change.
John Milton

CANCER
The world is full of small pleasures; art consists in knowing how to identify them.
Li Tai-Po

LEO
Doubt is a mountain that only faith can move.
French Quote

VIRGO
Events of great consequence often spring from trifling circumstances.
Livy

LIBRA
Crawling on your hands and knees will never keep you from walking vertically.
Kenyan Quote

SCORPIO
Whoever confronts paradox exposes himself to reality.
Friedrich Durrenmatt

SAGITTARIUS
A person can not make another happy, but he can make him unhappy.
Thomas Szasz

CAPRICORN
Love in its essence is spiritual fire.
Swedenborg

AQUARIUS
If a man has strong faith he can indulge in the luxury of skepticism.
Nietzsche

PISCES
Nine tenths of wisdom consists in being wise in time.
Theodore Roosevelt

9

MARCH

Real personal conviction can always draw a crowd.

ARIES
The best reformers in the world are those who begin with themselves.
Manu

TAURUS
What is character, if not determination of incidents.
Henry James

GEMINI
I have never hated a man enough to give him back his diamonds.
Zsa Zsa Gabor

CANCER
Hitch your wagon to a star.
Ralph Waldo Emerson

LEO
This "I and Mine" causes the whole
misery . . . we are made slaves by attachment.
Vivekananda

VIRGO
Trust in God, and keep your powder dry.
Oliver Cromwell

LIBRA
He who has health has hope, and he who has hope has everything.
Arabian Quote

SCORPIO
A tree depicts divinest plan, But God himself lives in a man.
Anonymous

SAGITTARIUS
Everybody possesses their own fears.
Mexican Quote

CAPRICORN
Every reform was once a private opinion.
Ralph Waldo Emerson

AQUARIUS
The feast of reason, and the flow of soul.
Alexander Pope

PISCES
If a man could half his wishes, he would double his troubles.
Benjamin Franklin

Silence will be your best reply.

ARIES
Carefully, you can do all you should do.
Burmese Quote

TAURUS
What is an incident, if not illustration of character.
Henry James

GEMINI
The secret of happiness is freedom, and the secret of freedom, courage.
Thucydides

CANCER
Generally we see things not the way they are, but the way we are.
Hungarian Quote

LEO
You can prove "a" truth with an epigraph, "the" truth, never.
Graffiti

VIRGO
The best man stumbles.
Anonymous

LIBRA
The poet is the priest of the invisible.
Wallace Stevens

SCORPIO
Don't play what's there, play what isn't there.
Miles Davis

SAGITTARIUS
Through others I am somebody.
African Quote

CAPRICORN
Lots of folks confuse management with destiny.
Kin Hubbard

AQUARIUS
A handful of patience is worth more than a bushel of brains.
Dutch Quote

PISCES
I am as free as I am within my own self.
Hegel

11
MARCH

Listen to yourself listening to others.

ARIES
Quality not quantity is my measure.
Douglas Jerrold

TAURUS
What should a man be like? I would say like himself!
Henrik Ibsen

GEMINI
A glass can be either half full or half empty.
Anonymous

CANCER
We carry our homes within us, which enables us to fly.
John Cage

LEO
Be thy own palace, or the world's thy jail.
John Donne

VIRGO
Measurement of life should be proportioned rather to the intensity of the experience than to its actual length.
Thomas Hardy

LIBRA
Asleep, nobody is a hypocrite.
William Hazlitt

SCORPIO
There is nothing worth more than this day!
Goethe

SAGITTARIUS
Ideal society is a drama enacted exclusively in the imagination.
Santayana

CAPRICORN
Secondary things are much more important than primary ones.
François Fénelon

AQUARIUS
Keep a thing for seven years and you will find use for it.
Irish Proverb

PISCES
I love to pray at sunrise before the world becomes polluted with vanity and hatred.
The Koreiser Rabbi

"Where are you? The Sun, the Moon, the day, the night; summer, winter, not in vain but in orderly succession do they march to their destined place, to their goal." Inca Prayer to a Cosmic God

ARIES
Egotism is the glue with which you get stuck in yourself.
Dan Post

TAURUS
There is nothing in Christianity or Buddhism that quite matches the sympathetic unselfishness of an oyster.
Saki

GEMINI
Though canst not stir a flower, Without troubling of a star.
Francis Thompson

CANCER
Would there be this eternal seeking if the found existed?
Antonio Porchia

LEO
Drink in the wind.
Tibetan Quote

VIRGO
Our insignificance is often the cause of our safety.
Aesop

LIBRA
A cold causes less suffering than an idea.
Jules Renard

SCORPIO
My time is TODAY.
George Gershwin

SAGITTARIUS
What we have never had, remains; It is the things we have that go.
Sara Teasdale

CAPRICORN
True religion will never oppose intellect.
Italian Quote

AQUARIUS
The true direction is that everyone must measure his way with his own ruler.
Horace

PISCES
I need few things, and the few things I need, I need them rarely.
Saint Francis of Assisi

13
MARCH

Deductive speculation at times works wonders that inductive reasoning cannot.

ARIES
The unknown always passes for the marvelous.
Tacitus

TAURUS
Men are neither good nor bad; they are born with instincts and abilities.
Honoré de Balzac

GEMINI
It was not of a time, it was for all times.
Leslie Caron

CANCER
Follow the gleam.
Alfred Lord Tennyson

LEO
The best way to please those around you is to listen to them.
Anonymous

VIRGO
Money is good for bribing yourself through the inconveniences of life.
Gottfried Reinhardt

LIBRA
Man's feet have grown so big that he forgets his littleness.
Don Marquis

SCORPIO
Explaining comes in many ways, as many as there are teachers and questions.
Anonymous

SAGITTARIUS
An idea can be invalid even though men have given their life for it.
Ikram Antaki

CAPRICORN
We say, "Time flies."
Time does not exist. We are the ones moving about.
The Talmud

AQUARIUS
I try to arrange my life to myself, and not my self to life.
Horace

PISCES
My heart is heavy with the life I am surpassing.
Nahuatl Quote

Coexistence is delicate, for it depends
on the fluttering of an idea.

14
MARCH

ARIES
If you cannot build a town, build a heart.
Kurd Quote

TAURUS
Analogies do not prove anything, this is true, but they make you feel better and at ease.
Sigmund Freud

GEMINI
Let us thank the fools. If it were not for them, the rest of us could not achieve.
Mark Twain

CANCER
What the imagination seizes as beauty must be true.
John Keats

LEO
The individual never asserts himself more than when he forgets himself.
André Gide

VIRGO
To oblige persons often costs little and helps much.
Baltasar Gracián

LIBRA
It is good to know the truth, but it is better to talk about palm trees.
Arab Quote

SCORPIO
When we say something is in a certain place, all we really mean is that it is at that place in relation to other things.
René Descartes

SAGITTARIUS
The best effect of fine persons is felt after we have left their presence.
T. S. Eliot

CAPRICORN
You are WHERE you eat!
Pamela Fiori

AQUARIUS
Freedom is only conceivable when it has to do with intelligence.
Johann G. Fichte

PISCES
When in doubt, consult your pillow.
Anonymous

15
MARCH

Get to know your limits. Just being comfortable
with them is a step outside of your own bounds.

ARIES
Sometimes, a smile passes like a bolt, but its memory lasts a lifetime.
Chazal

TAURUS
No one can understand unless, holding to his own nature, he respects the free nature of others.
Graffiti

GEMINI
To know happiness one must have the gall to swallow it.
Charles Baudelaire

CANCER
Age and time are but timidities of thought.
Eugene O'Neill

LEO
He who divides gets the worst share.
Spanish Quote

VIRGO
Inspiration could be called the inhalation of the memory of an act that has never been experienced.
Ned Rorem

LIBRA
Calumny is only the noise of madmen.
Diogenes

SCORPIO
By a small sample we may judge of the whole piece.
Cervantes

SAGITTARIUS
Anybody who is any good is different from anybody else.
Felix Frankfurter

CAPRICORN
We always like those who admire us, but we do not always like those whom we admire.
La Rochefoucauld

AQUARIUS
Glory comes from the unchanging din-din-din of one supreme gift.
F. Scott Fitzgerald

PISCES
Loneliness is a nest for the thoughts.
Kyrgyzstan Quote

"There is gold, and a multitude of rubies: but the lips of knowledge are a precious jewel." Proverbs 20:15

16
MARCH

ARIES
Bessie Smith showed me the air and taught me how to fill it.
Janis Joplin

TAURUS
Whatever we build, let us do it as if it were forever.
John Ruskin

GEMINI
The faster you go, the more control there is.
Gerald Arpino

CANCER
The happiest of all lives is a busy solitude.
Voltaire

LEO
Nothing but the astonishing is beautiful.
André Breton

VIRGO
If it is art, it is not for all. If it is for all, it is not art.
Arnold Schonberg

LIBRA
Hot can be cool, and cool can be hot.
Louis Armstrong

SCORPIO
Be yourself. The world worships the original.
Ingrid Bergman

SAGITTARIUS
Man is ready to die for an idea, provided that idea is not quite clear to him.
Paul Eldridge

CAPRICORN
Every story is completed by the reader.
Grace Paley

AQUARIUS
It is not good to be too free, nor to have everything one wants.
Blaise Pascal

PISCES
Greatness breaks laws.
Louise Nevelson

17
MARCH

The cosmic dance of planets will help to unfold
ideas for every sign of the Zodiac and bring
to each one of us something special.

ARIES
Success could consist in doing everyday things uncommonly well.
F. Crane

TAURUS
Just listen with the vastness of the world in mind. You can't fail to get the message.
Pierre Boulez

GEMINI
After truth, there is nothing as beautiful as fiction.
Antonio Machado

CANCER
All I mean by truth is what I can't help thinking.
Oliver Wendell Holmes

LEO
A bit of inaccuracy sometimes saves tons of explanations.
Saki

VIRGO
Great Time makes all things dim.
Sophocles

LIBRA
Any fool can make a rule, and all fools follow them.
Mexican Quote

SCORPIO
A point is a nexus of real entities with a certain form.
Alfred North Whitehead

SAGITTARIUS
Wood can be used to create carvings or to build a fire.
Anonymous

CAPRICORN
Men know each other by the company they avoid.
Anonymous

AQUARIUS
Whatever it is that you wish for as you pray, believe you'll get it and you will.
Saint Mark

PISCES
The salvation brought by Christ is not natural but personal.
Georgio Agamben

Trust your instincts, believe in yourself,
you are your own lucky star.

ARIES
Most people only do what they are asked to do; success comes to those who do a little more.
Karl Kraus

TAURUS
Time is the only critic that has no ambition.
John Steinbeck

GEMINI
If you cannot explain what you are doing, your work will not be worth anything.
Erwin Schrodinger

CANCER
No matter how many miles a man may travel, he will never get ahead of himself.
George Ade

LEO
Remember that the conquest of glory surpasses the glory of the conquest.
Leonardo da Vinci

VIRGO
What you cannot change, better forget.
Yugoslavian Quote

LIBRA
Man learns in two ways. By doing and by being done.
Anonymous

SCORPIO
A specific point is not necessary.
Aristotle

SAGITTARIUS
I asked for riches to be happy; I was given poverty to be able to get wise.
Spanish Quote

CAPRICORN
It is always easier to stay.
Anonymous

AQUARIUS
The most difficult plagiarism to avoid is autoplagiarism.
Marcel Proust

PISCES
It is very foolish to fear what cannot be avoided.
Publilius Syrus

19
MARCH

Ride the wave and rely on duality of temperament as we ease into another sign of the Zodiac.

ARIES
Words should be weighed and not counted.
Yiddish Quote

TAURUS
Dare to be wise.
Horace

GEMINI
It is as risky to believe everything as it is to believe nothing.
Denis Diderot

CANCER
I would love to spend the rest of my life traveling, if I could have another life to stay at home.
William Hazlitt

LEO
Never judge a book by its cover.
English Quote

VIRGO
Better to aim at the moon than shoot at the well.
Heard in Indiana

LIBRA
If you always tell the truth, nobody will trust you.
Ashleigh Brilliant

SCORPIO
Yet man is born unto trouble, as the sparks fly upward.
Job 5:7

SAGITTARIUS
I asked for all those things to enjoy life; I was given life so as to enjoy all things.
Spanish Quote

CAPRICORN
As you make your bed, so must you lie in it.
Anonymous

AQUARIUS
Memory is the diary that we all carry about with us.
Oscar Wilde

PISCES
The more civilized you are, the more unhappy you become.
Anton Chekov

*Do not discriminate in dispensing your love,
consciousness, and will. Persist and go forward.*

20
MARCH

ARIES
He who ties well unties well.
Mexican Quote

TAURUS
I'll not listen to reason. Reason always means what someone else has got to say.
Elizabeth Gaskell

GEMINI
In heaven, an angel is nobody in particular.
George Bernard Shaw

CANCER
Travel makes a wise man better but a fool much worse.
Anonymous

LEO
If you live long enough you live to see everything.
Anonymous

VIRGO
You can never really get away, you can only take yourself somewhere else.
Peter's Almanac

LIBRA
Men tire themselves in pursuit of rest.
Anonymous

SCORPIO
We are too late for the gods, too early for Being. Being's poem, just begun, is man.
Martin Heidegger

SAGITTARIUS
The biggest human temptation is to settle for too little.
Thomas Merton

CAPRICORN
Start every day with a smile and get it over with.
W. C. Fields

AQUARIUS
Error has its own logic, just as truth does.
Georg V. Plejanov

PISCES
We need a faculty that enables us to envision our objective from afar, and that faculty is intuition.
Jules-Henri Poincaré

21
MARCH

There are those who regard this day as the day of Creation, the one during which God made Sun, Moon, and stars. And so, begins measurable time.

ARIES
There is always more spirit in attack than in defense.
Livy

TAURUS
Nothing is a loss of time, if you enjoy the day.
Arthur Koestler

GEMINI
Saintliness is only acceptable in saints.
Pamela H. Johnson

CANCER
The traveler sees what he sees; the tourist sees what he came to see.
G. K. Chesterton

LEO
Fools who are in a hurry drink tea with a fork.
Chinese Quote

VIRGO
The fault, dear Brutus, is not in the stars, But in ourselves, that we are underlings.
William Shakespeare

LIBRA
Life begins on the other side of desperation.
Jean-Paul Sartre

SCORPIO
We do not change our locations, we change our nature.
Gaston Bachelard

SAGITTARIUS
Let heaven exist, even if our place results being in hell.
Jorge Luis Borges

CAPRICORN
Trivialities are the Sundays of stupidity.
Anonymous

AQUARIUS
I love everything that is old; old friends, old times, old manners, old books, old wines.
Oliver Goldsmith

PISCES
If you can spend a perfectly idle afternoon in a perfectly idle way, you have learned to live.
Lin Yu-T'ang

Each day carries a story that can be shared.

ARIES
The future is much like the present, only longer.
Don Quisenberry

TAURUS
It is impossible to enjoy idling unless there is plenty of work to do.
Jerome K. Jerome

GEMINI
We must learn to live together like brothers, or we will perish together like fools.
Martin Luther King, Jr.

CANCER
The best slogan for the traveler is: "let yourself go."
American Quote

LEO
When God wants something to happen, he puts things in motion so that you reach that something.
Babikr Bedri

VIRGO
If you can't be the first, make sure you are not the last.
English Quote

LIBRA
The only threat is inertia.
Saint John Pierce

SCORPIO
Renew yourself completely, each day; do it again, and again once more, and forever, again.
Chinese Quote

SAGITTARIUS
Spring: an experience in immorality.
Henry David Thoreau

CAPRICORN
Like all dreamers, I mistook disenchantment for truth.
Jean-Paul Sartre

AQUARIUS
If a problem has no solution, why worry?
Tibetan Quote

PISCES
A sparrow does not announce the spring.
Aristotle

23
MARCH

If you can look objectively at yourself, you can have a good day.

ARIES
Kind deeds begin with kind thoughts.
Leo Tolstoy

TAURUS
Whoever sees me, sees who sent me.
Saint John

GEMINI
He said true things, but called them by wrong names.
Robert Browning

CANCER
The day I read all the words that exist in Sanskrit to say "the absolute," I realized that I was living in the wrong country.
E. M. Cioran

LEO
Not even the bravest man can fight further than his strength allows him to.
Homer

VIRGO
Astuteness overcomes all difficulties.
Manlio

LIBRA
It's not true that life is one damn thing after another: it is one damn thing after another again and again.
Edna St. Vincent Millay

SCORPIO
I believe a leaf of grass is no less than the journey-work of the stars.
Walt Whitman

SAGITTARIUS
Lord, I believe; help thou mine unbelief.
Saint Mark

CAPRICORN
The art of living is more like wrestling than dancing.
Marcus Aurelius

AQUARIUS
It is unpleasant to go alone, even to be drowned.
Russian Quote

PISCES
Our remedies oft in ourselves do lie, which we ascribe to heaven.
William Shakespeare

Subordinate your ego and let inner serenity take over.

24
MARCH

ARIES
Actions are always the best interpreters of thoughts.
T. H. Huxley

TAURUS
God, any God, or God overpowering, communicates with man through nature.
Johannes Kepler

GEMINI
Equality is a useless search; equality of opportunities is what is noble.
Ian McLeod

CANCER
We can change our minds ten, twenty, thirty times a day, but let us look for the truth.
E. M. Cioran

LEO
God permits, but not forever.
Chilean Quote

VIRGO
If you have a job without aggravations, you don't have a job.
Malcom Forbes

LIBRA
Real life has no plot.
Ivy Compton-Burnett

SCORPIO
If nobody asks me, I know; if somebody asks me, I don't know.
Saint Augustine

SAGITTARIUS
Love is what you've been through with somebody.
James Thurber

CAPRICORN
If you think education is expensive, try ignorance.
Derek Bok

AQUARIUS
All men are fools for at least five minutes a day. Wisdom consists in not going past that limit.
La Rochefoucauld

PISCES
Let others praise ancient times; I am glad I was born in these.
Ovid

25
MARCH

On Earth we are framed by sunrise and sunset, but in space there is no up or down. Go beyond specifics.

ARIES
Good manners are shown by tolerating bad ones.
George Bernard Shaw

TAURUS
It is good that everyone finds their own comfort in whichever crutch they choose to use.
Jiddu Krishnamurti

GEMINI
All good books are alike in that they are truer than if they really happened.
Ernest Hemingway

CANCER
One can only see truthfully with the heart, what is essential is invisible to the eye.
Antoine de Saint-Exupéry

LEO
Some get pears without asking, and others don't even get alms, though they beg.
Indonesian Quote

VIRGO
We spend and we spend billing the future. And the future goes bankrupt.
Friedrich Hebbel

LIBRA
Cure sometimes, soothe frequently, comfort always.
Anonymous

SCORPIO
In humility, one must imitate Jesus and Socrates.
Benjamin Franklin

SAGITTARIUS
There are men who never make mistakes for they have never done anything.
Goethe

CAPRICORN
Better untaught than ill taught.
Anonymous

AQUARIUS
Everybody's stupidity can be like a caricature of their intelligence.
John Sterling

PISCES
If it weren't for the last minute, nothing would get done.
Anonymous

The best thing for you is to take yourself into account.

ARIES
Come quickly, I am tasting the stars!
Dom Perignon at the moment of discovering champagne

TAURUS
Even if you are on the right track, you'll get run over if you just sit there.
Will Rogers

GEMINI
It is easier to get forgiveness than permission.
Murphy's Law

CANCER
The fear of being deceived is a vulgar version of the search for truth.
E. M. Cioran

LEO
When there is a lot to put in them, a day has a hundred pockets.
Nietzsche

VIRGO
Psychoanalysis is that mental illness for which it regards itself a therapy.
Karl Kraus

LIBRA
Memory is that thing with which you forget yourself.
Alexander Chase

SCORPIO
Ninety percent of everything is crap.
Theodore Sturgeon

SAGITTARIUS
His absence is good company.
Scottish Saying

CAPRICORN
The best way to keep your word is not to give it.
Napoleon Bonaparte

AQUARIUS
Would you live with ease, do what you ought, and not what you please.
Anonymous

PISCES
A change of fortune hurts a wise man no more than a change of the moon.
Benjamin Franklin

Decide on one single goal, make it exclusive.

ARIES
We can only change the world by changing man.
Persian Quote

TAURUS
We need to see our fears and our resources as a net through which one needs to learn to navigate.
Jiddu Krishnamurti

GEMINI
No one exists who cannot teach something to someone.
Baltasar Gracián

CANCER
Think of three things—whence you came, where you are going, and to whom you must account.
Benjamin Franklin

LEO
Nobody loves himself too much.
Benjamin Whichcote

VIRGO
I was thrown out of NYU for cheating on my metaphysics final.
Woody Allen

LIBRA
All sins cast long shadows.
Irish Quote

SCORPIO
Hurry up, slowly.
Latin Quote

SAGITTARIUS
We need the free competition of minds.
Mikhail Gorbachev

CAPRICORN
The flea though he kill none, he does all the harm he can.
John Donne

AQUARIUS
Friendship is love without its wings.
Lord Byron

PISCES
Do as you will and keep what you see to yourself.
Spanish Quote

Forms, sensations, and symbols can have
brand new meanings if you allow them to.

28
MARCH

ARIES
The best thing is doing what others say cannot be done.
Anonymous

TAURUS
The human body is the best picture of the human soul.
Ludwig Wittgenstein

GEMINI
And there is no one who is so superior that he cannot be bettered.
Baltasar Gracián

CANCER
The "no meddling" is the other person's job.
African Quote

LEO
Egotism is the essence of a noble soul.
Nietzsche

VIRGO
On a metaphysician: A blind man in a dark room, looking for a black hat which is not there.
Lord Bowen

LIBRA
Your health comes first; you can always hang yourself later.
Yiddish Quote

SCORPIO
The stable wears out a horse more than the road.
Anonymous

SAGITTARIUS
This dark brightness that falls from the stars.
Corneille

CAPRICORN
Beware the fury of a patient man.
John Dryden

AQUARIUS
I don't believe in God but I do believe in His saints.
Edith Wharton

PISCES
What is the proof that I know something? Most certainly not my saying I know it!
Ludwig Wittgenstein

29
MARCH

Promote innovation and let yourself go.

ARIES
There will always be more opportunities than accomplishments.
Anonymous

TAURUS
Divide each difficulty into as many parts as is feasible and necessary to resolve it.
René Descartes

GEMINI
There are many things in your heart that you can never tell to another person.
Greta Garbo

CANCER
One is as good as the other, or one is as bad. It depends.
Graffiti

LEO
There is no wealth but life.
John Ruskin

VIRGO
Nothing so absurd can be said, that some philosopher has not already voiced.
Cicero

LIBRA
Early to bed and early to rise, makes a man healthy, wealthy and wise.
Benjamin Franklin

SCORPIO
Thy own importance know.
Alexander Pope

SAGITTARIUS
Never allow discouragement, laziness or impatience to take over the best part of our day.
Anonymous

CAPRICORN
Today must borrow nothing of tomorrow.
Anonymous

AQUARIUS
I am like all things, hated or loved.
Bhagavad Gita

PISCES
A clean mouth and an honest hand will take a man through any land.
Midwestern American Quote

Balance is the key. Enjoy the equal time that
night and day bestow at this time of year.

ARIES
I like men to behave like men, strong and childish.
Françoise Sagan

TAURUS
Generosity and good faith are first cousins.
Corneille

GEMINI
You cannot create experience. You have to submit to it.
Albert Camus

CANCER
The supreme faculty of man is not reason, but imagination.
Edmund O'Gorman

LEO
Power never takes a step backwards, except before another power.
Malcolm X

VIRGO
How many things can I do without?
Socrates

LIBRA
Morality is not respectability.
George Bernard Shaw

SCORPIO
In life, as in chess, foresight ends up winning.
Charles Buxton

SAGITTARIUS
All of life is like that, systole and diastole.
John F. Kennedy

CAPRICORN
What you have already eaten and what you have enjoyed is yours forever.
Anonymous

AQUARIUS
Striving to be better, oft we mar what's well.
William Shakespeare

PISCES
No intelligent man has ever said that a change of mind is inconsistency.
Cicero

31
MARCH

Your choices are the cause of everything else.
Choose wisely.

ARIES
Everything flows from Providence, and alongside it is Necessity, and whatever contributes to the entire universe of which you are a part.
Marcus Aurelius

TAURUS
He who does not look ahead remains behind.
Mexican Quote

GEMINI
Every blade of grass has its angel that bends over it and whispers, grow, grow.
The Talmud

CANCER
Try to be the best. But never believe you are the best.
Ansari de Herat

LEO
More than an army, it's a quotation who's time has come.
William Gates

VIRGO
God, before the creation, was a mystery unto himself: he had to create to know himself.
Friedrich Hebbel

LIBRA
A mature person is seen by the way love is given or received; with a sense of happiness and without guilt.
Leo Baek

SCORPIO
Nothing underneath the sun Merely happens; things are done.
Arthur Guiterman

SAGITTARIUS
A man possessed by peace never stops smiling.
Milan Kundera

CAPRICORN
It is not enough to wait for things to happen, at times they must be provoked.
Villaume

AQUARIUS
You want to rule the art of prolonging your life? Dedicate yourself to the art of bearing it.
E. Feuchtersleben

PISCES
Ideas move the world, but not before they are transformed into feelings.
Gustave le Bon

APRIL

APRIL

All things from eternity are of like forms and come round in a circle.
Marcus Aurelius

According to Plato, a man, to be a ruler, must be a philosopher as well as a king, and must govern unwillingly, because he loves philosophy better than dominion. Such a ruler has existed once. He was Marcus Aurelius, born under the sign of Taurus, on the 26th of April in 121 A.D. He was an adopted son who was given the perfect education of his time—a student of philosophy and rhetoric. He was unassuming and strict with himself until his death at the age of fifty-nine. Most important, he was a stoic who perfectly embodies the boldness of this month. This spirit is reflected in his quotes, which are used on All Fool's Day to loft us all to greater heights.

ARIES

The Zodiac's early bloomers might do well to hang on to their hearts and heed what a fantastic Indian writer said at the ripe young age of eighty-four: "With lust, you go kaput at a certain age." Arians should not *quite* keep their cool during this, their usual birthday month. Think of the oft-said quote, "The more, the merrier"; however, interpret it: "The more you do and plan for, the better." Even if you do not accomplish all that you had hoped this month, remember, that, as Albert Camus said, "To live is, in itself, a value judgment."
Keywords: Opportunities abound

TAURUS

Nothing new under the Sun? Not for you, this month, Taurus. All through the very interesting first part of April, you'll find day-by-day insights. Then, on the 21st or 22nd of the month, the Sun lights up your sign with an intensity you can't help but perceive. So prick up your ears and concentrate, for this month you could discover yourself.
Keyword: Perceptiveness

GEMINI

"With our thoughts we build the world" goes the ancient Buddhist aphorism, and this idea should fuel you all through April, quixotic Gemini. Pay extra mind to your own on-the-fly ponderings, and, if you have ever dreamt of knowing everyone else's little secrets, April just might be the month when your celestial fortune bestows the privilege on you. But bear in mind that knowing doesn't always mean understanding!
Keyword: Concentrate

CANCER

Cancer will always find something to learn from an Aries, and so, during this very "Martian" month (the planet Mars rules the sign Aries), Cancer will find out how even slight doses of unhappiness or anger can be conquered, tamed, and put to good use. With challenges, Cancer, you always grow. And then, you become absolutely fascinating.
Keywords: Remember substance

LEO

If things don't work out wonderfully the first time, Leo, try and try again. During April, give everything and everybody a second chance. In the end, what's been lost, everyone and everything will return to you. You could dive under the covers but that phone would still be ringing off the hook. April brings glorious rays, filled with those nanoparticles that you need to get you purring and help you find your own place in the sun, especially in your profession.
Keyword: Breakthrough

VIRGO

Time changes, religious festivities, even meteors streaking across the sky all make April a special month for Virgo. Just as a speck of dust weighing less than a gram can be either a sparkling, brilliant "house star" or just another household nuisance to get rid of, so can little matters light up your life—or drain you. April carries a "load of stuff" for Virgo, but realize that it is all there to get you this month to act and make things happen, before returning you to your old vital self.
Keywords: Things happen

LIBRA

Within a framework of subtleties, Libra will redefine and broaden his wishes, wants, ideas, vibes, and attitudes. Need an example, Libra? Have you ever felt music permeate your body and soul, making you twinge with indescribable responses that you didn't even know you were capable of feeling? Take it from there, Libra, to stretch out, extrapolate, and hear new sounds.
Keywords: Double meanings

SCORPIO

April is the perfect time for all Scorpios to remember that "life is what happens when you're making other plans." No repeating the same mistakes, since push-ahead Mars is Aries's confidence as well as yours! You need to come to your own aid by settling down a bit. Remember, exclamation marks are there for a purpose but can be platitudinous if overused.
Keywords: Take a hint

SAGITTARIUS

Dum inter homines sumus, colamus humanitatem—"while we live among men, we appreciate other men"—Latin for *you* Sagittarius, any day of any year, as long as it is in April. Now is the time for you to appreciate and to be appreciated, to value and to be valued, to read a bit more of ancient Seneca if you can, so you can say, "Yes, I am listening to my fellow men."
Keyword: Learn

CAPRICORN

Everything that is related to law, rules, discipline, codes, and opinions is touched by your special angels just now, and that now is April. Keep to the rules, bide your time, and don't be so goatishly stubborn, but give in a little. And in the midst of all this business, find a little pleasure, perhaps take in the Lyrid meteor shower (every April, for at least another twenty thousand years), and see how wonderful it feels to connect with the celestial sphere and its wonders.
Keywords: Manipulate within your bounds

AQUARIUS

Aquarians are like live wires—you can be wonderful or scary! Whenever there is an energy shift, whether due to a change of season, the phases of the Moon, sunspots, or the implosion of a white star, Aquarians feel it in their soul. You have the gift of being receptive to all that goes on in the world—in your own delightfully disorganized fashion. This is particularly true in April. So more than any other time of the year, let yourself go and thank your lucky stars that you were born under this incredibly tuned-in sign.
Keywords: Try anything

PISCES

The only thing you should not attempt in April, Pisces, is to count the waves in the sea. It really cannot be done. But don't let this dissuade you from trying something else, for there are scientists weighing the Universe, which goes to prove that anything is possible. Especially for you, Pisces, in April.
Keywords: Count on anything, even aftershocks

1

APRIL

ARIES
Nothing happens to any man that he is not formed by nature to bear.
Marcus Aurelius

TAURUS
Live with the gods. And he does so who constantly shows them that his soul is satisfied with what is assigned to him.
Marcus Aurelius

GEMINI
Every man is worth just so much as the things are worth about which he busies himself.
Anonymous — Attributed to Gustave Flaubert and Marcus Aurelius

CANCER
It is not death that a man should fear, but he should fear never beginning to live.
Marcus Aurelius

LEO
The implication of causes was from eternity spinning the thread of your being.
Marcus Aurelius

VIRGO
The universe is transformation; our life is what our thoughts make it.
Marcus Aurelius

LIBRA
Observe constantly that all things take place by change.
Marcus Aurelius

SCORPIO
Mind that which lies before you, whether it be thought, word, or action.
Marcus Aurelius

SAGITTARIUS
Satisfaction consists in doing the things we were made for.
Marcus Aurelius

CAPRICORN
Whatever this is that I am, it is a little flesh and breath, and the ruling part.
Marcus Aurelius

AQUARIUS
As to the case of good fortune, take it without pride, and resign it without reluctance.
Marcus Aurelius

PISCES
Whatever may happen to you was prepared for you from all eternity.
Marcus Aurelius

*Each day is an epic journey and
you are the hero of the saga.*

2
APRIL

ARIES
There is nothing under the sun that you cannot do.
Anonymous

TAURUS
From every good, there is something bad to be found; from everything bad, there is always some good.
Christiane Grautoff

GEMINI
With our thoughts, we shape the world.
Buddhist Quote

CANCER
One is born under the wrong sign and to live with dignity means to correct, day by day, our own horoscope.
Milan Kundera

LEO
I quote others only the better to express myself.
Michel de Montaigne

VIRGO
A sound mind in a sound body.
Juvenal

LIBRA
The little I know I own to my ignorance.
Sacha Guitry

SCORPIO
Think enough, and you will come to the conclusion that you know nothing.
Kenneth Patchen

SAGITTARIUS
I would rather appreciate what I can't have than have what I can't appreciate.
O. S. Marden

CAPRICORN
Money is the credit card of the poor.
Marshall McLuhan

AQUARIUS
You lose more of yourself than you redeem doing the decent thing.
Seamus Heaney

PISCES
That is happiness; to be dissolved into something completely great.
Willa Cather

3
APRIL

You are special enough to recognize that everyone else is special too.

ARIES
Every exit is an entry to somewhere else.
Tom Stoppard

TAURUS
You can be sure that you will have to pay a price for everything you love.
Agatha Christie

GEMINI
History, even one's own, is not mechanic, because man is free to transform it.
Ernesto Sabato

CANCER
The person who is not around to take advantage of his luck doesn't deserve it.
Mandino

LEO
Winning gave me a marvelous feeling of completeness.
Timothy Albright

VIRGO
The youth who has not shed tears is a savage, and the elder who does not laugh is a poor man.
Santayana

LIBRA
Life's tragedy is not so much how man suffers, but rather what he misses.
Thomas Carlyle

SCORPIO
The voyage of discovery lies, not in finding new landscapes, but in having new eyes.
Marcel Proust

SAGITTARIUS
Only the cheap things can be bought with money.
Anonymous

CAPRICORN
One must adjust laws to things, rather than things to laws.
Plutarch

AQUARIUS
The hour which gives us life begins to take it away.
Seneca

PISCES
Nobody can leave their individuality.
Arthur Schopenhauer

Sprinkle your quests with feelings
just as the cook seasons his broth.

4
APRIL

ARIES
Don't think that everyone will agree with you, even if you are a king.
Catalan Quote

TAURUS
No temptation can every be measured by the worth of its objective.
Colette

GEMINI
Talent does not hinder having obsessions, but it makes them notable.
Madame de Staël

CANCER
A hurtful act is the transference to others of the degradation which we bear in ourselves.
Simone Weil

LEO
Tension is a prerequisite to live creatively.
A. Meyer

VIRGO
An unsculpted piece of marble can sustain the form of each thought that the best artist in the world may have.
Miguel Angelo Buonarroti

LIBRA
Men's passions are so many roads by which they can be reached.
Marquis de Vauvenargues

SCORPIO
Dare to be inventive.
R. Buckminster Fuller

SAGITTARIUS
When one trains one's conscience, it kisses one while it bites.
Nietzsche

CAPRICORN
Law is a bottomless well.
John Arbuthnot

AQUARIUS
The very first king was a lucky soldier.
Voltaire

PISCES
Tell us your phobias and we will tell you what you are afraid of.
Robert Benchley

5
APRIL

There is a legend behind every sign of the Zodiac and over the ages it provides every soul with mythical support. Use it.

ARIES
We are what we think. Everything we are raises with our thoughts and with them we fabricate the world.
Buddha

TAURUS
Happiness is a net of love with which one can trap souls.
Mother Teresa

GEMINI
At times, the only way to be right, is not to be.
José Bergamin

CANCER
Anything invented is true.
Gustave Flaubert

LEO
When a man really sympathizes with all living beings, only then is he really noble.
Buddha

VIRGO
The unexpected and incredible belong in this world. Only then is life whole.
Carl Jung

LIBRA
My language is the universal whore whom I have to convert into a virgin.
Karl Kraus

SCORPIO
The best way out is always through.
Robert Frost

SAGITTARIUS
My satisfaction will be to know that on my way I have helped the world to be a better place.
H. B. Zachry

CAPRICORN
Marriage is not a word, it is a whole phrase.
Anonymous

AQUARIUS
Genius is nothing but a great aptitude for patience.
George-Louis de Buffon

PISCES
A good memory is the intelligence of fools.
Rainer Maria Rilke

*"A wise man says: everything is real so long as you
do not take it for more than it is."* Bernard Bosanquet

6
APRIL

ARIES
Self-trust is the essence of heroism.
Ralph Waldo Emerson

TAURUS
Sometimes, a caress is better than a career.
Shelley Winters

GEMINI
A thing might look specious in theory, and yet be ruinous in practice.
Edmund Burke

CANCER
The future is filled with pseudoimpossible possibilities.
Isaac Asimov

LEO
For the ant, a couple of drops of water is a deluge.
Japanese Quote

VIRGO
Where do I find all the time for not reading so many books.
Karl Kraus

LIBRA
The unexamined life is not worth living.
Socrates

SCORPIO
Society prepares the crime; the criminal commits it.
Buckle

SAGITTARIUS
Let us never confuse the power of strength with the strength of power.
Epictetus

CAPRICORN
Beverage quenches thirst; food satisfies hunger, but gold and silver never appease greed.
Plutarch

AQUARIUS
Because you are a human being, you want to make a difference.
Anonymous

PISCES
Painting is silent poetry, and poetry is a painting that speaks.
Simonides

7
APRIL

ARIES

Do not defy he whom you cannot overcome.
Attila the Hun

TAURUS

Failure must be but a challenge to others.
Amelia Earhart

GEMINI

A thing may look evil in theory, and yet be excellent in practice.
Edmund Burke

CANCER

Melancholy is the bliss of being unhappy.
Milan Kundera

LEO

There are no roses without thorns.
English Quote

VIRGO

Heaven and earth do nothing, and yet there is nothing they cannot do.
Chuang-Tse

LIBRA

What I was looking for was the rapture of dizziness, the second fall into nothing.
Samuel Beckett

SCORPIO

Money is not the root of all evil, no money is.
Anonymous

SAGITTARIUS

A learned person is not wise, a wise person is not learned.
Tao Te Ching

CAPRICORN

There's a period of life when we swallow a knowledge of ourselves and it becomes either good or sour inside.
Pearl Bailey

AQUARIUS

Marriage is half of the tradition, the other half is patience.
Mahoma

PISCES

A man who cannot seduce a man, cannot save him either.
Søren Kierkegaard

Make allowance for Buddha's birthday by finding the peace within you—by tapping your own inner source of relief.

8
APRIL

ARIES
There are those who always know what to do, until it happens to them.
Anonymous

TAURUS
Courage is having grace under pressure.
Ernest Hemingway

GEMINI
When something is well said, have no scruples; take it and copy it.
Anatole France

CANCER
Remember. Melancholy is the bliss of unhappiness.
Milan Kundera

LEO
There is no reason to fear the wind if your stack of hay is well tied.
Irish Quote

VIRGO
A baby is God's opinion that the world should go on.
Carl Sandburg

LIBRA
Solitude is impracticable, and society fatal.
Ralph Waldo Emerson

SCORPIO
Many are called and few are chosen.
Matthew 22:14

SAGITTARIUS
Man is designed to be a comprehensivist.
R. Buckminster Fuller

CAPRICORN
A house without books is a house without dignity.
Edmundo D'Amicis

AQUARIUS
Believe you will have it and you will have it.
Erasmus of Rotterdam

PISCES
The sum of all things is an infinite conjugation of the verb to do.
Thomas Carlyle

9
APRIL

Although your feet stand firmly on the ground, it does not always mean that you are upright.

ARIES
Do not ask God to make your life easier, ask him to show you how to be stronger.
Hindu Quote

TAURUS
My meditations, my musings are never more enchanting than when I am able to forget myself.
Jean-Jacques Rousseau

GEMINI
There is nothing new, except that which one has already forgotten.
Marie Antoinette

CANCER
Memory can be a fountain of wealth for the spirit, if it isn't poison.
Hugo Arguelles

LEO
There is a huge difference between "good," "good reasons," and "reasons that sound good."
Burton Hillis

VIRGO
The frog says, "I only have my jump."
Liberian Quote

LIBRA
In Hollywood, all marriages are happy ones. It's the living together afterwards that causes all the trouble.
Shelley Winters

SCORPIO
There is a basic cause in all effects.
Giordano Bruno

SAGITTARIUS
Who is not truthful to himself, will never see the truth.
Paracelsus

CAPRICORN
Rich and poor have this in common. The Lord made them both.
The Bible

AQUARIUS
Hot can be cool, and cool can be hot, and each can be both.
Louis Armstrong

PISCES
The real mystery in the world is the visible, not the invisible.
Oscar Wilde

Even if you know how to count,
your days are not numbered.

10
APRIL

ARIES
An unguarded object remains safe if protected by destiny.
Sanskrit Quote

TAURUS
Turn around and you will see that happiness is the shadow right behind you.
Felipe Villaespesa

GEMINI
Fervor without profound knowledge is fire without light.
Thomas Fuller

CANCER
As the clouds in an empty sky we become and squander over lost depths.
Marguerite Yourcenar

LEO
Learn to reason forwards, backwards and on the sides of any question.
Thomas Blandi

VIRGO
"Nothing" is something that is frequently good to do.
Will Durant

LIBRA
Leave well enough alone.
Anonymous

SCORPIO
It is always time to learn, even for the elderly.
Aeschylus

SAGITTARIUS
Remembering is for those who have forgotten.
Plotinus

CAPRICORN
Men carry their superiority inside, animals outside.
Russian Quote

AQUARIUS
How many teeth does love bite with?
Dante Alighieri

PISCES
Whatever is natural possesses variety.
French Quote

11
APRIL

Stand completely still and you may be lucky enough to feel the rush of the Earth as it whirls through space.

ARIES

Speed is the form of ecstasy the technical revolution has bestowed on man.
Milan Kundera

TAURUS

The man who never alters his opinion is like stagnant water, and breeds reptiles for the mind.
William Blake

GEMINI

Every dogma has its moment, but ideals are eternal.
Israel Zangwill

CANCER

To really see one must compare what one sees with what one has seen.
Octavio Paz

LEO

Success has made many men fail.
Cindy Adams

VIRGO

Learn to reject favors. It is a great art, besides being very useful.
Thomas Fuller

LIBRA

Man proposes, God disposes.
Anonymous

SCORPIO

In youth, the days are short and the nights are long; in old age, the years are short and the days are long.
Panin

SAGITTARIUS

This, our universe, is as much One as Many.
Dionysius of Halicarnassus

CAPRICORN

Strike while the iron is hot!
Anonymous

AQUARIUS

The stars speak of man's insignificance in the long eternity of time.
Edwin Way Teale

PISCES

As many opinions as there are men; each a law to himself.
Terence

Somewhere this day is called the day of Cosmic Optimism. Better still, use Einstein's adage: "If all things disappeared from the world, space and time would be left."

12
APRIL

ARIES
Oh God, while I stay on this earth, I want to be that which I am.
Epictetus

TAURUS
It is necessary that we survive, in spite of the crumbling of so many heavens.
Thomas Lawrence

GEMINI
Under certain circumstances the deed must be quicker than the thought.
Hernán Cortés

CANCER
Idealizing the past denies history its true self.
Moctezuma

LEO
We think in generalities, we live in detail.
Alfred North Whitehead

VIRGO
A person who has no inner life is a slave to circumstance.
Henry Frederic Amiel

LIBRA
Never trust a husband far away or a bachelor nearby.
Henry Rowland

SCORPIO
Knowledge is gained by learning; trust by doubt; skill by practice; and love by love.
Thomas S. Szasz

SAGITTARIUS
Meditate on knowing and not knowing, existing and not existing. Then put them aside so you can be.
Shiva Samahitâ

CAPRICORN
Doing wrong voluntarily is worse than doing it by force.
Aristotle

AQUARIUS
Every moment is nothing without end.
Octavio Paz

PISCES
Be a person, and treat everyone else as an individual person.
Attributed to Wilhelm F. Hegel

13
APRIL

The ancient Romans used this day to honor Jupiter.
There could be something lucky in the air
if you trust yourself and do the same.

ARIES
Let us receive the occult with an ovation and come out to contemplate the stars once again. . . . My sun sets to rise again.
Robert Browning

TAURUS
What I search for, I find. What we neglect escapes us.
Sophocles

GEMINI
A word wrongly put to use, spoils the most beautiful thought.
Voltaire

CANCER
Only he who accepts that the essence or meaning of his life is not material but spiritual can be free.
Anonymous

LEO
Change your mind and you change your world.
Norman Vincent Peale

VIRGO
To believe in certainty, we must believe by doubting.
Polish Quote

LIBRA
Could it be possible that blonds also prefer gentlemen?
Mamie Van Doren

SCORPIO
I lived in a city so huge that I needed the universe to fill it.
Robert Sabatier

SAGITTARIUS
Without leaving my home, I know the whole universe.
Lao-Tzu

CAPRICORN
The reward for virtue is the understanding of the good deed.
Cicero

AQUARIUS
Let go the things in which you are in doubt for the things in which there is no doubt.
Muhammad

PISCES
My favorite person? Myself.
James Boswell

Liberation comes from inside and we must learn
to share it with ourselves as well as with others.

14
APRIL

ARIES
Little by little, time draws out all things in sight and reason takes them to the shore of light.
Lucretius

TAURUS
The winds and waves are always on the side of the ablest navigators.
Anonymous

GEMINI
As soon as you let a word out, you are its slave. Until then, you rule it.
Arab Quote

CANCER
We mortals cross the ocean of this world, Each in his average cabin of a life.
Robert Browning

LEO
One of the biggest sources of energy is pride in what you do.
Senegal Quote

VIRGO
Only real life is the life one never lives.
Oscar Wilde

LIBRA
In mystery there is nothing profound.
Charles Caleb Colton

SCORPIO
A man with a soul will only obey the universe.
Gabriel Germain

SAGITTARIUS
There is nothing superfluous in nature.
Averroes

CAPRICORN
Optimist: a proponent of the doctrine that black is white.
Ambrose Bierce

AQUARIUS
And why not use the rain as your raincoat?
Daito

PISCES
I am what I am before God, and nothing else.
Saint Francis of Assisi

15
APRIL

Spiritual thirst is always a good thing.
Quenching it is better still.

ARIES
What are we on this earth for if it is not to grow?
Robert Browning

TAURUS
What is good can resist defeat, what is bad, cannot.
Rabindranath Tagore

GEMINI
We are such stuff as dreams are made on.
William Shakespeare

CANCER
Search in your past for what is good and beautiful. Build your future from there.
Paul Kruger

LEO
Some wise man will shape more opportunities than he finds.
Bantu Quote

VIRGO
After the first death, there is no other.
Dylan Thomas

LIBRA
To become old is life's parody.
Simone de Beauvoir

SCORPIO
Life is unbearable for the person who doesn't have some enthusiasm nearby.
Maurice Barres

SAGITTARIUS
If you contemplate the abyss for a long time, the abyss will also contemplate you.
Nietzsche

CAPRICORN
If you haven't got much education, you've got to use your brains.
Anonymous

AQUARIUS
You will always find an answer in the sound of water.
Chuang-Tse

PISCES
The heavenly bodies rule the destiny of men, but God rules the heavenly bodies.
Cellarius

ARIES
Those who lose for a noble cause never get frustrated.
Lord Byron

TAURUS
To stumble is allowed, to get up is mandatory!
Russian Quote

GEMINI
Conscience is the best interpreter of life.
Karl Barth

CANCER
If your feet are standing firmly on the ground, you can't fall from very high.
Anonymous

LEO
Use a dynamic dialogue that visualizes your words.
Radio U.S.A.

VIRGO
Have you ever tried to write your autobiography in advance?
Abraham Joshua Heschel

LIBRA
Happiness or misery is in one's soul. The whole universe is the home of a noble soul.
Democritus

SCORPIO
As far as we can discern, the sole purpose of human existence is to kindle a light in the darkness of mere being.
Carl Jung

SAGITTARIUS
Genius has limitations; stupidity is boundless.
Anonymous

CAPRICORN
As for titles, the way to defend them is to be worthy of them.
George Meredith

AQUARIUS
Between God and me, there is nothing in between.
Meister Eckhart

PISCES
Real goods, solid and eternal, are those that reason gives.
Seneca

17
APRIL

Clarify, reevaluate, and then accomplish.

ARIES
Rivalry is a good thing for mortals.
Hesiod Hestodus

TAURUS
Every blade of grass has its angel that bends over it and whispers, "grow, grow."
The Talmud

GEMINI
A man must not swallow more beliefs than he can digest.
Havelock Ellis

CANCER
Everybody should do at least two things that we hate a day, as good practice.
William James

LEO
Everything is worth what its buyer pays for it.
Publilius Syrus

VIRGO
We lie screaming when we lie to ourselves.
Eric Hoffer

LIBRA
As you are I saw myself; as you see me you will be seen.
Mexican Quote

SCORPIO
Art is the objectivity of feelings.
Susanne Langer

SAGITTARIUS
Regret is insight that comes a day too late.
Anonymous

CAPRICORN
All matter depends on movement.
René Descartes

AQUARIUS
If your mind is not clouded with unnecessary things, this is the best season of your life.
Wu-Men

PISCES
Man, as long as he is alive, can expect everything.
Seneca

Be as gracious when you're mistook
as you are when your mistaken.

ARIES
Nothing great has been done without enthusiasm.
Ralph Waldo Emerson

TAURUS
Something begun is something half done.
Horace

GEMINI
The majesty of duty has nothing to do with the enjoyment of life.
Immanuel Kant

CANCER
Poetry is the language in which man explores his own amazement.
Christopher Fry

LEO
I have not observed that honesty grows with man's riches.
Thomas Jefferson

VIRGO
The soul selects its own society-then-shuts the door.
Emily Dickinson

LIBRA
So many men, so many opinions.
Lord Samuel

SCORPIO
There is no security in this world; there is only opportunity.
Douglas MacArthur

SAGITTARIUS
Of words, not the sound, but the feeling.
Anonymous

CAPRICORN
There is, notwithstanding, a limit within which indulgence is no longer a virtue.
Edmund Burke

AQUARIUS
It is a huge event to have been born and to be; and the life of anybody is an unending and unique event.
Dhammapada

PISCES
Enough is never a little; enough is never a lot.
Seneca

19
APRIL

ARIES
Joy is even greater when it comes unexpected.
Théophile de Viau

TAURUS
Writing is only a guided dream.
Jorge Luis Borges

GEMINI
Our knowledge consists mostly in "thinking we know" and in believing that others know.
Paul Valéry

CANCER
What I can see with my eyes I can point to with my fingers.
Dominican Republic Quote

LEO
I prefer roses on my table than diamonds on my neck.
Emma Goldman

VIRGO
Nothing can give a man strength, when he is looking for salvation, other than his own effort.
Anonymous

LIBRA
The world is not run by thought, nor by imagination, but by opinion.
Elizabeth Drew

SCORPIO
In the beginning was the word, in the end the platitude.
Stanlislaw Lec

SAGITTARIUS
Politeness is to goodness what words are to thought.
Colombian Quote

CAPRICORN
Only within the law does liberty exist!
Oswald Spengler

AQUARIUS
Look, as if it was for the first time, at a beautiful person or at an ordinary object.
Shiva Samahitâ

PISCES
A man's paradise is his own good nature.
VI Dynasty, Massime degli antichi Egiziani

*Reality, someone said, is what is left when
one no longer believes in what is perceived.*

20
APRIL

ARIES
The finished man of the world must eat of every apple once.
Ralph Waldo Emerson

TAURUS
There is Buddha for those who do not know what he really is. There is not Budha for those who know what he really is.
Zen Proverb

GEMINI
There are many things, once and for all, that I do not want to know.
Nietzsche

CANCER
Evil is not the contrary, rather it is the lack of good.
Leibniz

LEO
There is no end. There is no beginning. There is only the infinite passion of living.
Federico Fellini

VIRGO
Fortune does not change men; it only takes off their mask.
Alfonso Teja Zabre

LIBRA
One single cloud can eclipse the Sun.
Thomas Fuller

SCORPIO
Survival is triumph enough!
Harry Crews

SAGITTARIUS
Pleasure is not within things, but in ourselves.
Richard Wagner

CAPRICORN
In a piranha infested river, the crocodile swims on his back.
Glauber Rocha

AQUARIUS
Blood boils without a fire.
Anonymous

PISCES
With each dawn and every dusk we connect with the world in its time.
Iranian Quote

21
APRIL

Every moment counts.

ARIES
Even seeing has to be learned.
Seneca

TAURUS
To play is an exultation of what is possible.
Martin Buber

GEMINI
Life is the art of drawing conclusions from insufficient premises.
Unknown

CANCER
This became a credo of mine: Attempt the impossible in order to improve your work.
Bette Davis

LEO
We are so made that we can derive intense enjoyment from a contrast and very little from a state of things.
Sigmund Freud

VIRGO
The story of a man's life dwells in his attitude.
Julio Torri

LIBRA
Too often we enjoy the commodity of opinion without the incommodity of a reflection.
John F. Kennedy

SCORPIO
Solitude, my mother, recount my life for me.
Czeslaw Milosz

SAGITTARIUS
Delinquents do less harm than a bad judge.
Cervantes

CAPRICORN
Ruling is not a privilege, it is a duty and an honor.
André Maurois

AQUARIUS
Pleasures and sorrows should be given free reign.
Anonymous

PISCES
One man with courage makes a majority.
Andrew Jackson

How much time do you need? Just enough to
believe, to anticipate, to assume, and to envision.

22
APRIL

ARIES
Earth's the right place for love; I don't know where it's likely to go better.
Robert Frost

TAURUS
A man is more complex, infinitely more so than his thoughts.
Paul Valéry

GEMINI
You are not as bright as you think if you light the candle at both ends!
Anonymous

CANCER
Different in life, men are all equal in death.
Lao-Tzu

LEO
If at first you don't succeed, you're running about average.
M. H. Alderson

VIRGO
Every sinner should be vouchsafed a future, as every saint has had a past.
Sarvepalli Radhakrishnan

LIBRA
The superior man understands what is fair; the inferior man understands how to sell.
Confucius

SCORPIO
Silence can't be misquoted.
Anonymous

SAGITTARIUS
What one thinks about during the daytime is dreamt about during the night.
Mexican Quote

CAPRICORN
Life would be so much easier if one could rule with quotes instead of laws!
Unknown

AQUARIUS
Talk is cheap, but you can seldom buy it back.
Anonymous

PISCES
Watch where you are going but never forget from where you have come.
Mexican Quote

23
APRIL

A response needs to be effective.

ARIES
Spirit, in love, consists in uniting perpetual innovation.
Salvador de Madariaga

TAURUS
The best and most beautiful things in life cannot be seen nor touched. They have to be felt with the heart.
Helen Keller

GEMINI
Nothing is good or bad but by comparison.
Anonymous

CANCER
Nature cannot be conquered, only followed.
Sir Francis Bacon

LEO
Work extends itself so as to be able to fill real time with the possibility of ending.
Kathryn N. Parkinson

VIRGO
Provision in season makes a comfortable house.
Anonymous

LIBRA
No man is an Island, entire of itself; every man is a piece of the Continent, a part of the main.
John Donne

SCORPIO
What is sensible today may be madness another time.
Yoruban Quote

SAGITTARIUS
The end justifies the means.
Latin Quote

CAPRICORN
One word, one anecdote, one quote, can frequently teach more than any public treatise.
Emil Ludwig

AQUARIUS
Ambition never fills itself up.
Anonymous

PISCES
Serious people have few ideas. People with ideas are never serious.
Paul Valéry

ARIES

All things stem from joy. They are held in joy and within joy they keep going and find their end.
Rabindranath Tagore

TAURUS

Who talks, spends; who is silent, keeps.
Anonymous

GEMINI

Example is not the most important thing to prove your point, it is the only thing.
Anonymous

CANCER

Selfishness is not living as one wishes to live. It is asking others to live as one wishes to live.
Oscar Wilde

LEO

Whatever is not worth doing is not worth doing well.
Donn Hebb

VIRGO

A wise man never says, "I didn't think."
Lope de Vega

LIBRA

Intelligence must follow faith, never precede it, and never destroy it.
Thomas à Kempis

SCORPIO

In the arithmetic of love, one plus one equals everything, and two minus one equals nothing.
Mignon McLaughlin

SAGITTARIUS

Everyone is the crafter of his own fortune.
Sallust

CAPRICORN

Things well thought out usually hit the mark.
Anonymous

AQUARIUS

Life is the childhood of our immortality.
Goethe

PISCES

It is absolute perfection to know how to get the most possible out of our own individuality.
Michel de Montaigne

25

APRIL

ARIES
He loved his dreams and cultivated them.
Colette

TAURUS
Choose what's best. Custom will make it soft and easy.
Pythagoras

GEMINI
It is best to rise from life as from a banquet, neither thirsty nor drunken.
Aristotle

CANCER
There is a little less trouble in governing a private family than a whole kingdom.
Michel de Montaigne

LEO
If you don't want to work, you have to work to earn enough money so that you don't have to work.
Ogden Nash

VIRGO
Ideas must work through the brains and the arms of good and brave men, or they are no better than dreams.
Ralph Waldo Emerson

LIBRA
A woman is more influenced by what she divines than by what she is told.
Ninon de L'Enclos

SCORPIO
The injury we do and the one we suffer are not weighed in the same scales.
Aesop

SAGITTARIUS
One refusal, no rebuff.
Lord Byron

CAPRICORN
Thinking is not knowing as looking is not seeing.
Anonymous

AQUARIUS
Ignorance never settles a question.
Benjamin Disraeli

PISCES
But you can be absolutely sure that you are terribly like others.
James Russell Lowell

ARIES
Important principles may and must be flexible.
Abraham Lincoln

TAURUS
Any eventfulness whatsoever is creative.
Attributed to Edgar Allan Poe

GEMINI
Grammar is the logic of speech, even as logic is the grammar of reason.
Trench

CANCER
Almost the entire world plays a part.
Petronius

LEO
Love me as if I were your brother, but do your bills with me as if I were your enemy.
Tunisian Quote

VIRGO
Sexuality is the lyricism of the masses.
Charles Baudelaire

LIBRA
I wish I could change my sex as I change my shirt.
André Breton

SCORPIO
Elegance is a degeneration.
Coco Chanel

SAGITTARIUS
There is no law that can make everyone happy.
Livy

CAPRICORN
Miracles do happen, but not often enough to be worth waiting up for.
Ashleigh Brilliant

AQUARIUS
The easiest way to catch a plane is to miss the one before.
Anonymous

PISCES
An intellectual is someone whose mind takes care of itself.
Albert Camus

27
APRIL

Give away some food, find somebody's keys,
believe in angels.

ARIES
You know as well as I do, that the best thing modern consciousness has is the torment of infinity.
Gustave Sorel

TAURUS
A work of art is a nook or cranny of creation as viewed through an individual temperament.
Émile Zola

GEMINI
Computers will only replace a human being when they laugh at a joke.
Graffiti

CANCER
Show me a sane man and I will cure him for you.
Carl Jung

LEO
A very greedy person is like a snake trying to eat an elephant.
Chinese Quote

VIRGO
I believe in sex and death, two experiences that come once in a lifetime.
Woody Allen

LIBRA
Let bygones be bygones.
Anonymous

SCORPIO
Don't hate. It is too heavy a burden.
Martin Luther King, Jr.

SAGITTARIUS
Whoever is a slave to the body is not really free.
Seneca

CAPRICORN
Drive your business, don't let your business drive you.
Anonymous

AQUARIUS
Some arguments only make a lot of noise.
Anonymous

PISCES
Enough of a good thing is plenty.
Anonymous

ARIES
It is the customary fate of new truths to begin as heresies and to end as superstitions.
Aldous Huxley

TAURUS
Where one door closes, another opens.
Cervantes

GEMINI
A real friend should strengthen you with his prayers, bless you with his love and encourage you with his hope.
Attributed to Voltaire

CANCER
One must not light the fuse of incongruence.
Mariano Azuela

LEO
I can't say I have ever gotten lost, but I was confused for a couple of days.
Daniel Boone

VIRGO
Psychiatry is the care of the id by the odd.
Unknown

LIBRA
We all have three characters: the one we show, the one we have, and the one we think we have.
Alphonse Karr

SCORPIO
Keep thy shop and thy shop will keep thee.
Anonymous

SAGITTARIUS
There are fixed limits.
Horace

CAPRICORN
There are some things that can't be helped, and they are many.
Mariano José de Larra

AQUARIUS
A lie may better the present, but it doesn't have much of a future.
Anonymous

PISCES
Every age wants its playthings.
Anonymous

This is the time to learn the sequence of the planets in our solar system and relate to who you are and where you fall among them.

ARIES
Still to ourselves in every place consigned, Our own felicity we make or find.
Oliver Goldsmith

TAURUS
Life shrinks or expands in proportion to one's courage.
Anaïs Nin

GEMINI
Better to cry with wise men than to laugh with fools.
Spanish Quote

CANCER
There is no great man who has never made a mistake.
Ernesto Sabato

LEO
If you want a rose you must respect the thorn.
Persian Quote

VIRGO
What is man in nature? Nothing in relation to the infinite, all in relation to nothing, a mean between nothing and everything.
Blaise Pascal

LIBRA
Some day you will understand what I mean.
Tom Thomson

SCORPIO
Man is an animal that makes deals.
Adam Smith

SAGITTARIUS
There is nothing great without melancholy.
Latin Quote

CAPRICORN
There are few ways in which a man can be more innocently employed than in getting money.
Samuel Johnson

AQUARIUS
We feel and know that we are eternal.
Spinoza

PISCES
You know more than you think you do.
Benjamin Spock

ARIES
Beginning things is the first sign of intelligence. Finishing what you have begun, is the second.
Panchatantra

TAURUS
I can always be distracted by love, but eventually I get horny for my creativity.
Gilda Radner

GEMINI
Whoever is happy will make others happy too. He who has courage and faith will never perish in misery.
Anne Frank

CANCER
The purpose of life is the expansion of happiness.
Maharishi Mahesh Yogi

LEO
Half a calamity is better than a whole one.
Lawrence of Arabia

VIRGO
I do not love a man who is zealous for nothing.
Oliver Goldsmith

LIBRA
Weak men can never be sincere.
La Rochefoucauld

SCORPIO
Home is not where you live, it is where you are understood.
Christian Morgenstern

SAGITTARIUS
Man is neither angel nor beast, and unfortunately he who would act the angel acts the beast.
Blaise Pascal

CAPRICORN
What is new just now was already old some time ago.
Anonymous

AQUARIUS
Whatever you do, there always will be someone to say, "I told you so!"
Anonymous

PISCES
Mischance makes men understand the world.
Pythagoras

MAY

MAY

Be not solitary. Be not idle.
Robert Burton

Venus, Goddess of Love, rules May. May is not all about hearts and flowers, but is about the deeper stuff that makes those flowers grow, those hearts beat. Consider that May is ruled for most of the month by Taurus. In ancient books of wisdom, this sign was related to the living Earth of the alchemist, the clay that was to be molded into a fitting vessel for the "Divine Life" within. It is a kind of interesting synchronicity that Sigmund Freud, himself a kind of "interior" designer, is a Taurus, May-born individual! Many believe the signs of the Zodiac are actually pictures of character that could help everyone. During May ponder Albert Einstein's words: "The true value of a human being can be found in the degree to which he has attained liberation from the self." More than that, give it a try, each in your own way, as May flies by.

ARIES

You dash-ahead Arians rarely look before you leap, which is both wonderfully exciting to watch but likely to have you crashing into walls. Try not to leap—into walls or to your usual conclusions. At least not so fast. You can better deal with your world this month if you stop to figure out what is getting your goat—even though you are the Ram—and getting you going. Tend to your own personal pastures and work to make them greener.
Keywords: Work things out

TAURUS

You birthday Bulls might notice that Venus, your guiding planet, is usually very visible in the sky during this month. Nature probably did this on purpose to remind all of you Taureans that due to Venus's guiding spirit you can be extra enticing this month. Glow yourself or give anything you choose your own special luster. Your personal magnetism is what counts during these days (until the 20, 21, or 22 of May), while the way you make yourself the center of attraction can become extremely creative.

Being free and easy may not be your forte, but, Taurus, this is your month to frolic!
Keywords: Fortune in any cookie

GEMINI

This May, airy Gemini, come down to earth—but only just a bit. Watch your wallet, your words, and your relationships, and be sure to keep a twinkle in your eye, no matter what comes to you during May. You love to learn, so take advantage of everything new that's in store for you—no matter how wild it may seem. Yours is such an eclectic sign that you usually have all your fingers in all the pies—and isn't that delicious? Just make sure you help others have a portion, too.
Keywords: Getting better

CANCER

The well-known psychoanalyst Erich Fromm said that there are two ways of existing: to have or to be. Choose, Cancer, choose. It is almost now or never, and this is the best month to give yourself a break from your own personal Sturm und Drang. Put yesterday's news in its place and start thinking about making today's headlines instead. All your fondest wishes are hanging from your own personal celestial tree. All you have to do is pick.
Keywords: Take your choice

LEO

"Oops" has a great sound, takes care of mistakes, and if said in the right way can help you in, and out of, a couple of situations, Leo. Not that you really have to be cautious (that doesn't go very well with your natural king-of-the-jungle persona), but here's something (yup, all month) that they say in Sweden that translates perfectly for you in May: "Good advice should be seen from behind." It'll be much easier for all other signs to "follow the leader" if you remember to give them all the room they need to do so!
Keywords: Give 'em a break

VIRGO

What now? and why? are the double questions in your celestial scale during May, Virgo. That's because you're ruled by Mercury, a double-breasted kind of guy who makes you take ages to decide on anything. But remember, you can turn things inside out or upside down, and still come out a winner (even with any double-whammy May happens to throw your way), if you let yourself loosen up and take advantage of all the encouraging vibes that this month would like to bestow upon you. Pay special attention to the whole first week of May, which should provide a real lesson in understanding. A good one.
Keyword: Out-with-it

LIBRA

Try as you might, Libra, you may not be able to strike just the right chords for creating harmony this month. Don't search for excuses as to why things are a little off-balance. Think instead of the wise Seneca, who said that there was nothing too bitter that a patient mind couldn't heal—and this is not a pun on what's in store for you during May, Libra! You could still get the best out of almost anything if you use your admirable sense of maneuvering. And if you start doing the groundwork now, in another three months, whatever dream you're dreaming could become a reality.
Keywords: Subtle nuances

SCORPIO

You should be able to make the most of May, Scorpio, even though it may sometimes seem as if all you are doing is plodding along. If your usually strong power supply seems a little dim, it's because, astrologically, the Sun is on your shadow side, in opposition to you (until it moves along to Gemini). Remember H. B. Hamilton's sage saying, "Man is an animal that would rather reason instead of being reasonable." So do your utmost not to be the rebel without a cause. Give yourself a couple of breaks. Relax. You have enough intensity to cast some light on the shadows.
Keyword: Faith

SAGITTARIUS

May sunshine could seem to shine a bit too strongly this month for you, fun-loving Sag, but don't despair! Being a melancholy baby is never for you, and if you seek, you can find some wonderful solutions to any problems. Healing arts, foresight, and suppositions are all on your side and guaranteed to get you back on target. Bless you, Sags, in May, because you, better than any other sign in the Zodiac, can turn almost any downer into an upper!

Keyword: Synergy

CAPRICORN

For you, Capricorn, all those April showers do indeed bring May flowers—and in great bouquets! You should definitely be reaping something that you have sown within the past thirty to forty days just now, and it should be making a long-term difference. But take some care, because your footing may not feel so sure, especially between the 120th and 142nd days of any year. Anything that can be done, you know you can do it better, but don't forget to offer a nod of your wise head to others who may not have it so good. Toward the end of the month, you may find yourself a bit more solitary than usual, but remember, it's only when you feel secure in your own space that people begin to gravitate toward you.

Keywords: Attain and achieve

AQUARIUS

Over a thousand years ago, an unknown Greek grandfather said that "he who does not heed advice is much more stubborn than he who gives it." So pay attention, Aquarius, because in May, this means you. Since you like to march to the beat of your own drum, not only don't you like being told what to do, but your ego needs constant cuddling. And in May, you (along with Scorpio and Leo) may feel yourself pushed around a bit. Maybe you think others are making mistakes or damming up your swift currents, but please, take a closer look. Don't assume anything. Listen. And you could be in for a buoyant May.

Keyword: Care

PISCES

This month, Pisces, don't just serve yourself with a silver spoon, go so far as to even polish it to perfection! In May, you can clear up things, ask for your heart's desire, and live 'n' learn the easy way. Or, use your lucky stars to wriggle your way out of situations that you just don't feel like dealing with anymore. Pisceans are usually more pessimistic than optimistic, but this month you should dare to believe that the glass you usually see as half empty is actually brimming over with good things. You may feel a little caught, but know you're still swimming, right in the same school as all of us, whether we're fish or not!

Keywords: Believe it or not

1
MAY

The brain should be the hardest muscle.

ARIES
Every fault that a Sultan pleases can be a quality.
Iranian Proverb

TAURUS
The smallest gift is enough if you have a big heart.
French Saying

GEMINI
Between two evils, I always pick the one I never tried before.
Mae West

CANCER
Hope is a waking dream.
Aristotle

LEO
Exasperation is the lover of the impossible.
French Quote

VIRGO
The world is my country, the human race is my race, man's future is my paradise.
Anonymous

LIBRA
With time and patience, the leaf of the juniper tree turns into a silk robe.
Chinese Proverb

SCORPIO
It is as simple as this. Between two flutterings, without any other explanation, the journey unfolds.
Eduardo Galeano

SAGITTARIUS
It is not quite enough to know how to escape restrictions.
Arthur Miller

CAPRICORN
Before you talk about it, understand it.
Mexican Saying

AQUARIUS
The follies of fathers are no lesson for the sons.
Bernard de Fontenelle

PISCES
If you are born without wings do nothing to prevent their growing.
Coco Chanel

Hoard your words, not your feelings.

ARIES
Do not think that fortune will give you what your work does not do.
Portuguese Saying

TAURUS
Possessions are usually diminished by possession.
Nietzsche

GEMINI
One should be happy just to BE alive.
Emily Dickinson

CANCER
Language is a social event.
Richard Rodriguez

LEO
A monk and a butcher fight it out within each desire.
E. M. Cioran

VIRGO
Man is a social animal.   Man is a political animal.
Spinoza   *Aristotle*

LIBRA
You cannot fight against the future, time is on our side.
William E. Gladstone

SCORPIO
Pretend you are seeing everything for the first time.
Anonymous

SAGITTARIUS
Sooner or later one also has to think of arriving somewhere.
Arthur Miller

CAPRICORN
Upon paying your debts, you start getting rich.
French Proverb

AQUARIUS
Too many people are too stubborn when following the path they have
chosen, and too few chose their aims.
Nietzsche

PISCES
Life is like boxing. We've all got this plan until we get knocked out!
Brenda Salmon

3
MAY

The best day can be just a normal day.

ARIES

If you don't climb to the top of the hill, there is no way to admire the view.
English Proverb

TAURUS

We feel free when we escape, even if it is from the frying pan into the fire.
Eric Hoffer

GEMINI

The essence of pleasure is spontaneity.
Germaine Greer

CANCER

I am never upset at what people ask me to do, only at what they deny me.
A. C. Castillo

LEO

Happy is the one who finds delight in his children.
Anonymous

VIRGO

Man is a being in search of reason.
Plato

LIBRA

Trust, but take care in whom.
Latin Quote

SCORPIO

Losing an illusion makes you wiser than finding some truth.
Ludwig Borne

SAGITTARIUS

Those who take a long time watching dreams, end up looking like a shadow.
André Malraux

CAPRICORN

There is no mirror that reflects the image of any man as his own words.
Luis Vives

AQUARIUS

Men are strange creatures: a combination of the nervousness of a horse,
stubbornness of a donkey and slyness of a camel.
Thomas H. Huxley

PISCES

If poverty is the mother of all ills, the lack of common sense is father of the
same!
Jean de La Bruyère

ARIES
To win without risk is to triumph without glory.
Corneille

TAURUS
A minute's success pays the failure of years.
Robert Browning

GEMINI
Our inventions mirror our secret wishes.
Lawrence Durrell

CANCER
If you are asked about "Tao" and somebody answers, they know nothing.
Chuang-Tse

LEO
Careful of purring over flattery murmured by unfamiliar people.
Oliver Wendell Holmes

VIRGO
Man is no more than his instinct adulterated by his intelligence.
Luis Maria Martinez

LIBRA
Never claim as a right what you can ask as a favor.
John C. Collins

SCORPIO
Bad moods are an invasion of reality, while good moods are an acceptance of the same.
Malcolm Muggeridge

SAGITTARIUS
Life is one journey, life is growing, life is a pilgrimage.
Joseph R. Sizoo

CAPRICORN
One thought can fill all eternity.
William Blake

AQUARIUS
Positive, adj. Mistaken at the top of one's voice.
Ambrose Bierce

PISCES
Man's main task in life is to give birth to himself.
Erich Fromm

5

MAY

ARIES
All decent people live beyond their incomes.
Saki

TAURUS
The most difficult thing to give is that which we give up.
Elizabeth Bibesco

GEMINI
When you obey all the rules, you miss all the fun.
Katharine Hepburn

CANCER
He that would know what shall be must consider what hath been.
Thomas Fuller

LEO
The absolute truth, in the next-to-last-case, is a lie.
Arthur Koestler

VIRGO
All self inflicted censure is a slanted self inflicted praise.
Samuel Johnson

LIBRA
The mind resorts to reason for want of training.
Henry Adams

SCORPIO
War is just like love, it always finds a way.
Bertolt Brecht

SAGITTARIUS
Life collects and life pays.
Anonymous

CAPRICORN
It is the disposition of the thought that altereth the nature of the thing.
John Lyly

AQUARIUS
They have a right to censure that have a heart to help.
William Penn

PISCES
Next to the joy of the egotist is the joy of the detractor.
Agnes Repplier

Search for a way to better your physical condition.

ARIES
It is a sign of contraction of the mind when it is content, or a sign of weariness.
Michel de Montaigne

TAURUS
It is easier to stay out than to get out.
Mark Twain

GEMINI
A pinch of probably is worth a pound of perhaps.
James Thurber

CANCER
If one could only leave now, and return ten years earlier.
Marlene Dietrich

LEO
The maxim "nothing avails but perfection" may be spelled "Paralysis."
Sir Winston Churchill

VIRGO
There is a pleasure in not being pleased.
Voltaire

LIBRA
Sleep, riches and health, to be really enjoyed, must be interrupted.
Jean-Paul Richter

SCORPIO
An old road can turn into a new path.
Anonymous

SAGITTARIUS
There are optical illusions in time as well as in space.
Marcel Proust

CAPRICORN
A finished product is one that has already seen its better days.
Art Linkletter

AQUARIUS
There are times when a battle decides everything, and there are times when the most insignificant thing can decide the outcome of a battle.
Napoleon Bonaparte

PISCES
Don't do everything today, save some mistakes for tomorrow.
Anonymous

7
MAY

Something unknown is doing something we know nothing about somewhere.

ARIES
Burning is quenched by fire.
Michel de Montaigne

TAURUS
It is better to do what you have to do than to have an honorable position.
Confucius

GEMINI
When in doubt, tell the truth.
Mark Twain

CANCER
Nothing is improbable until it moves into the past tense.
George Ade

LEO
I would rather worry without need than live without heed.
Beaumarchais

VIRGO
Man is but a reed, the weakest in nature, but a thinking reed.
Blaise Pascal

LIBRA
You all are what I once was: incredulous.
Thomas Merton

SCORPIO
Filth can be washed away; bad habits are much more difficult to get rid of.
Indonesian Saying

SAGITTARIUS
To be asked is not sin, and to be refused is no calamity.
Russian Proverb

CAPRICORN
There is life in the ground, it goes into the seeds.
Charles Dudley Warner

AQUARIUS
For I fear I have nothing original in me
Excepting Original Sin
Thomas Campbell

PISCES
The road that leads toward justice is mysterious.
Sanskrit Proverb

Fight your battles in your own way.

ARIES
The earth is filled with sky.
Elizabeth Browning

TAURUS
Success usually depends on knowing how long it will take to arrive.
Montesquieu

GEMINI
A smile is a curve that helps to see things straight.
Anonymous

CANCER
It's the job that's never started that takes longest to finish.
J. R. R. Tolkien

LEO
Every day I hear stupid people say things that are not stupid.
Michel de Montaigne

VIRGO
You are lost the very moment that you know what the outcome will be.
Juan Gris

LIBRA
Any and all cruelty comes from weakness.
Seneca

SCORPIO
Temptation is a woman's weapon and a man's excuse.
H. L. Mencken

SAGITTARIUS
One man's sunset is always another man's sunrise.
Anonymous

CAPRICORN
Nothing is ever completely done.
Horace

AQUARIUS
I have seen gross intolerance shown in support of tolerance.
Samuel Taylor Coleridge

PISCES
Broad-mindedness is the result of flattening out high-mindedness.
George Saintsbury

9

MAY

ARIES
The shortest answer sometimes is to do it.
Anonymous

TAURUS
Pick a winner; anyone can pick a loser.
Subway Knowledge

GEMINI
My philosophy is simple: fill what is empty, empty what is full, and scratch if it itches.
Alice Roosevelt Longworth

CANCER
Poison is in everything: the dosage makes it either a poison or a remedy.
Paracelsus

LEO
If it weren't for dilusions, many men would go out of their minds.
Anonymous

VIRGO
Whatever happens is a sign that something will happen.
Seneca

LIBRA
Reason respects differences, and imagination the similitudes of things.
Percy Bysshe Shelley

SCORPIO
Pride is the mask of one's own faults.
Jewish Proverb

SAGITTARIUS
Thus, miracles will follow miracles and the wonders will not cease.
Saint Francis

CAPRICORN
No matter how muddy it looks, never say you will not drink of that water.
Spanish Saying

AQUARIUS
Those who carry noble thoughts with them are never alone.
Phillip Sidney

PISCES
Better late than never.
Anonymous

Celebrate the human experience.

ARIES
Sometimes, all the early bird gets is up!
Anonymous

TAURUS
A mother is not to be leaned on, for she should teach you how not to lean.
Dorothy C. Fisher

GEMINI
I'll lie here and learn How, over their ground,
Trees make a long shadow And a light sound.
Louise Bogen

CANCER
The most important thing in the world is to hold your soul aloft.
Gustave Flaubert

LEO
Better to have a good conscience without knowledge than to have knowledge without a good conscience.
German Proverb

VIRGO
Every and any beetle is gorgeous in the eyes of his mother!
Moorish Proverb

LIBRA
Know thyself, but tell no one what you knowest.
Graffiti

SCORPIO
Cannot you see that you are the reason of what you blame.
Sor Juana Inés de la Cruz

SAGITTARIUS
Man is akin to God in having been endowed with a soul.
The Talmud

CAPRICORN
By labor, fire is got out of a stone.
Dutch Proverb

AQUARIUS
Always obey your superiors if you have any.
Mark Twain

PISCES
God cannot be everywhere, so he made mothers.
Anonymous

Find, feel, and adapt to your own heavenly breeze.

ARIES
For many, the happiest times occur within the family.
Joyce Brothers

TAURUS
Art is to get some fun out of sex without having to work for it.
Robert Frost

GEMINI
Some personal histories are either comedies or traumas.
Woody Allen

CANCER
The best time for planning a book is while you are doing the dishes.
Agatha Christie

LEO
One must learn to take a kick from a cow, as well as the milk, its skim and the cream.
Hindu Proverb

VIRGO
Satisfaction is calmness of the heart under the course of destiny.
Al-Muhasibi

LIBRA
Love your self's self where it lives.
Anne Sexton

SCORPIO
The key is all in our genes.
El Pais

SAGITTARIUS
Light is the task when many share the toil.
Homer

CAPRICORN
The child is father of the man.
Henry Wordsworth Longfellow

AQUARIUS
An expert is one who knows more and more about less and less.
Nicholas Murray Butler

PISCES
Brothers, be kind to your brothers for they are the other half of yourselves.
Nahuatl Proverb

It is a good thing to be able to ask for guidance.

ARIES
Be happy. It is a good way of being wise.
Colette

TAURUS
Don't be humble. You're not that great.
Golda Meir

GEMINI
God put pleasure so near to pain that sometimes one cries with joy.
George Sand

CANCER
The pain of the discipline is short, but the glory of the fruition is eternal.
Harriet Beecher Stowe

LEO
Discretion, the best part of valour.
Beaumont and Fletcher

VIRGO
Who says what he should not, listens to what he does not want to hear.
Ali

LIBRA
Madness, a perfectly rational adjustment in an insane world.
R. D. Lang

SCORPIO
When I have no work, I must keep on working.
Ruth Gabriel

SAGITTARIUS
Only a battle that is won can be as melancholy as a battle that is lost.
Arthur W. Wellington

CAPRICORN
Hitch your wagon to a star.
Ralph Waldo Emerson

AQUARIUS
Greatness is a zigzag streak of lightning in the brain.
Herbert Asquith

PISCES
I love an opposition that has convictions.
Frederick the Great

13
MAY

Kindheartedness always carries a message.

ARIES
Maturity is achieved when you understand that one has to decide.
Angela B. McBride

TAURUS
The table is set, the deed is done.
Anonymous

GEMINI
A person who has never done something silly will never do anything interesting.
Santayana

CANCER
Getting along with someone is to grant.
Mexican Proverb

LEO
United we stand, divided we fall.
Motto of Kentucky

VIRGO
Brothers and sisters are as close as hands and feet.
Vietnamese Proverb

LIBRA
Listen. What is it that is lacking at this moment?
Lin-Chi

SCORPIO
No man was ever great without a touch of divine afflatus.
Cicero

SAGITTARIUS
Youth lasts but a moment, yet it encloses a spark that is always carried in the heart.
Raisa Gorbachev

CAPRICORN
They can because they think they can.
Virgil

AQUARIUS
Whoever has patience, has it all.
Benjamin Franklin

PISCES
I am not now That which I have been.
Lord Byron

Consequences are weighed by actions.

14
MAY

ARIES
Everything should begin by thinking things over. Then you can emphasize deeper with other people.
Shirley MacLaine

TAURUS
A good spectator is also a creator!
Swiss Proverb

GEMINI
Poetry is written when poetry wants to be written.
José Hierro

CANCER
Be just before being generous; be human before being just.
Cecilia Bohl

LEO
Who does not know when he has enough is impecunious.
Japanese Proverb

VIRGO
Patience brings beauty to an elderly face.
Paul Elliot

LIBRA
Either men will learn to live like brothers, or they will die like beasts.
Max Lerner

SCORPIO
Few things are impossible to diligence and skill.
Samuel Johnson

SAGITTARIUS
The best is the enemy of the good.
Voltaire

CAPRICORN
Providence is the Christian name, the baptismal name of chance.
Alphonse Karr

AQUARIUS
A sense of wrongdoing is an enhancement of pleasure.
Oliver Wendell Holmes

PISCES
I believe that what we are really searching for is the experience of being alive.
Joseph Campbell

15
MAY

We are all a spark of divine light.

ARIES
Experience is the best teacher.
John Locke

TAURUS
I am a part of everything I have ever known.
Alfred Lord Tennyson

GEMINI
Generally, teachers teach more with what they are than with what they say.
Anonymous

CANCER
Nature is the grand doctor, and man posseses nature within.
Paracelsus

LEO
If you can look in the mirror and smile back at yourself, there's hope!
Andrea Valeria

VIRGO
What is modern is only modern for a time, and only for some place.
T. S. Eliot

LIBRA
I listen and I forget. I see and I remember. I do and I understand.
Chinese Proverb

SCORPIO
One can find everything in solitude except character.
Stendhal

SAGITTARIUS
We are never so happy, nor so unhappy, as we suppose ourselves to be.
La Rochefoucauld

CAPRICORN
Great thoughts reduced to practice become great acts.
William Hazlitt

AQUARIUS
Solitude is the nurse of the soul.
Anonymous

PISCES
Art, as does love, has roots in pain.
Jane Campion

Go to work on yourself.

16
MAY

ARIES
Whatsoever thy hand findeth to do, do it with thy might.
Ecclesiastes

TAURUS
To drink from the spirit of where you are, you must not only be alone, but also you must be without a hurry.
Santayana

GEMINI
Be yourself. Who else is better qualified?
Frank J. Giblin II

CANCER
Words have been invented to hide the feelings.
Voltaire

LEO
I think that somehow we learn who we really are and then live with that decision.
Eleanor Roosevelt

VIRGO
Any doubt is philosophy.
Michel de Montaigne

LIBRA
I am I plus my circumstances.
José Ortega y Gasset

SCORPIO
Luxury carries more danger than any enemy.
Juvenal

SAGITTARIUS
Saints are those sinner's who keep on walking.
Robert Louis Stevenson

CAPRICORN
When good people cease their vigilance and struggle, then evil men prevail.
Pearl S. Buck

AQUARIUS
Silence is as full of potential wisdom and wit as the unhewn marble of great sculpture.
Aldous Huxley

PISCES
We will always be surprised and enlightened by what our own lives have taught us about how to see.
Mary Lefkowitz

17
MAY

Tariki is Japanese for outside strength. Jiriki means power from within. Tap into them both and take a chance.

ARIES
To give love is a way of education.
Eleanor Roosevelt

TAURUS
We conquer only that which we assimilate.
André Gide

GEMINI
Compassion for myself is the most powerful healer of them all.
Yitzhak Rabin

CANCER
One may understand the cosmos, but never the ego; the self is more distant than any stary.
G. K. Chesterton

LEO
Laugh and the world laughs with you; weep and you weep alone.
Ella Wheeler Wilcox

VIRGO
Stupidity is the imitation that the weak make of the strong.
Eric Hoffer

LIBRA
How many capable men are children more than once during the day?
Napoleon Bonaparte

SCORPIO
It is easier to confess a defect than to claim a quality.
Max Beerbohm

SAGITTARIUS
If I can keep my good character, I will be rich enough.
Platitude

CAPRICORN
Stubborness is the energy of fools.
Anonymous

AQUARIUS
Fate is nonawareness.
Jan Kott

PISCES
Tell the truth and so puzzle and confound your adversaries.
Sir Henry Wotto

Define the wind beneath your wings.

ARIES
Before building a theory, clear what it is that requires explanation.
Stephan Toulman

TAURUS
We begin to promise things when hope dies out.
Leonardo da Vinci

GEMINI
It is far more valuable to hold respect from others than admiration.
Jean-Jacques Rousseau

CANCER
The most universal quality is diversity.
Michel de Montaigne

LEO
Rather the bite of a friend than a kiss from an enemy.
Solomon Aleichem

VIRGO
What is the test of good manners? To be able to bear patiently with bad ones.
Solomon ibn Gabirol

LIBRA
Better to lose a minute in your life than your life in a minute.
Uruguayan Proverb

SCORPIO
Where people drink, they spill.
Andrey Voznesensky

SAGITTARIUS
What is false in the science of facts may be true in the science of *values*.
Santayana

CAPRICORN
Time runs like colts, behind some, come others.
Mexican Proverb

AQUARIUS
To hope is to contradict the future.
E. M. Cioran

PISCES
Thinking clearly is worth it, even when you are inspired.
Gabriel Zaid

19

MAY

Abundance can be found in many ways and things.

ARIES
Autodiscipline yourself, so others do not have to do it for you.
Marcel Marceau

TAURUS
The great man is a man who does a thing for the first time.
Adam Smith

GEMINI
If each one of us could sell our experiences for all they are really worth, we would be, every one of us, millionaires.
Abigail Van Buren

CANCER
What perturbes men is not precisely things, but the opinion that they have of them.
Epictetus

LEO
Sir, I despise what you write but would give my life to allow you to write it.
Voltaire

VIRGO
Humanity bears only a bit of reality.
T. S. Eliot

LIBRA
A mistake in judgement is not fatal, but too much anxiety about it is!
Pauline Kael

SCORPIO
An era can be said to end when its basic illusions are exhausted.
Arthur Miller

SAGITTARIUS
You have never done enough while you may still contribute in some way.
Dag Hammarskjöld

CAPRICORN
Everything is worth what its purchaser will pay for it.
Publilius Syrus

AQUARIUS
Most people would succeed in small things if they were not troubled by great ambition.
Henry Wadsworth Longfellow

PISCES
After living and dreaming, the most important thing in this world is awakening.
Virgil

---

*To rise above your limitations you
must be gung ho about doing so.*

20
MAY

ARIES
The age of discretion comes when you do foolish things in a dignified way.
Hans Moser

TAURUS
Colors are the deeds and suffering of light.
Goethe

GEMINI
God gives every bird its food but they must fly for it.
Anonymous

CANCER
The bottom of a heart is further away than the end of the world.
Danish Proverb

LEO
Don't cross your bridges until you've burned them.
Dick Bower

VIRGO
The drop became a fountain, the fountain grew to become a river, a river was
united with the sea of all eternity.
Sheik Abulfaiz Faiyazi

LIBRA
Exuberance is better than taste.
Gustave Flaubert

SCORPIO
I was well; I could be better; here I am.
Anonymous Epitaph

SAGITTARIUS
Things are beautiful if you love them.
Jean Anouilh

CAPRICORN
The best prophet is the one who makes the best calculation.
Euripides

AQUARIUS
A perfectly normal person is rare in our civilization.
Karen Horney

PISCES
The end is important in all things.
Japanese Warrior, 18th Century

21
MAY

Sometimes a good struggle clears the air.

ARIES
Without an adversary prowess shrivels.
Seneca

TAURUS
Don't marry without love, but don't love without reason.
Anonymous

GEMINI
What is to be mine will fall into my hands.
José Saramago

CANCER
There is nothing more powerful in this world than an idea whose time has come.
Victor Hugo

LEO
Good fences make good neighbors.
Robert Frost

VIRGO
I consider myself a Hindi, a Christian, a Muslim, a Jew, a Buddhist, and a Confucian.
Mahatma Gandhi

LIBRA
At what point do we stop having real intentionality and have mere as if intentionality?
Daniel Dennett

SCORPIO
Heaven is equally distant everywhere.
Petronius

SAGITTARIUS
Age does not always bring wisdom. Sometimes it appears by itself.
Elena Garro

CAPRICORN
What is unity, so it is understood, is two diverse things made one.
Saint Theresa

AQUARIUS
After all, everything is a big joke on the outside of a script.
Charles Chaplin

PISCES
In quiet waters one finds the biggest fish.
Danish Proverb

Humility does not mean submission.

22

MAY

ARIES

Imagination is nature's equal, sensuality her slave.
Goethe

TAURUS

He who cannot interest himself in small things will take false interest in big ones.
Leibnitz

GEMINI

Success does not give or take away the reason of things.
A. C. Castillo

CANCER

Who lives without folly is not so wise as he thinks.
La Rochefoucauld

LEO

Modesty is the only sure bait when you angle for praise.
G. K. Chesterton

VIRGO

To love is human; to be indulgent is human, too.
Plautus

LIBRA

Justice delayed is justice denied.
William E. Gladstone

SCORPIO

Sweet milk of adversity, philosophy.
William Shakespeare

SAGITTARIUS

There are too many men in this world who don't know what world they are living in.
Bob Hope

CAPRICORN

Ambition is only vanity enobled.
Jerome K. Jerome

AQUARIUS

If you take big paces you leave big spaces.
Burmese Proverb

PISCES

Our ideals are the best part of our beings.
A. B. Alcott

23
MAY

Indulge in a moment of sybaritism—wassail!

ARIES
Happiness makes up in height what it lacks in length.
Robert Frost

TAURUS
Pain makes man think. Thought makes man wise. Wisdom makes life endurable.
John Patrick

GEMINI
A glass of wine at the right moment is worth more than all the riches in the world.
Gustav Mahler

CANCER
I am not an optimist. I want to be an optimist.
Émile Zola

LEO
We rarely trust those who are better than we are.
Anonymous

VIRGO
Nothing will ever be attempted, if all possible objections must first be overcome.
Samuel Johnson

LIBRA
When the music changes, so should the dance change.
Hausa Proverb

SCORPIO
Indulgences, not fulfillment, are what the world permits us.
Christopher Fry

SAGITTARIUS
It is worth being unhappy many times to be happy for a minute.
Jorge Luis Borges

CAPRICORN
Man's desires are limited by his perceptions: none can desire what he has not perceived.
William Blake

AQUARIUS
Organize the unorganized.
John L. Lewis

PISCES
It isn't what people think that is important, but the reason they think what they think.
Eugene Ionesco

ARIES

Many things that were something, upon leaving them are nothing.
Baltasar Gracián

TAURUS

Stars are the jewels of the night and possibly surpass anything that the day has to show us.
Johannes Kepler

GEMINI

Never confuse knowledge with wisdom. One helps you earn a living, the other helps you build a life.
Sandra Carey

CANCER

The greatest truths are the simplist, and so are the greatest men.
Julius Charles Hare

LEO

A kind word is worth three cold seasons.
Japanese Proverb

VIRGO

A basic investigation is what I do when I don't know what I am doing.
Werner von Braun

LIBRA

The eye always crosses the river before the body does.
Libian Quote

SCORPIO

You never can have fun with the things you haven't done.
Ogden Nash

SAGITTARIUS

Better bend than break.
Spanish Proverb

CAPRICORN

It can be useful to take the best of all the parts.
Cicero

AQUARIUS

Each truth we discover in nature or social life destroys the crutches on which we used to lean.
Ernst Toller

PISCES

Sight must learn from reason.
Johannes Kepler

25
MAY

Order, symmetry, and a bit of class are needed.

ARIES
If you do not enjoy what you have, how could you be happy with more?
Tibetan quote

TAURUS
Nothing without reason, nothing sterile, nothing dead exists, in the universe.
Dogen

GEMINI
The secret of business is to know something that nobody else knows.
Aristotle Onassis

CANCER
History is a pact between the dead, the living, and the unborn.
Edmund Burke

LEO
Being completely honest with oneself is a very good exercise.
Sigmund Freud

VIRGO
Each one of us must patiently bear the results of our own example.
Phaedrus

LIBRA
He who does not know one thing, always knows another.
Kenyan Proverb

SCORPIO
A barren tree pleads for substitute fruit.
Popular Mexican Saying

SAGITTARIUS
Going fast, although a great virtue, begets a vice: speed.
José Agustín

CAPRICORN
What loneliness is more lonely than distrust.
George Eliot

AQUARIUS
The bottom line of capitalism is "you or I," not "you and I."
William Liebknecht

PISCES
The insane open paths that the wise use later on.
C. Dossi

Let yourself feel the vitality of a protest.
Learn to conscientiously object.

ARIES
You always pass failure on the way to success.
Mickey Rooney

TAURUS
Whatso'er we perpetrate, We do but row, we are steered by fate.
Samuel Butler

GEMINI
There are two ways of spreading light: to be the candle or the mirror that reflects it.
Edith Wharton

CANCER
Golden words are often followed by heavy acts.
Dutch Proverb

LEO
Yet to be honest, one must be inconsistent.
Herbert George Wells

VIRGO
Lord, make me chaste—but not yet.
Saint Augustine

LIBRA
What belongs to everybody, belongs to nobody.
Anonymous

SCORPIO
Hunger is the teacher of all art and inspires invention.
Persian Quote

SAGITTARIUS
A man of words and not of deeds is like a garden full of weeds.
English Proverb

CAPRICORN
My own self is both my friend and my enemy.
Mahabarata

AQUARIUS
Things have a terrible permanence when people die.
Joyce Kilmer

PISCES
An intelligent person notices everything; a fool makes a remark about everything.
Heinrich Heine

27
MAY

Relate to the root emotions that give way to personal dignity.

ARIES
Not with what we have, but with what we enjoy, do we find our true abundance.
Tibetan Quote

TAURUS
Vision is the art of seeing things invisible.
Jonathan Swift

GEMINI
A professional is someone who can do his best work when he doesn't feel like it.
Alfred Alistair Cooke

CANCER
Clearness is the virtue of deep thoughts and thinkers.
Marquis de Vauvenargues

LEO
Man makes sacred what he believes in, as he makes beautiful what he loves.
Ernest Renen

VIRGO
There is something complacent in the calm recollection of a sad memory.
Cicero

LIBRA
Experience is fine, if it is not too expensive!
English Quote

SCORPIO
Not truth, but faith, it is, that keeps the world alive.
Edna St. Vincent Millay

SAGITTARIUS
Incompetence is much more frightening than competence.
Luis Marcet

CAPRICORN
A great battle-zone is man!
Victor Hugo

AQUARIUS
Bed is the poor mans opera.
Italian Proverb

PISCES
Nobody is born taught, if it isn't to cry.
Bolivian Proverb

Accept a challenge. Risk, juggle, and evolve.

ARIES
He who has no inner fire cannot warm others.
Richard Burton

TAURUS
What the world needs is more geniuses with humility. There are so few of us left.
Oscar Levant

GEMINI
Language most shows a man; speak that I may see thee.
Ben Jonson

CANCER
What is human is immortal!
Bulwer-Lytton

LEO
I present myself to you in the same way that I want my relationship with you to be.
Luigi Prandello

VIRGO
Tact is the intelligence of the heart.
Anonymous

LIBRA
Everyone has a talent. What is rare is the courage to follow the talent to the dark places where it leads.
Erica Jong

SCORPIO
It's better to be quotable than to be honest.
Tom Stoppard

SAGITTARIUS
Move emotions with poems. Assign ceremonies in the right way. Provide unity with music.
Confucius

CAPRICORN
The hardest work is to go idle.
Jewish Proverb

AQUARIUS
The universe is made up of stories, not of atoms.
Muriel Rukeyser

PISCES
Death twitches my ear. "Live," he says, "I am coming."
Virgil

*We exist within the Milky Way and
it is our link to time and space.*

ARIES
Clear your mind of can't.
Samuel Johnson

TAURUS
Words derive their power from the original word.
Meister Eckhart

GEMINI
Freedom must first be accepted, then planned and finally, enjoyed.
Paco Rabanne

CANCER
Lateness jeopardizes.
Popular Mexican Saying

LEO
Make yourself necessary to somebody.
Ralph Waldo Emerson

VIRGO
It's good to be without vices, but not to be without temptations.
Walter Bagehot

LIBRA
The best mirror is the eye of a friend.
Irish Proverb

SCORPIO
Immortality could be a much worse destiny than death.
E. A. Shoaff

SAGITTARIUS
The wise man is completely at ease. The insignificant man always complains.
Confucius

CAPRICORN
Fortune might take away your riches, but not your spirit or intention.
Seneca

AQUARIUS
Words use us just as we use words.
Lewis Carroll

PISCES
Credulity is man's weakness, but the child's strength.
Charles Lamb

ARIES
When fortune knocks, open the door.
Anonymous

TAURUS
There are two ways to confront difficulties. Either you alter them, or you alter yourself.
Santayana

GEMINI
A belief is not true because it is useful.
Henri Frederic Amiel

CANCER
Reality is what is left when one no longer believes what one perceives.
Michel Serres

LEO
I was born modest; not all over, in pieces.
Mark Twain

VIRGO
If you don't improve today you'll grow worse tomorrow.
Anonymous

LIBRA
To escape criticism, do nothing, say nothing, be nothing.
Elbert Hubbard

SCORPIO
The last drop makes the cup run over.
Anonymous

SAGITTARIUS
Clapping with the right hand only will not produce a noise.
Malay Proverb

CAPRICORN
Achievement has come to be the only real patent of nobility.
Woodrow Wilson

AQUARIUS
Just because he was born in a stable doesn't make a man a horse.
Anonymous

PISCES
For every credibility gap there is a gullibility fill.
Richard Clopton

31
MAY

ARIES
Experience is what you get from being inexperienced.
Franklin P. Jones

TAURUS
Man's heart is the central point
And heaven the circumference
Shabistari

GEMINI
Sometimes, I've believed six impossible things before breakfast!
Lewis Carroll

CANCER
Man is what he believes.
Anton Chekhov

LEO
The more you let yourself go, the less they will let you go.
Nietzsche

VIRGO
If the sky falls, we shall catch larks.
Anonymous

LIBRA
In literature as in love, we wonder at the choice of others.
André Maurois

SCORPIO
Last but not least.
Anonymous

SAGITTARIUS
Integrity simply means a willingness not to violate one's identity.
Erich Fromm

CAPRICORN
There are limits to self-indulgence, none to self-restraint.
Mahatma Gandhi

AQUARIUS
Love dies only when growth stops.
Pearl S. Buck

PISCES
Knowledge does not take up much space.
Anonymous

JUNE

JUNE

There once was a man from Peru
Who wrote limericks that end at line two.
Anonymous

Either the Gods have power to assist us, or they have not.
Marcus Aurelius

"June is a migraine above the eyes. Strict auras and yellow blots," writes Charles Wright in his marvelous *Black Zodiac*. This book has nothing to do with astrology, yet everything to do with cycles and wisdom. June is yellow, the color that pertains to birthday-boy or -girl Gemini's aura. June is also a month, as Karl Jaspers put it, for "awakening to myself, in my situation. . . . I must search for being if I want to find my real self. But it is not till I fail in this search for intrinsic being that I begin to philosophize." June should make all of us smile in complicity at ourselves. By the end of the month, when the Sun moves into Cancer, everyone should have resolved something important—even if it is simply how to enjoy a color, a word . . . a migraine.

ARIES

Aries, it all depends on you this month. The Sun moves into Gemini the last week in May and will shed new light on all the subjects that intrigue you. This month there is both certainty and uncertainty. For once, give yourself the option not to rush into things like any old fool, but to stop, look, and listen to the wisdom you carry within. And try to let your wool-gathering include someone else who can help you to knit things—or relationships—together. Just try to know what to ask, as well as to whom.

Remember . . . "Ask, and thou shalt be told."

Keywords: Learn to think positivily

TAURUS

The summer solstice (the winter solstice for those living in the Southern Hemisphere) is a wonderful gift for every Taurus, giving a lift during the last week of June. Lucky you! Now is the time to build up your fortunes. But do take it easy. Look around. Give others the right of way before you stampede. Everything has a deeper meaning than you think, and the zillions of electromagnetic influences now shining down on you are on your side.

Keywords: Look and connect inward

GEMINI

Although you Geminis are always quick to change, others often never are! This can be imponderable, yet this is your month to ponder the human soul. Take a few risks, no matter what the outcome. Make any moves with a longer view (your decisions will be good until the year 2999) shape the years to come—and yourself—with positive action. And remember, as the Buddhists say, "We are what we think." So think what is best for the grand old *you.*

Keywords: Push yet ponder

CANCER

This is the perfect month for all you Moonchildren to do a little reflective Moon gazing. Though you might find yourself caught offguard, no matter how choppy your sea becomes, try to float. Toughen your soft shell with a gloss of good humor. And remember, you Cancers are never sure of anything until it is over, and that includes the month of June.

Keywords: Lighten up

LEO

Anything that you can do better than before—reappraise or improve on, besides really leaning on the "let's-have-some-fun" side of the coin—is what is best for you in June, Leo. Last month's little tensions should be blown away by this month's solstice, and any decision you make now works like catnip. So be playful as a pussycat, and let yourself be surprised.
Keywords: Smile and surprise

VIRGO

Virgo will not always breathe a sigh of relief in June. Take your time just now, adjust, move into place with thoughts on the larger scheme of things, and don't take too much for granted. Try to repair your inner discontent, maybe by paying less attention to your distress signals. And until the last eight days of June, be *"qui vive"*—alert, on the go, and appreciative.
Keyword: Enlightenment

LIBRA

This month, supply your demands! Convey, reach for, and require whatever you feel like to satisfy your hidden dreams or downright necessities, no matter how wild they might be! Breaking new ground definitely is advised. Work to keep your balance, for June could topple you with surprises—some good, some that may require a little adjustment on your part. Just know, you're on the right path.
Keywords: Imagine and paradoxes

SCORPIO

You Scorpios like to have your cake and wolf it down with gusto, but this month, you may have to leave a little on your plate. So try to adapt. Tailor your needs and your appetites. Learn to be more productive in new ways. It's all a matter of perfect timing: when to talk, when to think, and when to think about what you can't decide on!
Keywords: Adapt to both sides of the story

SAGITTARIUS

You are the target this month! So get out there and practice. Try to find out more about yourself. Do this by watching yourself as you interact with others, visiting, sharing, imitating, correcting, or even enjoying. Your mind is being given a message, so don't make excuses. Ask about anything, listen to everything, and try to figure out why you are supposed to be the philosopher your sign says you are, even as the last sultry days of June wind down.

Keywords: Measure and query

CAPRICORN

This is the month to climb new mountains. Try to look at yourself—and others—in a fresh new way. You usually are the perfect example of responsibility, but in June, you could lose your surefootedness and stumble on your own words and deeds. Now is the time to sort things out in your usual slow-and-steady-wins-the-race sort of pace, and even if you do live to be 999 (Noah's age of 999), remember, there actually is always something new under the sun. And this is just the month when you could be constantly reminded of it.

Keyword: Decisions

AQUARIUS

You water-bearers could find yourselves especially buoyant all through June. Laugh and have a good time, Aquarius, but do not drown out other peoples' feelings, especially those in your immediate family. It really *is* hard to please everyone, starting with yourself. Dwell more on your choice of words and remember that you can be misunderstood. Don't feel guilty about having fun, but do try to be New and Improved—an easy task for most Aquarians.

Keywords: Subtlety and considerations

PISCES

A picture isn't always worth a thousand words, Pisces. Sometimes words are more priceless than a Picasso. So try, during this summer's solstice, to take a little extra care in making your words perfect this month, in particular on the full moon. By month's end, your freedom of speech is yours once again!

Keywords: Meanings and thoughts

1

Look for the wisdom—then speak.

JUNE

ARIES
. . . how serious a matter human life is . . .
Harriet Martineau

TAURUS
Things don't change, but by and by, our wishes change.
Marcel Proust

GEMINI
Speech is the small change of silence.
George Meredith

CANCER
Man is an animal of solitudes.
Rosario Castellanos

LEO
To be successful, always have a tan, live in an elegant building . . . let yourself be seen in the trendiest restaurants . . . and if you borrow money, ask for huge amounts.   *Aristotle Onassis*

VIRGO
There is a crack in everything God has made.
Ralph Waldo Emerson

LIBRA
Imagination is not the talent of some men, but the well-being of all men.
Ralph Waldo Emerson

SCORPIO
Every new adjustment is a crisis in self-esteem.
Eric Hoffer

SAGITTARIUS
Nature plays with nature, and nature contains nature, and nature knows how to surpass nature.
Hermetic Formula

CAPRICORN
I belong to this day and to yesterday, but there is something within me that is about tomorrow and the next day, and the future.
Attributed to Nietzsche

AQUARIUS
Words should be dressed as a goddess and soar like a bird.
Tibetan Proverb

PISCES
A poet is a liar who always speaks the truth.
Jean Cocteau

Experience breeds opportunity.

2

JUNE

ARIES
If you really respect yourself, you can do others no harm.
Hindu Proverb

TAURUS
Every man's life is a fairy tale written by God's fingers.
Hans Christian Andersen

GEMINI
With our thoughts alone, we can build the world.
Buddha

CANCER
Reason is like a pot with two handles: it can be taken by the right side or by the left side.
Michel de Montaigne

LEO
Laughter is the shortest distance between two people.
Victor Borge

VIRGO
Until death, all is life.
Cervantes

LIBRA
A supposition is much better than the truth.
Sir Francis Bacon

SCORPIO
Perhaps out of all of man's creations, language is the most astounding.
Lytton Strachey

SAGITTARIUS
There are things as futile as a clock in an empty house.
James Thurber

CAPRICORN
Any machine can do the work of fifty ordinary men. No machine can do the work of one extraordinary man.
Henry Ford

AQUARIUS
I love such mirth as does not make friends ashamed to look upon one another next morning.
Izaak Walton

PISCES
How long a time lies in one little word!
William Shakespeare

3

Life should work for people. Make it work for you.

ARIES
Whatever you do, it must have at least some little grams of love.
Harriet Martineau

TAURUS
He who owes least to fortune is in the strongest position.
Machiavelli

GEMINI
True thankfulness might be the finest of man's feelings, also the rarest.
Hermann Hesse

CANCER
He rose without a friend and sat down without an enemy.
Henry Grattan

LEO
First deserve it, then desire it!
Anonymous

VIRGO
Nostalgia is no longer what it used to be.
Stendhal

LIBRA
Practice does not always produce perfection: perfect practice brings perfection.
Vincent Lombardi

SCORPIO
Stick with the good guys, and you will become one of them.
Anonymous

SAGITTARIUS
The ass endures the load, but not the overload.
Cervantes

CAPRICORN
Never trust appearances.
Horace

AQUARIUS
If you can't be good, be careful.
Anonymous

PISCES
Silence is sometimes also an opinion.
Anonymous

Individual fulfillment casts heroic molds.

ARIES
Who is the wisest man? He who studies. Who is the strongest man? He who has limits. Who is the richest? He who is content with what he has.
The Talmud

TAURUS
Out of two wrongs, pick the prettiest.
Orson Welles

GEMINI
When you stop thinking, do not forget to begin again.
Heraclitus

CANCER
Everyone interprets in their own way heaven's harmony.
Chinese Proverb

LEO
One of the paramount reasons for staying attractive is so you can have somebody to go to bed with.
Helen Gurley Brown

VIRGO
Money costs too much!
James Ramsay MacDonald

LIBRA
The only thing one really has to know is how to make good use of your own neurosis.
Arthur Adamov

SCORPIO
So . . . is God the good guy or the bad guy?
Eli Moskowitz [five years old]

SAGITTARIUS
There is nothing permanent except change.
Anonymous

CAPRICORN
Fire tests gold, misfortune brave men.
Seneca

AQUARIUS
Happiness is a gift. It comes like a butterfly in the winter woods. Let it sit with us a while.
Edith Wharton

PISCES
Reading is for the mind what exercise is for the body.
Richard Steele

5
JUNE

Become your very own source of inspiration.

ARIES
Nature needs few things, your imagination many.
Buddhist Scripture

TAURUS
If God dishes your rice in a basket, you should not wish to eat soup.
Mende of Sierra Leone

GEMINI
Thinking brings us to the foot of the mountain; faith brings us to the top.
Lin-Chi

CANCER
There are those who make things happen, there are those who see how things happen, while there are others who ask, what is happening?
Anonymous

LEO
God's finger never leaves the same fingerprint.
Stanislaw Lec

VIRGO
Always forget your enemies, nothing could bother them more.
Oscar Wilde

LIBRA
Maturity is the capacity to stand any uncertainty.
John Finley

SCORPIO
. . . and he that revealeth secrets maketh known to thee
what shall come to pass . . .
Daniel 2:29

SAGITTARIUS
Asking costs nothing.
Anonymous

CAPRICORN
For mortal to aid mortal—this is God.
Pliny the Elder

AQUARIUS
Name the greatest of all inventors: Accident.
Mark Twain

PISCES
The human race would perish from the face of the earth if people would stop helping each other.
Sir Walter Scott

ARIES
A bit of sound sense is what makes men; the rest is rubbish.
Petronius

TAURUS
People change, and forget to tell that to other people.
Lillian Hellman

GEMINI
Carpe diem . . . (Seize the day . . .)
Attributed to Horace

CANCER
The fundamental deception of humanity is to suppose that I am here, and you are there outside.
Yasutani Roshi

LEO
If the goat had a longer tail he could wipe the stars clean.
Czech Saying

VIRGO
The world uncertain comes and goes.
Ralph Waldo Emerson

LIBRA
Who knows how to learn knows enough.
Henry Adams

SCORPIO
Silence always brings with it some part of eternity.
Thomas Carlyle

SAGITTARIUS
He who wants to, can make things easy.
Graffiti

CAPRICORN
There is nothing so adverse that the just soul does not find some solace for.
Seneca

AQUARIUS
The best prophet of the future is the past.
Lord Byron

PISCES
Life is just a dream—but don't wake me.
Yiddish Proverb

7

JUNE

ARIES
Beware of people carrying ideas. Beware of ideas carrying people.
Barbara Grizzuti Harrison

TAURUS
With time, we grow and believe that our own future will answer us.
Ruth Benedict

GEMINI
. . . And trust tomorrow as least as possible.
Second Part of Yesterday's Proverb

CANCER
What one does not talk about, should be left in silence.
Ludwig Wittgenstein

LEO
Among cultivated minds, the first interview is the best.
Ralph Waldo Emerson

VIRGO
Not even God can change what has already happened.
Agathon

LIBRA
Women never have the same success that men do, because they don't have wives to tell them what to do.
Dick Van Dyke

SCORPIO
The most powerful of men is he who has power over himself.
Seneca

SAGITTARIUS
The human being is a composite of all that is spiritual.
Ezra Ben Solomon

CAPRICORN
Sometimes it is wise to play the fool.
Horace

AQUARIUS
God forgives those who invent what they need.
Lillian Hellman

PISCES
Let the stubborn man cure you of himself.
Hisam al-Lajmi

ARIES
Intellect is what differentiates us from animals.
Asian Proverb

TAURUS
Humans are beings born to believe.
Benjamin Disraeli

GEMINI
A good life is a main argument.
Ben Jonson

CANCER
It should be just as easy to find the truth as it is to find a lie.
Cicero

LEO
Civilization can only be understood by those who are civilized.
Alfred North Whitehead

VIRGO
God may not change the past, but historians do!
Samuel Butler

LIBRA
You are remembered by the rules you break.
General Douglas MacArthur

SCORPIO
If you shut up, nobody can repeat what you say.
Anonymous

SAGITTARIUS
The first democratic doctrine is that all men are interesting.
G. K. Chesterton

CAPRICORN
To hear somebody else talk well about oneself makes for a second heritage.
Publilius Syrus

AQUARIUS
You can't change the world. The best you can do is learn to live with it.
Henry Miller

PISCES
We never miss the water 'til the well runs dry.
Anonymous

9
JUNE

Dreams never slip away, they just rest.

ARIES
Morning will still come with or without the crowing of the cock.
Burundi Proverb

TAURUS
Remember that art is "me," science is "us."
Claude Bernard

GEMINI
The wise man knows very well when he doesn't know; the stubborn man thinks he knows.
Fen-Yang

CANCER
Life is like throwing dice: if they don't turn up as you hoped, you have to make the most of how they did.
Terence

LEO
Proof of your fame comes when some crazy person thinks that he is really you.
Graffiti

VIRGO
When the talker and the listener do not agree, it becomes metaphysics.
Voltaire

LIBRA
Man will always be in need of man.
Theocritus

SCORPIO
If you are quiet, nobody can tell you to shut up.
Anonymous

SAGITTARIUS
The perpetual obstacle for man's advancement is habit.
John Stuart Mill

CAPRICORN
There is nothing that is of no interest; only those who are not interested.
G. K. Chesterton

AQUARIUS
Change by itself is eternal, perpetual and immortal.
Arthur Schopenhauer

PISCES
Each one of us defends himself according to the way the finger is pointing.
English Proverb

Disclose your aims and then you will be able to achieve.

10
JUNE

ARIES
Every natural power exhilarates; a true talent delights the possessor first.
Ralph Waldo Emerson

TAURUS
If you investigate, and try to find out where the clear light mind is, you will be able to find it within an individual person.
The Dalai Lama

GEMINI
The young man knows the laws, but the old man understands the exceptions.
Oliver Wendell Holmes

CANCER
It would be fun to go for a day to a "no place."
Ogden Nash

LEO
Celebrity has the advantage of being known by those who don't know you.
Nicolas Chamfort

VIRGO
Poverty makes you sad as well as wise.
Bertolt Brecht

LIBRA
Whatever the heavens create, the earth can find use for.
Chinese Proverb

SCORPIO
If it isn't erotic, it is not interesting.
Fernando Arrabal

SAGITTARIUS
A man never knows how to be a son until he becomes a father.
American Indian Proverb

CAPRICORN
In all things, its measure is perfect usage.
Plautus

AQUARIUS
A sword may conquer for a while, but the spirit conquers forever.
Sholem Asch

PISCES
Each one of us can be the enemy of oneself.
Anacarsis

11
JUNE

That "something special" IS in the air!

ARIES
The spirit never dies. This is how a spiritual person liberates himself from death.
Said-Ben-Hamed

TAURUS
We feel and must understand that somehow, we are all eternal.
Spinoza

GEMINI
You just put your hand over your heart and keep going.
Giuseppe Verdi

CANCER
In a "no place" one could conquer anonymity if one would have proof of identity.
Max Aube

LEO
The best thing I got out of the Nobel prize was not having to stand in line at the cinema.
Gabriel García Márquez

VIRGO
The whole world is a door that opens towards liberation, but few want to walk in.
Hui-Wu

LIBRA
Natural man has only two primal passions: to get and to beget.
Sir William Osler

SCORPIO
Sex is at the basis of most problems and sometimes spoils everything.
Andreas Landshoff

SAGITTARIUS
The language of friendship is not words but meanings.
Henry David Thoreau

CAPRICORN
All stupidity suffers the irritation of itself.
Seneca

AQUARIUS
What is life if not what we think about all day? What is life if not an angle of vision.
Ralph Waldo Emerson

PISCES
The matter does not appear to me now as it appeares to have appeared to me then.
Baron George W. Bramwell

Give yourself some credit.

ARIES
I've been trying . . .
Tiger Woods

TAURUS
If it doesn't stem from yourself, where will you go to find it?
Zen Proverb

GEMINI
Study the sentences that seem to say the truth and doubt them.
D. Reisman

CANCER
To be wrong is human, and anyone can make a mistake.
Anonymous

LEO
Among those whom I like, I can find no common denominator, but among those whom I love, I can: all of them make me laugh.
W. H. Auden

VIRGO
Getting past the past, a leitmotif.
Alfred Corn

LIBRA
If we are not able to live to be happy, let us at least live to deserve happiness.
Fichte

SCORPIO
I am on a search for a huge maybe.
Rabelais

SAGITTARIUS
. . . to find the point where hypothesis and fact meet . . .
Lillian Smith

CAPRICORN
As I converse, time passes.
Ovid

AQUARIUS
There may be one problem after another, but in their resolution we find our greatest pleasure.
Karl Augustus Menninger

PISCES
Silence is deep as Eternity; speech shallow as Time.
Thomas Carlyle

13
JUNE

Listen to the back-country sounds. To the crickets and the trees and trucks on the distant highway.

ARIES
The body is the first pupil of the soul.
Henry David Thoreau

TAURUS
The pessimist complains about the wind: the optimist waits for it to change its course; the realist hoists the sails.
William Arthur Ward

GEMINI
During a game of chess, sometimes the best player gives up.
Norbert Guterman

CANCER
There are many more fools in this world than people.
Heine

LEO
There are many roads that lead to the top, but the scenery is always the same.
Chinese Proverb

VIRGO
Intuition is the result of the fusion of a pure heart with an illuminated intelligence.
Swami Ramdas

LIBRA
The history of a love affair is not really important; what is important is that one has the capacity to love.
Helen Hayes

SCORPIO
Money may buy you a good dog, but it will never make the dog wag its tail.
Josh Billings

SAGITTARIUS
Anyone is as young as he feels, but rarely as important.
Voltaire

CAPRICORN
All of us cannot do everything.
Virgil

AQUARIUS
Life is not as important as life's duties.
W. Cabell Bruce

PISCES
Charm is the way of getting the answer "yes" without having asked any clear question.
Albert Camus

ARIES
The mind of man is capable of anything—because everything is in it, all the past as well as all the future.
Joseph Conrad

TAURUS
A great many open minds should be closed for repairs.
Toledo Blade

GEMINI
Too much talk will include errors.
Burmese Proverb

CANCER
Keeping peace begins with autosatisfaction of each individual.
The Dalai Lama

LEO
Fame may be the stepmother of death and ambition, could be the excrement of glory.
Pietro Arentino

VIRGO
Children are the riches of the poor.
English Proverb

LIBRA
There are no illegitimate children, only illegitimate parents.
Judge Yankwich

SCORPIO
Pride is the mask of one's own faults.
Jewish Proverb

SAGITTARIUS
I have no expectation of making a hit every time I come to bat.
Franklin D. Roosevelt

CAPRICORN
Rest restores the body and the spirit's strength.
Ovid

AQUARIUS
Courage is the ladder on which all other virtues mount.
Anita Loos

PISCES
When you watch fire, when you look at the sky, never forget that the spirits of the past are within them.
Nanahuatzin (Aztec)

15

JUNE

"A bunch of hogwash" is always a good expression.

ARIES
One can always "better" the existent order of anything.
Lichtenstein

TAURUS
Words should be the mirror of actions.
Solon

GEMINI
Therefore, the cause of attainment is attainment itself.
Hujwiri

CANCER
It is the nature of all greatness not to be too exact.
Edmund Burke

LEO
Our actions are like rhyme games: we fill out the rest of the lines with whatever motives for the actions we please.
La Rochefoucauld

VIRGO
We often forgive those who bore us, but cannot forgive those whom we bore.
La Rochefoucauld

LIBRA
Think twice, act once.
Anonymous

SCORPIO
All animals, except for man, know that the best thing in life is to enjoy it.
Samuel Butler

SAGITTARIUS
I seem to have an awful lot of people inside of me.
Dame Edith Evans

CAPRICORN
Posterity will give to each and every one the honor that corresponds him.
Tacitus

AQUARIUS
Listen to the call of dawn which takes you towards the rest of the day.
Sanskrit Proverb

PISCES
Advice are those things that wise men don't need and fools don't use.
Anonymous

NOW could just be the time!

16
JUNE

ARIES
One can't give a firefly to a child if one hasn't caught it yet.
Anonymous from Madagascar

TAURUS
We all have silly ideas, but a wise person will not use them.
Wilhelm Busch

GEMINI
Before telling others what to do, one must be an instructor to oneself.
Zen Koan

CANCER
Nothing exists beyond man's contradictions.
Jesus Reyes Heroles

LEO
To do a great right do a little wrong.
William Shakespeare

VIRGO
Keep cool in bad times, and wait for the good times.
French Proverb

LIBRA
Fashion fades, style is eternal.
Yves Saint Laurent

SCORPIO
Life is short, art is long, opportunity fleeting, experience chancy, judgment difficult.
Hippocritus

SAGITTARIUS
Fill yourself once a day with some joy of creativity: there is the reward.
Anonymous

CAPRICORN
I only know that what is moral is what you feel good after, and what is immoral is what you feel bad after.
Ernest Hemingway

AQUARIUS
Insignificant things can make for
perfection . . . and perfection is never insignificant.
Miguel Angel Buonarroti

PISCES
Be careful of planning for the future, when it is already in the past.
Anonymous

17
JUNE

A day to encourage your own voice.

ARIES
Frivolity is the species' refusal to suffer.
John Lahr

TAURUS
One needs a long, long time to be young.
Pablo Picasso

GEMINI
Who has confidence in himself will gain the confidence of others.
Lazerov

CANCER
Energy is eternal delight.
William Blake

LEO
We must make our garden grow.
Voltaire

VIRGO
The supreme reality of our time is the vulnerability of our planet.
John F. Kennedy

LIBRA
Who, except the Gods, can live time through forever without any pain?
Aeschylus

SCORPIO
An artist never really finishes his work, it is simply abandoned.
Paul Valéry

SAGITTARIUS
Everybody has a friend in need.
Irish Proverb

CAPRICORN
We wait for what we want, but we take what comes.
Cicero

AQUARIUS
The future struggles against being mastered.
Anonymous

PISCES
Whoever wills the end, also wills . . . the means.
Immanuel Kant

Any form of spirituality will do, so long as you believe.

ARIES
The gods do not give mortals everything at the same time.
Homer

TAURUS
You cannot drive straight on a twisted lane.
Russian Quote

GEMINI
There is nothing so powerful as truth—and nothing so strange.
Daniel Webster

CANCER
Generosity does not consist in giving much but in giving at the right time.
Elsa Cross

LEO
Love, is above all, the gift of oneself.
Jean Anouilh

VIRGO
It is useless attacking the insensible.
Aesop

LIBRA
One lives with the hope of becoming a memory.
Antonio Porchia

SCORPIO
If we want to make a new world, the material is all there: after all, the first one was made out of chaos.
Robert Quillen

SAGITTARIUS
Better be happy with the fruitful grape than sadden after none, or bitter fruit.
Omar Khayyam

CAPRICORN
All experience is an arch to build up.
Henry Brooks Adams

AQUARIUS
Turn on. Tune in. Drop out.
Timothy Leary

PISCES
May all your pleasures become habits.
Latin Toast

19
JUNE

ARIES
The raft of knowledge ferries the worst sinner to safety.
Bhagavad Gita

TAURUS
When Fortune comes, seize her in front with a sure hand, because behind she is bald.
Leonardo da Vinci

GEMINI
To understand is to forgive, even oneself.
Alexander Chase

CANCER
Darkened by time, the masters, like our memories, mix and mismatch.
Charles Wright

LEO
What really counts, is what you learn after you know.
John Wooden

VIRGO
Hold on tight to the words of your ancestors.
Maori Quote

LIBRA
The superfluous is extremely necessary.
Voltaire

SCORPIO
Paradise is exactly like where you are now, except much, much better.
Laurie Anderson

SAGITTARIUS
Ask the gods nothing excessive.
Aeschylus

CAPRICORN
Men acquire a particular quality by constantly acting in a particular way.
Aristotle

AQUARIUS
We all carry a new world within our hearts.
Buenaventura Berruti

PISCES
God promises a good landing, but not a calm journey.
Anonymous

All rules do not apply to all circumstances.

ARIES
An error is simply a failure to adjust immediately from a preconception to an actuality.
John Cage

TAURUS
Every exit is an entry to somewhere.
Tom Stoppard

GEMINI
The tongue goes full speed ahead when the brain is in park.
Graffiti

CANCER
Only imbeciles never contradict themselves.
André Gide

LEO
Humor is nothing more than another defense against the universe.
Mel Brooks

VIRGO
Confidence is a slow growing plant.
William Pitt

LIBRA
I generally avoid temptation, unless I can't resist it.
Mae West

SCORPIO
Men willingly believe what they wish.
Julius Ceaser

SAGITTARIUS
Love your neighbor, but don't make love to the person.
French Proverb

CAPRICORN
If a man gives no thought to what is distant, he will find sorrow near at hand.
Confucius

AQUARIUS
Every fact that is learned becomes a key to other facts.
E. I. Youmans

PISCES
Everything comes if a man will only wait.
Benjamin Disraeli

21
JUNE

Care for someone.

ARIES
Search for a reason for evil and you will find that you carry it within.
Jean-Jacques Rousseau

TAURUS
The most important thing is not what destiny does to us, but what we do with it.
Florence Nightingale

GEMINI
It takes all sorts to make a world.
English Proverb

CANCER
The theory that has no practical application in life is an acrobatic thought.
Swami Vivekananda

LEO
Conquer your heart, then you will be somebody!
Ansari de Herat

VIRGO
There are certain defects, that when well used, shine more than virtue itself!
La Rochefoucauld

LIBRA
If I go to heaven I want to take my reason with me.
Ingersoll

SCORPIO
Gods live and die, but the atom remains.
Alexander Chase

SAGITTARIUS
Better be wise by the misfortunes of others than by your own.
Aeschylus

CAPRICORN
Peace rules the day where reason rules the mind.
William Collins

AQUARIUS
ALL generalizations are false, including this one.
Alexander Chase

PISCES
The slightly mad find their most eloquent spokesmen in the ranks of the eminently sane.
Attributed to Pierre Boulez

ARIES
By using every minute of our life we can understand what it is to be eternal.
Meister Eckhart

TAURUS
The real secret of looking good is to believe that one looks good.
Lily Tomlin

GEMINI
If you add five new words a month to your vocabulary, in a year your friends won't recognize you.
Subway Graffiti

CANCER
There is a mother at the beginning of all great things.
Anonymous

LEO
When the heart cries because of what it has lost, the spirit laughs for what it has found.
Sufi Proverb

VIRGO
The winds and waves are always on the side of the ablest navigators.
Gibbon

LIBRA
In bed, my real love has always been the sleep that rescued me by allowing me to dream.
Luigi Pirandello

SCORPIO
Credulity is the man's weakness, but the child's strength.
Charles Lamb

SAGITTARIUS
We learn from experience that we never learn from experience.
George Bernard Shaw

CAPRICORN
A mind all logic is like a knife all blade. It makes the hand bleed that uses it.
Rabindranath Tagore

AQUARIUS
Protest long enough that you are right, and you will be wrong.
Yiddish Proverb

PISCES
Use your radiance but shade your splendor.
Tao-Te Ching

23
JUNE

*Concern should be the inside of a sandwich made
with slices of helpfulness and tranquility.*

ARIES
Kindness should be an addiction.
C. C. Vigil

TAURUS
Better bend than break.
Anonymous

GEMINI
I begin where the last man stood.
Thomas Alva Edison

CANCER
What a home needs, most of all, is a family.
Anonymous

LEO
The banalities of great men pass for wit.
Alexander Chase

VIRGO
A friend may well be reckoned the masterpiece of nature.
Ralph Waldo Emerson

LIBRA
There is only a slight difference between total innocence and absolute
degradation.
Marguerite Yourcenar

SCORPIO
I am never bored, anywhere: being bored is an insult to myself.
Jules Renard

SAGITTARIUS
Life is a surprise. I do not see why death should not be an even bigger
surprise!
Vladimir Nabokov

CAPRICORN
I never know how much of what I say is true.
Bette Midler

AQUARIUS
It is much more important to be human than to be important.
Thomas Jefferson

PISCES
The moment you arrived in the world of being, a ladder was put in front of
you so as to be able to escape.
Ivani Shamsi Tabriz

We all have a sense of inevitability and destiny.

ARIES
Kindness is the best quality of the soul.
Confucius

TAURUS
The mind ought sometimes to be amused, that it may the better return to thought, and to itself.
Phaedrus

GEMINI
An optimist counts his blessings, a pessimist thinks his blessings do not count.
Anonymous

CANCER
The worst vice of a fanatic is his sincerity.
Oscar Wilde

LEO
From the invisible he made all visible, being himself invisible.
Enoch

VIRGO
A sensible man can obtain more from his enemies than the stubborn one from his friends.
Baltasar Gracián

LIBRA
Most of the change we think we see in life is due to truths being in and out of favor.
Robert Frost

SCORPIO
The meaning of things lies not in the things themselves, but in our attitude towards them.
Antoine de Saint-Exupéry

SAGITTARIUS
If we have our own why of life, we can get along with almost any how.
Nietzsche

CAPRICORN
Where the will is ready the feet are light.
Anonymous

AQUARIUS
If you search for the truth, you run the risk of finding it.
Manuel Vincent

PISCES
A lucky bastard is still a bastard; fortune doesn't change his luck.
Anonymous

25
JUNE

Endurance is the ability to sustain prolonged stressful activity. It is your body on trial.

ARIES
If God did not exist, we would have to invent him.
Voltaire

TAURUS
Money often costs too much.
Ralph Waldo Emerson

GEMINI
It is better to have loved and lost, then to be married and engaged!
H. L. Mencken

CANCER
We make our own fortune and call it destiny.
Benjamin Disraeli

LEO
Better to quarrel than to be alone.
Irish Proverb

VIRGO
Allow me to smile with the knowledgeable and eat with the rich.
Samuel Johnson

LIBRA
It is much easier to keep one's character than to get it back!
Thomas Paine

SCORPIO
The ocean is nothing more than a collection of drops.
Tibetan Proverb

SAGITTARIUS
Men are what their mothers made them.
Ralph Waldo Emerson

CAPRICORN
I am the inferior of any man whose rights I trample underfoot.
Horace Greely

AQUARIUS
If it is good to live, it is even better to dream, and best of all to awaken.
Antonio Machado

PISCES
You can't seek Lady Luck; Lady Luck seeks you.
Anonymous

Protect yourself with positive thoughts.

ARIES
If you are not doing anything, you are doing bad things.
Goethe

TAURUS
The same thing happens with money as does with toilet paper: when it is needed, it is urgent.
Upton Sinclair

GEMINI
The noisiest drum has nothing in it but air.
English Proverb

CANCER
It is easier to make some things legal than legitimate.
Chamfort

LEO
Charm: that quality in others of making us more satisfied with ourselves.
Henri F. Amiel

VIRGO
Simple pleasures are the last refuge of the complex.
Oscar Wilde

LIBRA
Any man I have once loved, becomes a kind of soul-kin.
Jeanne Moreau

SCORPIO
The mind resorts to reason for want of training.
Henry Adams

SAGITTARIUS
All for one, and one for all!
Alexandre Dumas Pére

CAPRICORN
The only truths we can point to are the ever-changing truths of our own experience.
Peter Weiss

AQUARIUS
If you are not respected as subtle, you will be regarded as sure.
Baltasar Gracián

PISCES
An idea is a feat of association.
Robert Frost

Support someone else's needs.

ARIES
Anyone has a place of peace and quiet in difficult moments, and that place is his own soul.
Leo Tolstoy

TAURUS
Every thing is of the nature of no thing.
Parmenides

GEMINI
Would it be called progress, teaching a cannibal the use of knife and fork?
Ogden Nash

CANCER
Don't ask the doctor, ask the patient.
Yiddish Proverb

LEO
Men's men: gentle or simple, they're much of a muchness.
George Eliot

VIRGO
Most females will forgive a liberty before a slight.
Charles Caleb Colton

LIBRA
It is the little things that sum up life.
Charles Dickens

SCORPIO
Happiness has a bearing, it is not just something.
Mexican Proverb

SAGITTARIUS
From a little spark, follows a flame.
Dante Alighieri

CAPRICORN
All problems can be solved with a proverb. A proverb will always help you grow.
Persian Proverb

AQUARIUS
One should never be the judge in one's own home.
Publilius Syrus

PISCES
He who conquers others is strong. He who conquers himself is powerful.
Lao-Tzu

Security comes from nurturing.

ARIES

The eagle suffers little birds to sing.
William Shakespeare

TAURUS

If men wish to draw near to God, they must seek him in the hearts of men.
Abu Said ibn Abi l-Khayr

GEMINI

An ace in the hand is worth more than two in a pack.
Manual of the Gambler

CANCER

When gossip grows old, it becomes a myth.
Stanislaw Lee

LEO

Ah, if only once, one could really know oneself!
Edward Boehmer

VIRGO

Woman are equal because they are not different anymore.
Erich Fromm

LIBRA

As if one could kill time without wounding eternity.
Henry David Thoreau

SCORPIO

Stoicism is the wisdom of madness, and cynicism, the madness of wisdom.
Bergan Evans

SAGITTARIUS

This is the way the world ends. Not with a bang but a whimper.
T. S. Eliot

CAPRICORN

Be a chess player, not a chessman.
Turkish Proverb

AQUARIUS

In America one says, "How are you?" In Europe one says, "Who are you?"
Subway Graffiti

PISCES

Duty is lighter than a feather and heavier than a mountain.
Japanese Proverb

29
JUNE

An inner resourcefulness can be most delightful.

ARIES

If you really understand what God is all about, you can talk to all men.
Berber Phrase

TAURUS

Too many people study the Bible instead of putting its words into practice.
Daniel Webster

GEMINI

Too many people on the "who's who" list, don't know what is what.
Elsa Maxwell

CANCER

We can designate the condition of energy, universal energy, in no other way than by time.
Carl Jung

LEO

I count only the sunny hours.
Motto on Sundial

VIRGO

Human action is what gives life to this planet.
José Vasconcelos

LIBRA

The bad thing about being too nice, is that people think you are a hypocrite.
F. P. Jones

SCORPIO

Non-cooperation with evil is as much a duty as is cooperation with good.
Mahatma Gandhi

SAGITTARIUS

We read the world wrong and say that it deceives us.
Rabindranath Tagore

CAPRICORN

The rose is a friend of the thorn.
Afghani Saying

AQUARIUS

A face can be the most beautiful of spectacles: understanding
Jean de La Bruyère

PISCES

Defense is one's duty; agression an act of madness.
Anonymous

ARIES
You may sell your work, but not your soul.
John Ruskin

TAURUS
We should never assume that people will behave as we wish them to.
Huang-Po

GEMINI
We have, I fear, confused power with greatness.
Steward L. Udall

CANCER
Whatever you ask me that I don't know, I will not answer.
Yogi Berra

LEO
Fight with anyone, except the cook!
François Avernin

VIRGO
Man is circumference and center, means and end, irradiation and enlightenment of himself.
Jesus Silva-Herzog

LIBRA
Paradoxes are useful to attract attention to ideas.
Mandell Creighton

SCORPIO
The only good is knowledge and the only evil is ignorance.
Socrates

SAGITTARIUS
It is wise to always wait for the end.
Jean de la Fontaine

CAPRICORN
While we are thinking what decision to make, it escapes us.
Publilius Syrus

AQUARIUS
Life is a cap; some put it on, others take it off.
Yiddish Proverb

PISCES
In love with silence, the poet can only speak.
Octavio Paz

JULY

JULY

Do the laws of nature evolve? Or does only physical reality evolve and are the laws of nature eternally fixed? What do we really mean when we talk about "the laws of nature"?

Rupert Sheldrake

July starts off with fireworks—much like Independence Day in America. Take this as your cue to develop some new independent thinking of your own, just don't do it with too loud a bang! Let July be your own personal "midsummer's night dream," by fitting in a little synchronicity and extrasensory perception into your soul. Try to be a part of something magical and mystical and celestial—such as the fireworks in the sky, the Perseid meteor shower. That is a first big step toward understanding and planning for something even more ethereal to come—be it next month or the next millennium—all of which will build up your spiritual being.

ARIES

This month, you Rams may find yourselves a little rundown. You need a change, and the best way to do this during July is to graze around for little distractions, such as counting the raindrops that fall on your head! Become a little more unconventional. Help others get a little unconventional right along with you, and you might see how everything and everyone is connected.

Keyword: Connections

TAURUS

July is one of the best months in the year (especially the first three weeks) for you to get a fresh new outlook. Spruce up your persona, your person, your home, or your workplace. But don't let your natural bullheadedness make you feel that unless the change is big, it is a waste of your time. By the end of the month, Taurus, you'll see how little things can mean a lot. If others try to break your new spirit or tether you, just remember to rely on your thick skin!

Keywords: Freshen up!

GEMINI

As long as you are not caught with your fingers in the door, and as long as that fine line you love to walk between truth and fiction stays firmly in place, Gemini, July could be double the fun for you. Others may want to offer advice, but the only person you should be listening to this month is you. Let some of the fool in you out! Spin, pause, swing, and plunk, quick-changing Geminis. Then land and start all over again, while the month zips by, no matter how hot it gets. Or doesn't.

Keyword: Enjoy

CANCER

Happy birthday, Moonchild! Composed, elegant, and sparkling is what you should be this month. Frazzled, harried, and in dire straights is what you could be if you do not seize the day—each of the thirty-one in July. Crabs may walk backward, but this doesn't mean you should give in to your usual tendency to live in the past! The Sun is in Cancer this month, which means that you can use your super-sensitivity to your advantage. You'll feel more, you'll realize more, you'll connect on deeper levels. So make a wish, take a plunge, and let the good times roll.

Keywords: Sensitivity is a plus

LEO

Used to ruling, you may balk a little at joining your subjects this month, but try to be more of a pussycat about this than usual, Leo, because it's really what could get you purring. Celebrate the cub in you as well as the adult and be ready for anything—even getting your whiskers pulled a bit. Take your time, keep calm, believe in the unbelievable, and you'll enjoy the lion's share in all your activities.

Keywords: New bounty

VIRGO

Worrywart Virgos should take a rain check from their usual downpouring of self-criticism this month—despite how articulate they are at it! Soak up some sun for a change—like Leo! Quickly read up on this top cat's sign, just to get a taste of what you could be doing instead! Try savoring the day. Instead of thinking, just do or be. The *pleasure* factor is what should be paramount for you, Virgo, even if it means letting go a bit more this month than you usually do. Know that you have the full support of the stars on your side.

Keywords: Keep striving

LIBRA

Librans love all things being equal, but this July, your scales are tipped a bit. Although you are usually careful to weigh everyone's feelings, this month may find you off balance. But don't fret. The best thing that could happen to you would be for you to lose something, sacrifice an idea, get in touch with anything that previously seemed unattainable, or simply learn to let go. Have patience. By the end of July, you should have learned a real lesson, Libra, something that actually makes you a better person.

Keyword: Tolerance

SCORPIO

It should be really fun to be you, passionate, provocative Scorpio, during the whole month of July, with special emphasis on the first twenty-three days. For once this year, your life can be a real open book (usually you are more of a shuttered window), as you show others how to tune in to the celestial delights you adore. But take heed: By the 24th, the sun is in Leo, and you may feel as if you've spun off your axis. Just remember, you are not alone. Others are also feeling the celestial sting, and you would be wise to reflect on that, too.

Keyword: Reflection

SAGITTARIUS

Get ready, take aim, fire yourself up, Sagittarius, for this is going to be a planned-for-quiet-yet-damned-for-outbreak month for you! You may want to do nothing more than bask in the sun and keep all things calm, but little events will pop up unpredictably. The main target for July is to dig deep into your psyche and make choices about things very dear to you. Have you ever visited a psychic? A shaman? A holy person? Now is the time to book your appointment. Open up and understand.

Keywords: Dig deeper

CAPRICORN

This month, if you dare, you might actually find out exactly what others think about you, Capricorn, even if you claim that you couldn't care less! You could also find out what others want from you, even if you have decided that you know already and are not going to oblige! Speed up your steady trot and polish your image. Notice, reflect, and connect. And remember that this July, you Goats can scale greater heights and do greater things, especially for yourself.

Keywords: Climb every mountain

AQUARIUS

You can't just float by this month, Aquarius! Keep your mind's eye (or at least a corner of it) focused on a bright yellow flag to remind you to heed your health. Pay attention to counting your assets and watching your spending, as well as your private space. Your soul needs a bit of settling down, without curbing your much-loved independence. Do this, and your long-range prospects could shine as brilliantly as the sun itself!

Keyword: Take care

PISCES

This month, you Fishes might find yourselves much obliged. Paying back what you owe and otherwise fulfilling any of your other obligations, in particular to yourself, are on the top of your July list, Pisces, as well as at the tip of your iceberg. Strive for perfect timing, for like perfect pitch, this can help you find the best way in and out of any situation—not only those situations that you have already encountered, but brand-new ones that will seem to float to the surface just because it is July!

Keyword: Persevere

1
JULY

Naiveté is cute but capricious. Be bold,
reach out eagerly for new meanings.

ARIES
Just make sure that your intentions are not pretensions.
Emile Ludwig

TAURUS
One must always go about with the head held high but remember the nose must be at an accessible level.
Natalia Makarova

GEMINI
To understand what one should NOT think about is a great virtue.
Jackson Holbrook

CANCER
Feel thoughts, think about feelings.
Miguel de Unamuno

LEO
It is better to be happy at home than to be a chieftain.
Yoruba Saying

VIRGO
Nobody does anything for anybody that reduces nothing to nothingness.
Peter Lord

LIBRA
Our obligation to survive is owed not just to ourselves but also to that cosmos, acient and vast, from which we spring.
Carl Sagan

SCORPIO
Up to a certain point every man is what he thinks he is.
F. H. Bradley

SAGITTARIUS
You will never learn enough looking for only the good things in life; doing that you will always be a pupil.
Japanese Proverb

CAPRICORN
I am a man. Nothing human is alien to me.
Terence

AQUARIUS
Choose the best way to live, and habit will make it agreeable.
Pithagoras

PISCES
It is the belief of all mankind that they must pray to God for fortune but obtain wisdom for themselves.
Cicero

You can't help everyone, so you do the best you can.

ARIES
Discontent is the first step in the progress of a man or a nation.
Oscar Wilde

TAURUS
Every day, in every way, I am getting better and better.
Emile Coué

GEMINI
Any man can see much further than what he can get, but this does not mean that he should stop himself from trying.
Ives Tanguy

CANCER
What else is man, but a memory of himself?
Juan José Arreola

LEO
And upon waking, you will see that the whole world, above as well as below, is no more than an observation of itself.
Hakuin

VIRGO
Variety is the very soul of pleasure.
Aphra Behn

LIBRA
There are two tragedies in life. One is not to get your heart's desire. The other is to get it.
George Bernard Shaw

SCORPIO
If you understand the world, you don't like it. If you like it, you don't understand it.
American Proverb

SAGITTARIUS
. . . Get wisdom. And with all thy getting, get understanding.
Proverbs 4:7

CAPRICORN
Nothing lasts more than change; nothing is perpetual except death.
Ludwig Borne

AQUARIUS
Man is a pliable animal, a being who gets accustomed to everything!
Dostoyevsky

PISCES
The mind's direction is more important than his progress.
Joseph Joubert

3
JULY

Forgive someone. Tell them they
are wonderful and mean it.

ARIES
A meeting is a conference during which people discuss what they should
actually be doing.
George Gissing

TAURUS
Instead of loving your enemies, treat your friends a little better.
Ed Howe

GEMINI
As you get more winnings, you get more wishes.
Rumi

CANCER
There is nothing either good or bad, but thinking makes it so.
William Shakespeare

LEO
Though ambition may be a fault in itself, it is often the mother of virtues.
Quintilian

VIRGO
A little rebellion now and then is a good thing.
Thomas Jefferson

LIBRA
All should be done in decency and all should be done with order.
Saint Paul

SCORPIO
If you can imagine it, you can achieve it; if you can dream it,
you can become it.
William Arthur Ward

SAGITTARIUS
The wish is father to the thought.
Latin Proverb

CAPRICORN
There is a land of the living and a land of the dead and the bridge is love, the
only meaning.
Thorton Wilder

AQUARIUS
From the day of your birth / 'til you ride in a hearse
There's nothing that's happened / that couldn't have been worse
Anonymous

PISCES
Man partly is and wholly hopes to be.
Robert Browning

Let nature nurture your spirit—let it make you feel free.

JULY

ARIES
Courage is not freedom from fear: it is being afraid and going on.
Author Unknown

TAURUS
Believing will always be a good opportunity.
André Gide

GEMINI
The white man knows how to make everything, but he does not know how to distribute it.
Sitting Bull

CANCER
Those who cannot remember the past are condemned to repeat it.
Santayana

LEO
It is because of the devotion or sacrifice of individuals that the causes become of value.
Julian Huxley

VIRGO
Humor is emotional chaos remembered in tranquility.
James Thurber

LIBRA
I affirm that I have controlled events, but I frankly confess that events have controlled me.
Abraham Lincoln

SCORPIO
Give the historians something to write about!
Propertius

SAGITTARIUS
Take me, make what you will of me, I have joy in my submission.
Ruth Prawer Jhabvala

CAPRICORN
History is the boat that takes living memories towards the future.
Stephen Spender

AQUARIUS
Some like one thing and some like another.
Latin Quotation

PISCES
To remember is a form of meeting. To forget is a form of freedom.
Kahlil Gibran

5

JULY

Forgive someone. Tell them that they are wonderful and mean it.

ARIES
Begin with another's to end with your own.
Baltasar Gracián

TAURUS
One idea can only be defined with another.
Bertrand Russell

GEMINI
I find it more difficult to take care of my money than to acquire it.
Michel de Montaigne

CANCER
In order to be able to draw a limit to thought, we should have to find both sides of the limit thinkable. We would have to be able to think what cannot be thought.
Ludwig Wittgenstein

LEO
It is necessary for you to reencounter the soul of the child within you.
Erik Erikson

VIRGO
I could go on like this, but I will not.
Luis Buñuel

LIBRA
The past is a foreign country; things there are done in another way.
Anonymous

SCORPIO
It is better to be hated for what you are than to be loved for what you are not.
André Gide

SAGITTARIUS
Do not permit the events of your daily lives to bind you, but never withdraw yourself from them.
Huang Po

CAPRICORN
A great man left a password that we can all repeat, "there is nobody who is indispensable."
Franklin D. Roosevelt

AQUARIUS
Health is not a condition of matter, but of mind, nor can the material senses bear reliable testimony on the subject of health.
Mary Baker Eddy

PISCES
No man should be judged by what he doesn't know. He should be judged only by how quickly and sensibly he assumes new duties.
Maxwell Struthers Burt

Unremitting alertness can be a gift. Use it.

6

JULY

ARIES
In case of dissension, never dare to judge 'til you've heard the other side.
Euripides

TAURUS
To desire something or someone is wonderful if one isn't making a mistake.
Hindu Proverb

GEMINI
Do not forget that there are three kinds of personalities: those who are unmovable, those who are movable and those who really move.
Don Marquis

CANCER
Not to call a thing good a day longer or a day earlier than it seems good to us is the only way to remain really happy.
Nietzsche

LEO
Your children are not dead. They are just waiting until the world deserves them.
Robert Browning

VIRGO
Fun is the happiness of the non-thinkers.
Alexander Pope

LIBRA
So long as we live among men, let us cherish humanity.
Seneca

SCORPIO
This eternal beginning in you has always existed, it exists now, and it will always exist; its time will never end.
Brahmin's Wisdom

SAGITTARIUS
The whole world is tormented by words, and there is no one who does without words. But in so far as one is free from words, does one really understand words?
Saraha

CAPRICORN
Who is wise? He who learns from all. Who is powerful? He who governs his passions. Who is rich? He who is content. Who is he? Nobody.
Benjamin Franklin

AQUARIUS
There will be sex after death, we just won't be able to feel it.
Lily Tomlin

PISCES
The trouble with the world is that the stupid are cocksure and the intelligent full of doubts.
Bertrand Russell

7
JULY

Face the northeast and wish yourself
into a perpetual spring.

ARIES
Most things bleed, including hearts. The lessons of life amount not to wisdom, but to scar tissue and callus.
Wallace Stegner

TAURUS
Each molecule could predict a perfect law.
Shutaku

GEMINI
The heart is a muscle, and when you think that you are in love, in reality you've got a twisted muscle.
Attributed to Ogden Nash

CANCER
At the age of 25, everyone has talent. The difficult thing is to conserve it at fifty.
Edgar Degas

LEO
Bad is never good until worse happens.
Danish Proverb

VIRGO
Tell me and I'll forget. Show me, and I may not remember. Involve me and I'll understand.
Native American Saying

LIBRA
Of two evils, choose the lesser.
Plato

SCORPIO
We are healthy in so far as the humanitarian ideas that we have.
Kurt Vonnegut

SAGITTARIUS
The most beautiful thing in the world is, of course, the world itself.
Wallace Stevens

CAPRICORN
What does not destroy me makes me stronger.
Nietzsche

AQUARIUS
What is a fact today, does not appear as one tomorrow.
G. W. Bramwell

PISCES
To really enjoy the better things in life, one must first have experienced the things they are better than.
Oskar Homolka

ARIES
Material gravity makes gold precious. Moral gravity does the same for people.
Peruvian Proverb

TAURUS
A fleeting thought can be eternal.
Shutaku

GEMINI
Man is a being who has unlimited needs but never needs all that he wants.
C. H. Parkhurst

CANCER
One needs to have good taste to know what good taste is.
Spanish Proverb

LEO
Proud within their humility, they are proud of not being proud.
Ben Jonson

VIRGO
Nobody is a hypocrite in their own pleasures.
Samuel Johnson

LIBRA
I have no knowledge of myself as I am, but merely as I appear to myself.
Immanuel Kant

SCORPIO
It is within human nature to think intelligently and to act foolishly.
Anatole France

SAGITTARIUS
Sameness is differentiation, differentiation is sameness.
Zen Formula

CAPRICORN
Never give up, never give up, never, never, never, never. Never give up unless you are convinced with honor and common sense.
Sir Winston Churchill

AQUARIUS
One man in his time plays many parts.
William Shakespeare

PISCES
Without a rush, but without a rest . . .
Machiavelli's Motto

9
JULY

*Any sacred symbol helps you now in
your personal growth.*

ARIES
Loyalty to a petrified opinion never yet broke a chain or freed a human soul.
Mark Twain

TAURUS
Liberation is nothing new that is acquired.
Sri Sankaracharya

GEMINI
Nothing risked, nothing gained.
Alexander Woollcott

CANCER
Nothing is repeated and everything is unparalleled.
Goncourt Brothers

LEO
I prefer to be profoundly wrong than weakly right.
Talulah Bankhead

VIRGO
The brighter you are, the more you have to learn.
Don Herold

LIBRA
The punishment of success is realizing that you are bored with the attention
given to you by those who used to ignore you.
Mary W. Smith

SCORPIO
Neither men nor countries can live without a sublime idea.
Dostoyevsky

SAGITTARIUS
To live is to be born every minute.
Erich Fromm

CAPRICORN
Look up and not down, look ahead and not behind, look towards the outside
and not towards the inside. Lend a hand.
E. E. Hand

AQUARIUS
Experience fine-lines the rules of each of the arts.
A. Perez

PISCES
Time is a circus always packing up and moving away.
Ben Hecht

Enthusiasm is kinder than any other dynamic process.

ARIES
Likes and dislikes are only in the mind.
Calderon de la Barca

TAURUS
One sole strand of hair can stir the sea.
Shutaku

GEMINI
As long as a thought does not make you its prisoner, it is worth it.
Rumi

CANCER
The body, she says, is subject to the forces of gravity. But the soul is ruled by levity, pure.
Saul Bellow

LEO
A good mind possesses a kingdom; a great fortune is a great slavery.
Seneca

VIRGO
God cannot be solemn, or he would not have blessed man with the incalculable gift of laughter.
Sydney Harris

LIBRA
Absence in a knowledgeable way is a weapon.
Charles Reade

SCORPIO
We are all ignorant, only on different subjects.
Will Rogers

SAGITTARIUS
To do the opposite is also a form of imitation.
Lichtenberg

CAPRICORN
One should never promise what one should not, in case we are asked to do what we cannot.
Attributed to Abraham Lincoln

AQUARIUS
Character calls forth character.
Goethe

PISCES
A single sentence will suffice for modern man: he fornicated and read the papers.
Albert Camus

11
JULY

Your mother is only responsible
for 25 percent of who your are.

ARIES
There is no failure except in no longer trying.
Elbert Hubbard

TAURUS
The head sublime, the heart pathos, the genitals beauty, the hands and feet proportion.
William Blake

GEMINI
For a man to really understand what a woman wants, he has to marry her.
Sholem Aleichem

CANCER
The Word will always come first, and if it is a poetic word, so much the better.
Efrain Huerta

LEO
Think like a man of action. Act like a man of thought.
Henri Bergson

VIRGO
We are more interested in making others believe that we are happy than in trying to be so.
La Rochefoucauld

LIBRA
The thing is to be able to outlast the trends.
Paul Anka

SCORPIO
The mystic bond of brotherhood makes all men one.
Thomas Carlyle

SAGITTARIUS
Think with your whole body.
Taisen Deshimaru

CAPRICORN
There's none without a fault.
Scottish Proverb

AQUARIUS
Wine brings light to the secrets of the soul.
Horace

PISCES
A man has generally the good or ill qualities which he attributes to mankind.
William Shenstone

Measure your responsibilities and defy them.
Enjoy yourself.

ARIES
Be careful of what you say and to whom you say it.
Horace

TAURUS
The soul is the female of the body. They do not have the same pleasure sense. In other words, they infrequently enjoy together.
Paul Valéry

GEMINI
Almost every fine quotation has an opposite one, not less intelligent, that balances.
Santayana

CANCER
The great cathedral place which was childhood.
Virginia Woolf

LEO
Turbulence is a vital power. It is opportunity. Let us love turbulence and use it for change.
Ramsay Clark

VIRGO
He who reflects upon himself reflects on his own original.
Plotinus

LIBRA
Abundance changes the value of things.
Terence

SCORPIO
An excellent memory is the intelligence of fools.
Angel C. Sanchez

SAGITTARIUS
To be moral is to discover, fundamentally, our own being.
Simone de Beauvoir

CAPRICORN
Moral courage is a more rare commodity than bravery in battle or great intelligence.
Robert F. Kennedy

AQUARIUS
A good half of psychoanalysis is anal.
M. Indik

PISCES
Note for this and whatever. The only cure for seasickness is to sit on the shady side of an old church in the country.
Anonymous

13
JULY

*The child you were wants to play
with who you are now.*

ARIES
Bad weather is always worse through a window.
Weather Lore

TAURUS
It is much more difficult to hide the feelings we have than to pretend to have those we do not have.
La Rochefoucauld

GEMINI
Opinion is ultimately determined by the feelings and not by the intellect.
Herbert Spencer

CANCER
Vision is the art of seeing the invisible.
Johnathan Swift

LEO
It's bad to be wise all the time, like being at a perpetual funeral.
D. H. Lawrence

VIRGO
Anyone can, in this life, get a certain and infallible happiness.
Confessio Fraternitatis

LIBRA
Limited in his nature, infinite in his desires, man is but a fallen god who remembers Heaven.
Alphonse de Lamartine

SCORPIO
An idea is a prowess of associations.
Robert Frost

SAGITTARIUS
The first problem for all of us, men and women, is not to learn, but to unlearn.
Gloria Steinem

CAPRICORN
There are those who study to be able to ignore.
Sor Juana Inés de la Cruz

AQUARIUS
A wise man sets requirements only for himself; an unwise man makes requirements for others.
Chinese Wisdom

PISCES
Nothing will bring you peace except yourself.
Ralph Waldo Emerson

Practical concerns can be helpful reinforcements.

14
JULY

ARIES
Every beginning is a consequence—every beginning ends something.
Paul Valéry

TAURUS
We boil at different degrees.
Ralph Waldo Emerson

GEMINI
I much prefer to be a man of paradoxes than a man of prejudices.
Jean-Jacques Rousseau

CANCER
The philosopher must be the bad conscience of his time.
Nietzsche

LEO
A royal crown can not cure a headache.
Spanish Quote

VIRGO
What is patriotism if not the love of the good things we are in our youth?
Lin Yutan

LIBRA
Liberté, egalité, fraternité. (Liberty, equality, fraternity.)
Motto of the French Republic

SCORPIO
The danger of success is that it makes us forget the world's dreadful injustice.
Jules Renard

SAGITTARIUS
Peace comes to the souls of human beings as they realize that they are one with the universe.
Black Elk

CAPRICORN
When you do a good deed, be grateful that you have had the chance to do it.
Anonymous

AQUARIUS
In the United States, there is more space where nobody is than where anybody is.
Gertrude Stein

PISCES
It is necessary to have been defeated two or three times to become something.
Marshal Turenne

15
JULY

All encompassing tenderness makes anything possible.

ARIES
Nobody has any idea about what goodness is until they start doing it.
Harriet Martineau

TAURUS
Vanity plays strange games with our memories.
Joseph Conrad

GEMINI
Order brings us closer to all virtues, but what brings us to order?
Lichtenberg

CANCER
Jupiter from on high smiles at the perjuries of lovers.
Ovid

LEO
Any one person should not swallow more beliefs than can be digested.
Brooks Adams

VIRGO
When you can't have what you choose, you just choose what you have.
Owen Wister

LIBRA
Let there be spaces in your togetherness.
Kahlil Gibran

SCORPIO
There are as many preferences as there are men.
Horace

SAGITTARIUS
To be, not to do, is my foremost bliss.
Theodore Roethke

CAPRICORN
Look for the truth, it wants to be found.
Blaise Pascal

AQUARIUS
The cautious seldom err.
Confucius

PISCES
Woe to the people who look without understanding, who do not know their foundations.
The Talmud

*There is a message in the weather. Look at the
barometer, the thermometer, the vane.*

16

JULY

ARIES

I will follow the best side to the fire, but not into it, if I can choose.
Michel de Montaigne

TAURUS

Tact is the intelligence of the heart.
Anonymous

GEMINI

The course of a river is almost always disapproved of by its source.
Jean Cocteau

CANCER

A mistake could be, taken by itself, good luck.
Alfred North Whitehead

LEO

Everyone is a genius at least once a year; a real genius has his original ideas closer together.
Lichtenberg

VIRGO

No man needs curing of his individual sickness; his universal malady is what he should look to.
Djuna Barnes

LIBRA

Human actions are what trace the maps of time.
Montgomery

SCORPIO

Let our life bee a sea, and then our reason, and even passions, are wind enough to carry us whither wee should goe . . .
John Donne

SAGITTARIUS

You do not have to enter the hiding place in the mountain . . . but in your own mind; construct your own hiding place in that which is yet unknown
Shido Munan

CAPRICORN

Analysis makes for unity, but not necessarily for goodness.
Sigmund Freud

AQUARIUS

Colourless green ideas sleep furiously.
(Sentence to illustrate grammatical structure as independent of meaning.)
Noam Chomsky

PISCES

The gods plant reason in mankind, of all good its the highest.
Sophocles

17
JULY

ARIES
The king feared the great lords; what he wanted were errand boys.
Saint-Simon

TAURUS
I can promise to be sincere, but not impartial.
Goethe

GEMINI
A fool and his money are soon giving a party.
African Proverb

CANCER
. . . Hear your nakedness, the owner of your dreams.
Cesar Vallejo

LEO
Those absent are always in the wrong.
Destouches (Philippe Nericault)

VIRGO
You cannot fly like an eagle with the wings of a hummingbird.
W. Henry Hudson

LIBRA
Distance is a great promoter of admiration.
Denis Diderot

SCORPIO
The richness of life lies in memories we have forgotten.
Cesare Pavese

SAGITTARIUS
Nothing was, nothing will be, everything has a reality and a presence.
Herman Hesse

CAPRICORN
Study prophecies when they become histories.
Sir Thomas Browne

AQUARIUS
All expectation hath something of torment.
Benjamin Whichcote

PISCES
Realism is a corruption of reality.
Wallace Stevens

You can give in a little, so long
as you never stop dreaming.

18

JULY

ARIES
Great talent has always a little madness mixed with it.
Anonymous

TAURUS
It is well sometimes to fool ourselves.
And very often illusion is happiness supreme.
Destouches (Philippe Nericault)

GEMINI
Man considers the actions, but God weighs the intentions.
Thomas à Kempis

CANCER
But perhaps the universe is suspended on the tooth of some monster.
Chekov

LEO
Nothing is more mine than I myself.
Max Stirner

VIRGO
Bees are not as busy as we think they are. They just can't buzz any slower.
Kin Hubbard

LIBRA
Adversity presents man to himself.
Anonymous

SCORPIO
Man is in love and loves what finishes, What more is there to say?
William Butler Yeats

SAGITTARIUS
Finally, all you have is yourself. The sun is thousands of beams on your belly.
Everything else is nothing.
Pablo Picasso

CAPRICORN
I am only a part of everything that I have found on my way.
Lord Alfred Tennyson

AQUARIUS
The Slave knows that life is in essence unpredictable.
Rebecca West

PISCES
Discontent is the first step in the progress of a man or a nation.
Oscar Wilde

19
JULY

There is an oasis within every day.
Find it and jump in.

ARIES

She was a lure, a light, an intimate flame, a secret kept.
Hilda Doolittle

TAURUS

Even stones have a love, a love that seeks the ground.
Meister Eckhart

GEMINI

The value of money is that with it, we can tell any man to go to the devil. It is the sixth sense which enables you to enjoy the other five.
W. Somerset Maugham

CANCER

Love, and do what you like.
Saint Augustine

LEO

It's better to be looked over than overlooked.
Mae West

VIRGO

'Tis easy enough to be pleasant / When life flows by like a song / But the one worth while / is the one who will smile / When everything goes wrong.
Ella W. Wilcox

LIBRA

So much has already been written about everything that you can't find out anything about it.
James Thurber

SCORPIO

Wonder is what the philosopher endures most; for there is no other beginning of philosophy than this.
Plato

SAGITTARIUS

The frenzy of birds is of no interest to the trees.
Henri Michaux

CAPRICORN

True friendship is never serene.
Madame de Sévigné

AQUARIUS

Ideally, the two members of a pair in love liberate each other towards different and new worlds.
Anne M. Lindbergh

PISCES

Nothing can make a person's soul softer than the understanding of his own blame, and nothing can make one harder than the desire to always be right.
The Talmud

To be able to operate in tune with your natural functions is real sophistication.

ARIES

One man's profit is another man's loss.
Anonymous

TAURUS

Who sees inaction in action and action in inaction, is intelligent among all; a person of established wisdom and a true performer of all actions.
Bhagavad Gita

GEMINI

If you will always pay your debts as well as your compliments, you will surely be successful.
English Proverb

CANCER

Good humor is one of the best articles of dress one can wear in society.
William Makepeace Thackeray

LEO

The material always comes before the work. The hills are full of marble before the world blooms with statues.
Phillips Brooks

VIRGO

There are three kinds of men—lovers of wisdom, lovers of honor, lovers of gain.
Plato

LIBRA

Today is yesterday's pupil.
Thomas Fuller

SCORPIO

Slowly make a good friend, but when you are one, continue fast and constant.
Attributed to Socrates

SAGITTARIUS

Error itself may be my happy chance.
Alfred North Whitehead

CAPRICORN

If your ship doesn't come in—swim out to it.
Jonathan Winters

AQUARIUS

When you see well being coming your way, get him into your home.
Cervantes

PISCES

It is part of the cure to wish to be cured.
Seneca

21
JULY

A moment of awe is as good as a prayer.

ARIES
Although there is an exception to every rule, fools rush in where angels fear to tread.
Anonymous

TAURUS
Beauty is an agreement between content and form.
Henrik Ibsen

GEMINI
Only the person who has faith in himself is able to be faithful to others.
Erich Fromm

CANCER
Real unselfishness consists of sharing the interests of others.
Santayana

LEO
Subtlety may deceive you. Integrity never will.
Oliver Cromwell

VIRGO
I don't want to be immortalized because of my work . . . I want to attain immortality by never dying.
Woody Allen

LIBRA
When nothing can be done, what can you do? There is nothing to be done. Time will tell.
Zen Koan

SCORPIO
Explaining is generally half confessing.
Marquess of Halifax

SAGITTARIUS
Generosity gives assistance, rather than advice.
Marquis de Vauvenargues

CAPRICORN
No pain, no palm; no thorns, no throne; no gall, no glory; no cross, no crown.
William Penn

AQUARIUS
The flame is not far from the smoke.
Anonymous

PISCES
The world globes itself in a drop of dew.
Ralph Waldo Emerson

You must not become a captive of your basic instincts.

ARIES
In search of my mother's garden, I found my own.
Alice Walker

TAURUS
Character building begins in our infancy and continues until death.
Eleanor Roosevelt

GEMINI
Never fear perfection, for it is something you will never attain.
Salvador Dalí

CANCER
Sometimes I think . . . and sometimes I am.
Paul Valéry, paraphrasing Descartes

LEO
I believe it simply because it is unbelievable.
Tertullian

VIRGO
Every single creator has, in human nature, a stake in the eternal.
Meister Eckhart

LIBRA
The happiest people seem to be those who have no particular reason for being happy except that they are so.
W. R. Inge

SCORPIO
Look for the ridiculous in everything, and you will find it.
Jules Renard

SAGITTARIUS
The wise man rejects what he thinks, not what he sees.
Huang-Po

CAPRICORN
He who wishes to be a leader must be a bridge.
Welsh Proverb

AQUARIUS
Do not believe everything told you, nor tell everything you know.
Italian Proverb

PISCES
To have realized your dream makes you feel lost.
Oriana Fallaci

23
JULY

Use something that you have preserved for a long time. Use time as a symbol.

ARIES

Tell me what you boast of, and I will tell you what you lack.
Anonymous

TAURUS

Ideally, couples need three lives. One for him, one for her, and one for both together.
Jacqueline Bisset

GEMINI

Seeing through is rarely seeing into.
Elizabeth Bibesco

CANCER

I myself must supply the theme of my writing.
Ovid

LEO

The most impressive title addressed to you, should be your own name.
Anonymous Czech Saying

VIRGO

The saddest thing I can imagine is to be accustomed to luxury.
Charles Chaplin

LIBRA

Such is the irresistible nature of the truth, that all it asks for and all it wants is the freedom of appearing.
Thomas Paine

SCORPIO

The material universe only exists in the mind.
Jonathan Edwards

SAGITTARIUS

One does not have enough wisdom to know how to make good use of prosperity.
Confucius

CAPRICORN

All rivers run into the sea; yet the sea is not full.
Ecclesiastes 1:7

AQUARIUS

The striving by which each thing strives to persevere in its being is nothing but the actual essence of the thing.
Spinoza

PISCES

Don't compromise yourself. You're all you've got.
Janis Joplin

Envision any moment getting better, and it will.

ARIES
You can fool too many of the people too much of the time.
James Thurber

TAURUS
Myself and other human beings . . . no difference.
Ikkyu

GEMINI
Truth is such a rare thing, it is delightful to tell it.
Emily Dickinson

CANCER
You can go wherever you want, anywhere, but finding the path, that is the difficult thing.
Zen Mondo

LEO
It is patience which gets you out of the net.
Nyanya of Malawi Proverb

VIRGO
Without a reader, I cannot write. It's like a kiss: they cannot be done alone.
John Cheever

LIBRA
Man is condemned to be free.
Jean-Paul Sartre

SCORPIO
The only race that exists is the human race.
Grace Moore

SAGITTARIUS
The greatest mystery is oneself.
Oscar Wilde

CAPRICORN
I need something else very badly, but I can't think what it is.
Norma Jean Harris

AQUARIUS
The sun is the universal medicine of the celestial pharmacy.
August Von Kotzebue

PISCES
The best trip is the one you carry with you.
Shirley MacLaine

25
JULY

There is an original thought migrating through every day. Catch it.

ARIES
Men with good judgment very infrequently trust their own.
Anonymous

TAURUS
Better ask twice than lose your way once.
Danish Proverb

GEMINI
The old saying "there is nothing new under the sun" can also be applied under the moon.
Graffiti

CANCER
Any mental activity is easy if one does not need to count on reality.
Marcel Proust

LEO
All conquests are born when we dare to begin.
Anonymous

VIRGO
We shall have to use flattery to recognize what we are not.
Elias Canetti

LIBRA
Who is he that knows if the gods will add tomorrow to the present time?
Horace

SCORPIO
Life is a jigsaw puzzle with missing pieces.
Anonymous

SAGITTARIUS
Lose an hour in the morning and you will be all day hunting for it.
Leslie Whately

CAPRICORN
There are victories of the spirit. Sometimes, even if you lose, you win.
Elie Weisel

AQUARIUS
If an urn does not have the characteristics of an urn, how can we call it an urn?
Confucius

PISCES
Allow me to listen to myself.
Gertrude Stein

ARIES
It is a mistake to judge a person by the opinion that he has of himself.
Marcel Pagnol

TAURUS
There are those who enjoy the smell of their own winds.
Islandic Proverb

GEMINI
Actually we are slaves to the cost of living.
Carolina Marin de Jesus

CANCER
To think is much more interesting than to know, but much less interesting than to see.
Goethe

LEO
A little but for a long time is better than a lot just for a while.
Morrocan Proverb

VIRGO
If you can enjoy the unfavorable, the rest is easy.
John Cage

LIBRA
We all need some good lies. There are too many bad ones.
Kurt Vonnegut

SCORPIO
Good looking apples are sometimes sour.
Dutch Proverb

SAGITTARIUS
Nobody can avoid what is going to happen.
Anonymous

CAPRICORN
There are no complete blessings.
John Updike

AQUARIUS
Look before you leap.
Anonymous

PISCES
Sorrow is tranquillity remembered in emotion.
Dorothy Parker

27

It's all about attitude.

JULY

ARIES
Worries are part of life, and if you don't share them, you don't let your mate love you enough.
Dinah Shore

TAURUS
There is one who kisses, and the other who offers a cheek.
French Proverb

GEMINI
Take away egoism, and you will castrate a lot of benefactors.
Ralph Waldo Emerson

CANCER
Possibly, our most important thoughts are those that contradict our feelings.
Paul Valéry

LEO
The best vengeance is the one that wasn't taken.
Spanish Quote

VIRGO
The greatest power in the world is the human being.
Anonymous

LIBRA
Friends are born, not made.
Henry Adams

SCORPIO
The wrong we do and the wrong we suffer are weighed on different scales.
Aesop

SAGITTARIUS
Whoever can do more, could also do less.
Guatemalan Proverb

CAPRICORN
Your footprint might be erased along the way, but the step you made will be forever printed within the memory of time.
Anonymous

AQUARIUS
To each his own.
Anonymous

PISCES
If you cannot be a good example, you will have to resign to be an awful example.
Catherine Airlie

ARIES
These are strange and marvelous times in which we live, that such transformations are wrought in our view of the nature of things.
Johannes Kepler

TAURUS
Those who lose dreaming are lost.
Australian Aboriginal Proverb

GEMINI
It is vain to do with more what can be done with less.
William of Occam

CANCER
People are very much like the moon, they always have a dark side that they never show to anybody.
Mark Twain

LEO
There is a time to work. There is a time to love. That allows us little time for anything else!
Coco Chanel

VIRGO
Anxiety is the dizziness of freedom.
Søren Kierkegaard

LIBRA
We go to such lengths—why? To become again what we were before we were.
E. M. Cioran

SCORPIO
Knowledge comes, but wisdom lingers.
Lockley Hall

SAGITTARIUS
The most perfect among men is he who loves his neighbor without thinking about whether the person is good or bad.
Mohammad

CAPRICORN
A promise is a cloud. Fulfillment is the rain.
Arabian Proverb

AQUARIUS
Every man shall bear his own burden.
Galatians 6:5

PISCES
That only thing that makes this life viable is the permanent, intolerable uncertainty: not knowing what is going to happen.
Ursula K. Le Guin

29
JULY

Yearning is a good thing.

ARIES
I unraveled all the knots along the way, except the knots of death and of destiny.
Omar Khayyam

TAURUS
The worst thing about inferiority complexes is that usually the wrong person has them.
Alain Delon

GEMINI
A book is a mirror: if an ass peers into it, you can't expect an apostle to look out.
Lichtenstein

CANCER
Wanting to forget something is thinking about it.
French Proverb

LEO
Goodness! Life is so everydayish . . .
Jules Laforgue

VIRGO
The best thing God did was to make one day follow another.
Puerto Rican Proverb

LIBRA
A vacuum can only exist, I imagine, by the things that enclose it.
Zelda Fitzerald

SCORPIO
A life: a sparkle of time in-between two eternities.
Thomas Carlyle

SAGITTARIUS
Persevere and there will always be a better tomorrow.
Virgil

CAPRICORN
Nothing is so difficult that diligence cannot master it.
Madagascan Proverb

AQUARIUS
Distracted by what is far away, he does not see his nose.
African Proverb

PISCES
We could never learn to be brave and patient if there were only joy in the world.
Helen Keller

ARIES
Take a good look at the moon before the refection disappears into the river.
Japanese Haiku

TAURUS
One can trust in a bad person. They never change.
William Faulkner

GEMINI
Blissful is he who does not look like others but like himself.
Rumi

CANCER
Feelings are swift dreams.
Santayana

LEO
It is not the years of your life, it is the life in your years that counts.
Adlai Stevnson

VIRGO
The toughest thing about being a success is that you've got to keep on being a success.
Irving Berlin

LIBRA
An intelligent woman is a woman with whom one can be as stupid as one wants.
Paul Valéry

SCORPIO
There is a passion for hunting something deeply implanted in the human breast.
Charles Dickens

SAGITTARIUS
I began to understand that mind is no more than mountains and rivers and the great wide earth, and the Sun and the Moon and the Stars.
Dogen

CAPRICORN
There is always a better way to do things.
J. A. Raxzo

AQUARIUS
When in Rome do as the Romans do.
Anonymous

PISCES
Age only matters if you are a cheese.
Billie Burke

31
JULY

A good day to say "what the hell!"

ARIES
When everything is coming your way, you're probably in the wrong lane.
Anonymous

TAURUS
In a moment, in the twinkling of an eye . . . we shall be changed.
1 Corinthians 15:52

GEMINI
Discovery consists of seeing what everybody has seen and thinking what nobody has thought.
Albert Bon Szent-Gyorgyi

CANCER
One can live in this world on predictions only, but not on truths.
Lichtenstein

LEO
A quotation is not a quotation until your life has illustrated it.
John Keats

VIRGO
Happiness is a by-product of function. You are happy when you function.
William Burroughs

LIBRA
Those who sleep are the workers and collaborators of the things that happen within the cosmos.
Heraclitus

SCORPIO
Lost time can never be found again.
John Aughey

SAGITTARIUS
The best way to start the day is to think about the possibility of doing something to help another human being.
Nietzsche

CAPRICORN
When you believe in yourself, then you will know how to live.
Goethe

AQUARIUS
Experience is not what happens to you. It is what you do with what happens to you.
Aldous Huxley

PISCES
There is either no freedom at all, or it is in the very asking about it.
Karl Jaspers

AUGUST

AUGUST

Each one of us comes into the world with her or his unique possibility—which is like an aim, or, if you wish, almost like a law. The job of our lives is to become, day by day, year by year, more conscious of that aim so that it can, at last, be realized.

John Berger and Nella Bielski

Ah, August! The blissful fun-and-sun of summer doesn't officially cool into fall until late September, but most consider August the last month of the season. In August, the Sun, in the fire sign of Leo, creates the most intense rays. Temperatures climb—and so do our hopes!—but take care, because things can appear to be not quite what they are in the shimmering heat. Remember, no matter where you are right now in your life, embrace love, luck, and the pursuit of happiness because the summer Sun makes things grow—and this means you too! One thing is assured, you will find what you need in August—be it the perfect sun hat or good advice—and you'll feel as if the Sun is shining its approval on everything you do.

ARIES

At any time during the first three weeks of this month, being wrong could make a wonderful right, because it would light a new fire in your life and set you on the path to self-revelation. There is absolutely no better month to heed Descartes' famous urge to "know thyself" than in August. But, as you look within do not forget to leave a door open so you can feel for, and do for, others as well.

Keywords: Prove yourself

TAURUS

"Criticize yourself, but do not despair," Epictetus said, and this quotation should color the whole month of August for you, Taurus, all the way up to the year 2999! Take heed, be careful, and let nothing bulldoze any plans you have. Remember, your particular magic symbol, the planet Venus, has not only been considered the queen of the constellations but also was the primary symbol of holiness. You, too, can become the lord of your domain, so push, pull, accommodate, structure, and perform.

Keyword: Sparseness

GEMINI

You talk fast, Gemini, but this month listen, too. Indulge in the month's pleasures, but remember that things like money can slip through your fingers as fast as lightning, so try not to want more than you can afford. It has been written by sages that yours is the sign that unites spirit to matter, so don't waste this gift and make the most of every minute. An easy task for you, Gemini, because you alone can follow Rudyard Kipling's exhortation, "To fill the unforgiving minute with sixty seconds worth of distance run."

Keywords: Pull your punches

CANCER

Only if there are two full moons in August do you really have cause to worry, you tantalizing Crab you! That won't be until 2012, 2023, or 2042, so no need to worry yet, for in this month in those years you could find yourself slightly out of synch. Knowing you can soften your hard shell a bit yet still be protected will help you weather any turn of the tides. This month, think of yourself as walking a special path of your choosing and set yourself the intention to enjoy it no matter what.

Keyword: Reconciliation

LEO

The Sun, your ruler, Leo, not only governs our solar system, but the echoes of sunspot cycles have been found even in the growth rings in trees! The Sun, your Sun, hurls five million tons of matter into energy each second and travels at 220 kilometers per second around its galactic orbit, bedazzling us, just as you do. There is nothing more you need to know about August other than that the first 500 hours of the month should help you get most of what you want and crave so personally.

Keywords: Developing insights

VIRGO

Now is the time to kindle that cool and quiet enthusiasm of yours, Virgo, even though your tendency to worry can turn you into a brick wall sometimes. The Sun moves into your sign during the last week of this month, allowing you, Virgo, to find new ways in and out of any situation as you explore, discover, and question—all things in which you excel, anyway. This is the time of year when you can begin your own personal quest for esteem, whatever esteem means to you in particular! Sympathize with others and you will find yourself either glowing or aglow. You choose.

Keyword: Compensations

LIBRA

You could, especially if you find a Leo to point things out, find new ways in and out of situations during August, *dauntless* Libra. Reflect on all you see, what you think you understand, and how you digest information. Once you have done this, the month will probably be over already, and you will have to wait another 365 days to get to be as precise about yourself as you should. And so it goes—all the way through these next thousand years up to the ensuing millennium. There is a chain of being, and you beat a big path as part of it.

Keywords: Wider horizons

SCORPIO

From the 212th to the 213th day of the year as the Sun moves into Virgo, you should be busier than you had planned—or would actually like! Scorpios are usually so good at knowing what they want, but it just might be your turn to be slightly stung by criticism. Slow down a bit, relax. August is the eighth month, yours is the eighth sign, so if nothing else works, numerology might. Go ahead, indulge, and let others around you also be as mysterious, passionate, and powerful as you are!

Keyword: Achieve

SAGITTARIUS

Cozy up to Mother Nature, in any individual way you can, even if she is only a patch of sky, and remind the constellation Draco, seen in our northern hemisphere, that you ARE on your way to conquer whatever. "Dream and reality resemble each other, and influence our lives equally," said A. Schnitzler, and that should inspire you to give your goals extra power.
Keyword: Assemble

CAPRICORN

Make up your mind that, even if you lose your usually sure footing, you will not yield an iota of your formidable faith, enthusiasm, tenure, face, or vigor, Capricorn. Remember, whenever you need to, that yours is the sign that in the Maha-Nidâna Sutta is perceived as the gateway through which all souls descend to the Earth. With enough quality time for yourself, you can climb any mountain, no matter how rocky.
Keyword: Realignments

AQUARIUS

There is a 180-degree separation between your sign and the Sun's place in our celestial firmament during August for Aquarians. Keeping things status quo just won't hold water, so try to keep your cool and use your eclectic experiences to float past any troubles and just simply enjoy! You could, if you put your mind to it, because yours is the sign that can do anything, even if you drive others or yourselves nuts as you pass through. Knowing you is always worth everything!
Keyword: Cruise

PISCES

Yin and yang, masculine and feminine, the Sun and the Moon, in and out. Pisces, during August you should take definite sides; for example, by paying special attention to the feminine side of your persona. "I am capable of conceiving infinity, and yet I do not accept finity. I would like this adventure, which is the context of my life, to go on without an end." So said Simone de Beauvoir, and so, I bet, say you.
Keyword: Stoicism

1

AUGUST

ARIES
Knowledge, as food, is much better when it has a good dose of seasoning.
American Proverb

TAURUS
Stubbornness by birth is an incurable disease.
Ben Jonson

GEMINI
No idea but in things.
William Carlos Williams

CANCER
He that would jest must take a jest, else to let it alone were best.
American Proverb

LEO
Within a man of light, there is light, and he illuminates the whole world.
When he does not shine, there is darkness.
Saint Thomas

VIRGO
Eye for eye, tooth for tooth, hand for hand, foot for foot . . .
Exodus 21:24

LIBRA
He who has nothing to assert has no style and can have none.
George Bernard Shaw

SCORPIO
There is a lot of difference in pioneering for gold and pioneering for spinach.
Will Rogers

SAGITTARIUS
Nature is an infinite sphere whose center is everywhere and whose
circumference is nowhere.
Blaise Pascal

CAPRICORN
If I am not for myself, who is for me? If I am only for myself, who am I? And, if
not now, when?
The Talmud

AQUARIUS
A paradox is no more than a conflict between reality and your feeling of what
reality should be.
Richard Feyneman

PISCES
Some men plant opinions they ought to pull up.
English Proverb

Every situation has its own spirit.

2

AUGUST

ARIES
Kind words do not use up the tongue, so use them.
Richard Whately

TAURUS
I prefer a tolerant vice to an obstinate virtue.
Molière

GEMINI
The secret of success is constancy to purpose.
Benjamin Disraeli

CANCER
Don't jump from the frying pan into the fire.
Popular Knowledge

LEO
Heaven is the daily bread of our eyes.
Ralph Waldo Emerson

VIRGO
Fame is the last evil for a novel mind.
John Milton

LIBRA
Every person is original and has his own solitary character. Nobody can understand or feel the book of their own life as oneself.
William Cecil, Minister to Elizabeth I

SCORPIO
X . . . is so ignorant that he feels superior to all other human beings.
John Ciardi

SAGITTARIUS
Pray to god and pry the hammer.
Cervantes

CAPRICORN
May your food be your medicine and your medicine be your food.
Hippocrates

AQUARIUS
Most men are about to become mad.
Diogenes

PISCES
Mistakes are not physical wounds, but we immediately feel their pain.
Jean-Paul Richter

3

AUGUST

A test of strength and courage brings abundance.

ARIES
Your brain becomes mind when it is strengthened by knowledge.
Rumi

TAURUS
The Will which says . . . "Hold on."
Rudyard Kipling

GEMINI
Grow a smile where there used to be a complaint.
Elbert Hubbard

CANCER
Darned if you do and darned if you don't.
Anonymous

LEO
Egoism puts feelings in line.
Chazal

VIRGO
Fame is something which must be won; honor is something which must not be lost.
Arthur Schopenhauer

LIBRA
The wings of good luck are made from the feathers of time.
Lyly

SCORPIO
If you wish to drown, do not torture yourself with shallow water.
Bulgarian Proverb

SAGITTARIUS
The art of seeing nature is a thing almost as much to be acquired as the art of reading the Egyptian hieroglyphics.
John Constable

CAPRICORN
It is the stars as not known to science that I would know, the stars which the lonely traveler knows.
Henry David Thoreau

AQUARIUS
Our Father, who art in Heaven, stay there. And we will stay upon the face of the earth, which is at times so beautiful.
Jacques Prevert

PISCES
Opportunity is sometimes hard to recognize if you're only looking for an lucky break.
Monta Crane

States of excitement can help you
on your spiritual journey.

ARIES
Your knowledge becomes wisdom after putting it to work.
Sri Ramakrishna

TAURUS
A bad mood gives people problems, but pride leaves them there.
Charles Caleb Colton

GEMINI
Grow two smiles where there was only a complaint.
Elbert Hubbard

CANCER
Do not drown in a glass of water.
Anonymous

LEO
He who listens and learns will know how to acknowledge and be still.
Sor Juana Inés de la Cruz

VIRGO
Amusement is the happiness of those who cannot think.
Alexander Pope

LIBRA
He who can do without a friend is like someone who can do without his life.
Sophocles

SCORPIO
The ability to fill moments of leisure intelligently is the ultimate product of civilization.
Bertrand Russell

SAGITTARIUS
There is always an open book for all eyes: nature.
Jean-Jacques Rousseau

CAPRICORN
If you are a good musician, you can play on one string.
Mexican Proverb

AQUARIUS
The objective of life is not to be on the side of the majority, but to escape and find oneself in the lines of the madmen.
Marcus Aurelius

PISCES
Losing is not as bitter when the winner is noble.
Eugene O'Neill

5
AUGUST

ARIES
Love is a game where two people end up winning.
Eva Gabor

TAURUS
The heaviest load in life is not to have anything to carry.
Confucius

GEMINI
To describe happiness is to diminish it.
Stendhal

CANCER
A little inaccuracy sometimes saves tons of explanation.
Saki

LEO
Fortune is like glass. It is most breakable when it shines brightest.
Publilius Syrus

VIRGO
He who knows how to be poor, knows everything.
Michelet

LIBRA
Friendship is always beneficial; love sometimes causes pain.
Seneca

SCORPIO
Do not judge so as not to be judged.
Anonymous

SAGITTARIUS
Man is like the sun, and the feelings his planets.
Novalis

CAPRICORN
Time heals all deeds, but deeds can be spoilt by heels.
Mae West

AQUARIUS
We hope that the world will not narrow into a neighborhood before it has broadened into a brotherhood.
Lyndon Baines Johnson

PISCES
If it sounds good it is good.
Duke Ellington

One word could change your outlook in an instant.

6

AUGUST

ARIES
No man can be held through the day by what happens through the night.
Sally Stanford

TAURUS
Watch your step, everybody else does.
Unknown

GEMINI
Look out for the fellow who lets you do all the talking.
Kin Hubbard

CANCER
Best to leave well enough alone.
Unknown

LEO
Moderation is a fatal thing. Enough is as bad as a meal. More than enough is as good as a feast.
Oscar Wilde

VIRGO
It takes the whole of life to learn how to live, and what will perhaps make you wonder more, it takes the whole of life to learn how to die.
Seneca

LIBRA
Friendship is a marriage of the soul, and this marriage is subject to divorce.
Voltaire

SCORPIO
One learns a lot teaching.
Seneca

SAGITTARIUS
A kind heart does not help the chess player whatsoever.
Chamfort

CAPRICORN
Only by trying a lesser thing, can we achieve a larger thing.
Hebrew Saying

AQUARIUS
It is a bad bridge that is shorter than its stream.
German Saying

PISCES
To be wise, you should say little and doubt even more.
Mexican Saying

7
AUGUST

Remember your heart.

ARIES
You can seduce a man without taking anything off, without even touching him.
Rae Dawn Chong

TAURUS
Do not cross any bridge unless you are sure it really exists.
Lin Chi

GEMINI
If time is money, why is it that rich executives never have extra time to spend?
George Gissing

CANCER
A variety of "nothings" is superior to a monotony of "somethings."
Jean-Paul Richter

LEO
What once was a vice is now in fashion.
Seneca

VIRGO
Men, at some moments, are owners of their destiny.
William Shakespeare

LIBRA
The happiest moments of my life have been the few which I have past at home in the bosom of my family.
Thomas Jefferson

SCORPIO
Plants do have a soul.
Dario Fo

SAGITTARIUS
Is it progress if a cannibal uses a knife and fork?
Stanislaw Lec

CAPRICORN
He who has little, and spends less, is rich without knowing it.
Unknown

AQUARIUS
You cannot hide behind your own finger.
Greek Saying

PISCES
Enthusiasm is that state of the soul within which imagination has triumphed over one's rational self.
W. Warburton

ARIES
Waiting for gratitude should be part of our calculations.
Friedrich Schiller

TAURUS
Reputation is appreciated, but character has no price.
Thomas Fuller

GEMINI
I have a point of view on many matters, and I am ready, as a politician, to change most of them.
James Agate

CANCER
Could sleeping be mating with oneself?
Novalis

LEO
I don't sing a song unless I feel it. The song don't tug at my heart, I pass on it. I have to believe in what I'm doing.
Anonymous

VIRGO
I would rather have a fool make me happy than experience bring the gift of sadness.
William Shakespeare

LIBRA
It is no tragedy to do ungrateful people favors, but it is unbearable to be indebted to a scoundrel.
La Rochefoucauld

SCORPIO
It is not a good thing to awaken the sleeping lion.
Philip Sidney

SAGITTARIUS
The world is the best of all possible worlds, and all that is in it is a necessary evil.
James Bradley

CAPRICORN
Out of every hundred people who know how to earn money, only one knows how to spend it.
English Proverb

AQUARIUS
Even the best cooking pot will not produce food.
African Proverb

PISCES
It is corrupt not to be able to be self-sufficient.
Gustave Flaubert

9
AUGUST

Search for your will to create.

ARIES
Material gravity turns gold into a precious metal. Moral gravity does the same to human beings.
Peruvian Proverb

TAURUS
Discontent is wont of self-reliance. It is infirmity of will.
Ralph Waldo Emerson

GEMINI
We shape our dwellings and afterwards our dwellings shape us.
Sir Winston Churchill

CANCER
To quarrel with a man of good speech is better than to converse with a man of rude address.
Sanskrit Proverb

LEO
Be careful of counting on an improbable truth.
Thomas Fuller

VIRGO
Please everyone and you will please no one.
Aesop

LIBRA
God has given you one face and you show another.
William Shakespeare

SCORPIO
There is no running away from either humanity or the cosmos.
Christiane Grautoff

SAGITTARIUS
Nature is filled with infinite causes that have never happened because of experiences.
Leonardo da Vinci

CAPRICORN
Take your time to make a promise, be quick to carry it out.
Persian Proverb

AQUARIUS
"If" married "But" and they had a son called "Maybe."
Persian Proverb

PISCES
To make mistakes is tolerable; to construct them is not.
Spanish Proverb

ARIES
To justify our likes and dislikes, we generally say that the work we don't like is really nothing serious.
Walter Sickert

TAURUS
It is much better to have common sense without an education than to have education without common sense.
Elbert Hubbard

GEMINI
Language is a human reason whose reasons are unknown to man.
Claude Levi-Strauss

CANCER
Let me smile with the wise and eat with the rich.
Samuel Johnson

LEO
To know oneself is to prevent; to prevent means that we choose our actions.
Paul Valéry

VIRGO
The errors of a wise man make your rule, rather than the perfections of a fool.
William Blake

LIBRA
Virtue must have limits.
Montesquieu

SCORPIO
We are all offspring of our pasts.
Edna G. Rostow

SAGITTARIUS
If the Sun and the Moon would have doubts, they would immediately disappear.
William Blake

CAPRICORN
If the mountain will not come to Mohammed, Mohammed will come to the mountain.
Arabic Proverb

AQUARIUS
Anger is a short madness.
Horace

PISCES
All you have to do is to write one true sentence, and then go on from there.
Ernest Hemingway

11

AUGUST

ARIES
The first forty years of life give us the text, the next thirty, the commentary.
Arthur Shopenhauer

TAURUS
"Yes" and "no" are the oldest and simplest words, but they require the most thought.
Pythagoras

GEMINI
I used to believe that anything was better than nothing. Now I know that sometimes nothing is better.
Glenda Jackson

CANCER
Use words that soak up life.
Virginia Woolf

LEO
You must be willing to accept the simple fact that you have flaws and will need to work every day to become a better chieftain than you were yesterday.
Attributed to Attila the Hun

VIRGO
The fault, dear Brutus, is not in our stars but in ourselves.
William Shakespeare

LIBRA
Nature does not provide us with virtue; to be a good person is an art.
Seneca

SCORPIO
The real constitution of things is accustomed to hide itself.
Heraclitus

SAGITTARIUS
Night does not have a bedroom; it sleeps wherever it falls.
Chazal

CAPRICORN
One day of worry is much more tiring than one week of hard word.
Armenian Proverb

AQUARIUS
All that glitters is not gold.
Cervantes

PISCES
He who fears is a slave.
Seneca

Enjoy a moment of freedom—however impermanent.

ARIES
It is never too late to be what you might have been.
George Eliot

TAURUS
Everyone thinks of changing the world, but no one thinks of changing himself.
Leo Tolstoy

GEMINI
You see things and say, "Why?" But I dream things that never were, and I say, "Why not?"
George Bernard Shaw

CANCER
My country is the world. My countrymen are all mankind.
William Lloyd Garrison

LEO
Action without a name, a "who" attached to it, is meaningless.
Hannah Arendt

VIRGO
Every man is a borrower and a mimic; life is theatrical and literature a quotation.
Ralph Waldo Emerson

LIBRA
Virtue is not left to stand alone. He who practices it will have neighbors.
Confucius

SCORPIO
Selfishness is the only true atheism.
Israel Zangwill

SAGITTARIUS
Each human being is a more complex structure than any social system to which he belongs.
Alfred North Whitehead

CAPRICORN
Understanding others is knowledge. Understanding oneself is enlightenment.
Tao Te Ching

AQUARIUS
Too many cooks spoil the broth, but it takes only one to burn it.
Julia Child

PISCES
An oversharp conscience is more often than not a bad thing, and very bad for the health as well as the spirit.
Euripides

13
AUGUST

A little nonsense can be a splendid, delicious thing.

ARIES
Talent is born in silence, but character is born within the struggle of life.
German Saying

TAURUS
From the tree of silence hangs the fruit of confidence.
Arabic Proverb

GEMINI
To have doubted one's own first principles is the mark of a civilized man.
Oliver Wendell Holmes

CANCER
He who does not reason is intolerant; he who cannot reason, is a fool; and he who does not dare to reason is a slave.
W. H. Drummond

LEO
The way to love anything is to realize that it might be lost.
G. K. Chesterton

VIRGO
Win without boasting. Lose without excusing yourself.
Albert Payson Terhune

LIBRA
Nothing's more revealing than movement.
Martha Graham

SCORPIO
If you have built castles in the
air . . . that is where they should be. Now put foundations under them.
Henry David Thoreau

SAGITTARIUS
My personal hobbies are reading, listening to music, and silence.
Edith Sitwell

CAPRICORN
Chaos often breeds life, when order breeds habit.
Henry Adams

AQUARIUS
Don't use no double negatives.
William Safire

PISCES
Without knowing the force of words, it is impossible to know men.
Confucius

Intoxicate yourself with an ecstatic experience.

Be weird.

14
AUGUST

ARIES
We need to haunt the halls of history and listen anew to the ancestor's wisdom.
Maya Angelou

TAURUS
Nothing is really work unless you would rather be doing something else.
Attributed to Sir James M. Barrie

GEMINI
If plagiarism were really a sin, there would be no sermons allowed.
Anonymous

CANCER
Accident: an inevitable occurrence due to the action of immutable, natural laws.
Ambrose Bierce

LEO
Do not allow your feelings to make a playing field of your mind.
Tibetan Proverb

VIRGO
It is preoccupation with possession more than anything else, that prevents men from living freely and nobly.
Bertrand Russell

LIBRA
Every man has his follies and they are often the most interesting things he has got.
Josh Billings

SCORPIO
Ten minutes of planning can save you hours of squandered time.
Arabic Proverb

SAGITTARIUS
The landscape belongs to the man who looks at it.
Ralph Waldo Emerson

CAPRICORN
I live on good soup, not fine words.
Molière

AQUARIUS
People demand freedom of speech to make up for the freedom of thought which they avoid.
Søren Kierkegaard

PISCES
Time goes, you say? Ah no! Alas, times stays, we go.
Austin Dobson

15
AUGUST

On this day, a sunny, blue sky could mean a mild winter.

ARIES
Good memories are lost jewels.
Paul Valéry

TAURUS
What is a fool? Perhaps simply an undemanding mind which is satisfied with little. Could it be that the fool is really wise?
Paul Valéry

GEMINI
It is not best to swap horses while crossing the river.
Abraham Lincoln

CANCER
Who runs from reason is a real fugitive.
Marcus Aurelius

LEO
There are two kinds of egotists: those who admit it, and the rest of us.
Laurence Peter

VIRGO
I am here. I am present. I, the singer. I have come at the right time, so come and approach me, those of you who have an aching heart. I lift up my song.
Popular Nahuatl Song

LIBRA
Truth can be understood only by waiting and watching, and when you get one truth, two more will appear before you.
John Ruskin

SCORPIO
This thing we call "failure" is not the falling down, but the staying down.
Mary Pickford

SAGITTARIUS
Repetition is the only form of permanence that nature can achieve.
Santayana

CAPRICORN
We must amuse ourselves to be able to accomplish good habits.
Hindu Proverb

AQUARIUS
If there is a winter, and there is a summer, what's the hurry?"
Persian Proverb

PISCES
To deny, to believe, and to doubt well, are to a man as the race is to a horse.
Blaise Pascal

Break out of your niche. Sing another's song.

ARIES
We are the hero of our own story.
Mary McCarthy

TAURUS
The purpose of psychology is to give us an entirely different idea of the things we know best.
Paul Valéry

GEMINI
Be nice to people until you make a couple of millions, then people will be nice to you.
Anonymous

CANCER
Most of us have enough strength to bear the misfortunes of others.
La Rochefoucauld

LEO
Human endeavor is what gives life to our planet.
J. Vasconcelos

VIRGO
The only interesting project is liberation from life's daily toil.
Jose Eznl

LIBRA
Any moderation need not be an excess.
Anonymous

SCORPIO
Learning makes a man fit company for himself.
Edward Young

SAGITTARIUS
Swans seem to be arrogant, foolish, and
mischievous . . . three qualities that make a fine combination.
Denis Diderot

CAPRICORN
The best way to do things is to do them one at a time.
Hindu Proverb

AQUARIUS
Out of clutter, find simplicity. From discord, find harmony. In the middle of difficulty lies opportunity.
Albert Einstein

PISCES
The wolf depends on the lamb, who depends on the grass.
Paul Valéry

17
AUGUST

ARIES
How many cares one loses when one decides not to be something but to be someone.
Coco Chanel

TAURUS
You should only complain if you have nothing else to do.
Popular Saying

GEMINI
No man is a hypocrite in his pleasures.
Samuel Johnson

CANCER
An emotion ceases to be a passion as soon as we form a clear and distinct idea of it.
Spinoza

LEO
Man equals an atom, but an atom that not only reflects the whole universe, but also thinks.
Justo Sierra

VIRGO
If you don't make mistakes, you are doing nothing.
Anonymous

LIBRA
The devil never stays around a place where there is music.
Martin Luther

SCORPIO
It is better to be hated for what you are than to be loved for what you are not.
André Gide

SAGITTARIUS
The father of geology is he who when, upon seeing some fossil shells on a mountain, conceived the theory of the deluge.
Samuel Butler

CAPRICORN
You can know about ten things by learning about one.
Japanese Proverb

AQUARIUS
Poverty is painful, but it certainly is not shameful.
Scottish Proverb

PISCES
The countless inspiring examples which we find in our books, our philosophy, our history, would all have been buried in darkness had not the light of literature fallen on them.
Cicero

To reach real self-sufficiency you need some help.

18
AUGUST

ARIES
I start where the last man left off.
Thomas A. Edison

TAURUS
The limits of my language are the limits of my world. All I know is what I have words for.
Ludwig Wittgenstien

GEMINI
We can believe in a thing, we can know that it exists, even if we cannot understand it with our intellect or explain it with words.
Unknown

CANCER
We can do noble acts without ruling earth and sea.
Aristotle

LEO
Man is but an instinct adulterated by intelligence.
Luis M. Martinez

VIRGO
Man's distress is God's opportunity.
Popular Mexican Saying

LIBRA
After silence, that which comes nearest to expressing the inexpressible is music.
Aldous Huxley

SCORPIO
The history of the world is the relation of man searching for his daily bread.
Hendrik W. Van Loon

SAGITTARIUS
Little strokes fell great oakes.
English Proverb

CAPRICORN
Those who ask, must be taught.
Japanese Proverb

AQUARIUS
Every day we have, each one of us, some opportunity of transformation.
Jane Bugalow

PISCES
No one needs to study to be a fool.
Popular Mexican Saying

19
AUGUST

Trust the spirits that roam.

ARIES
You mustn't force sex to do the work of love or love to do the work of sex.
Mary McCarthy

TAURUS
Good judgment comes from experience, and experience comes from bad judgment.
Anonymous

GEMINI
The anticipation of any pleasure is also a pleasure.
Friedrich F. Schiller

CANCER
It's all in how you look at it.
Anonymous

LEO
Men are really nothing, principles are everything.
Benito Juárez

VIRGO
Don't whistle what should be sung.
Popular Mexican Saying

LIBRA
There are ten commandments, right? Well, it is like an exam. You get eight out of ten, you're just about top of the class.
Mordecai Richler

SCORPIO
Fear reason, or she'll make you feel her.
Benjamin Franklin

SAGITTARIUS
The art of seeing nature is something almost as acquired as the art of reading Egyptian hieroglyphics.
John Constable

CAPRICORN
Once we realize that imperfect understanding is the human condition, there is no shame in being wrong, only in failing to correct our mistakes.
George Soros

AQUARIUS
There is no proof needed for what our eyes see.
Hindu Proverb

PISCES
A man cannot leave his wisdom or his experience to his heirs.
Popular Italian Saying

ARIES
Fear was the first mother of the gods.
Lucretius

TAURUS
We are born to quest and seek after truth; to possess it belongs to a greater power.
Michel de Montaigne

GEMINI
Courtesy should be contagious enough to produce epidemics.
Anonymous

CANCER
Things are in the saddle, and ride mankind.
Ralph Waldo Emerson

LEO
Ah, but a man's reach should exceed his grasp—
Or what's a heaven for?
Robert Browning

VIRGO
If society would never have been invented, man would have continued to be a savage beast, or what is actually the same thing, a saint.
Mikhail Bakunin

LIBRA
Do not choose to be wrong for the sake of being different.
Lord Samuel

SCORPIO
There is only one success—to be able to spend your life in your own way.
Christopher Morley

SAGITTARIUS
Medicine is my lawful life and literature my mistress; when I get tired of one, I spend a night with the other.
Anton Chekov

CAPRICORN
Our perception of the world is one of many that could be parallel to any other.
Douglas Adams

AQUARIUS
A hypocrite is a person who—but who isn't?
Don Marquis

PISCES
I know what I can know, and I do not worry about what I cannot know.
Fichte

21
AUGUST

ARIES
Life itself is the proper binge.
Julia Child

TAURUS
Do not forget. Man is a metaphysical animal.
Arthur Schopenhauer

GEMINI
Many a man's ambition is to be able to afford to spend what he is already spending.
Unknown

CANCER
Only the truth is revolutionary.
Graffiti on a Parisian Wall

LEO
We can fashion a ladder for our vices by trampling them underfoot.
Saint Augustine

VIRGO
All men advise patience, though few are disposed to practice it themselves.
Thomas Kempis

LIBRA
I invent nothing, I rediscover.
August Rodin

SCORPIO
Spotless, unobstructed, silent / Like the vast expanse of space / Who in truth does really see Thee?
Rahulabhadra

SAGITTARIUS
Nature is great in grand things, but it is greater in the small things.
Jacques Henri B. Saint-Pierre

CAPRICORN
Less than fifteen percent of the people do any original thinking on any subject.
Luther Burbank

AQUARIUS
Humans have two ears and one mouth so as to hear a lot and speak little.
German Proverb

PISCES
Life consists in penetrating the unknown, and fashioning our actions in accord with the new knowledge thus acquired.
Leo Tolstoy

Feel the beat. It could come from the stars.

22
AUGUST

ARIES
Change is an easy panacea. It takes character to stay in one place and be happy there.
Elizabeth Clarke Dunn

TAURUS
Existence is the reef upon which pure thought can be shipwrecked.
Attributed to Søren Kierkegaard

GEMINI
A man is quite dishonorable to sell himself
For anything other than quite a lot of pelf.
Ogden Nash

CANCER
When I choose a word, it means precisely what I want it to mean, neither more nor less.
Lewis Carroll

LEO
How life catches up with us and teaches us to love and forgive each other.
Judy Collins

VIRGO
The ones who live are the ones who struggle. / The ones whose soul and heart are filled with high purpose. / Yes, these are the living ones.
Victor Hugo

LIBRA
God still speaks to those who take the time to listen.
Popular Saying

SCORPIO
From each according to his abilities, to each according to his needs.
Karl Marx

SAGITTARIUS
A dog will always be a dog, even if bred among lions.
Lebanese Saying

CAPRICORN
To lengthen your life, shorten your dinners.
Popular Mexican Saying

AQUARIUS
Managing silence is much more difficult than managing words.
Georges Clemenceau

PISCES
Life's the best bargain. We get it for free!
Yiddish Proverb

23
AUGUST

You need more time for yourself.

ARIES
Better to be criticized than ignored.
Popular Saying

TAURUS
Between wishes and their being fulfilled flees all humanity.
Arthur Schopenhauer

GEMINI
We keep on talking, even when we don't have something to say.
Mary McGrory

CANCER
God casts no soul away, unless it cast itself away. Every soul is its own judgment.
Jacob Boehme

LEO
In the long run, people achieve only that which they have set as goals for themselves; therefore, set the highest possible goals for yourself.
Unknown

VIRGO
Tradition is the illusion of permanence.
Woody Allen

LIBRA
The best virtue that I possess has a slight taste of vice.
Montaigne

SCORPIO
Everything is worth exactly as much as a burp, with the difference that the burp is much more satisfactory.
Ingmar Bergman

SAGITTARIUS
All human actions have one or more of these seven causes: chance, nature, compulsions, habit, reason, passion, desire.
Aristotle

CAPRICORN
The ability to concentrate and use time well is everything.
Lee Iacocca

AQUARIUS
Nothing is so easy as to deceive oneself, for what we wish, that we readily believe. We believe whatever we want to believe.
Demosthenes

PISCES
Life is a series of surprises.
Ralph Waldo Emerson

ARIES
No pessimist ever discovered the secrets of the stars, or sailed to an uncharted land or opened a new heaven to the human spirit.
Helen Keller

TAURUS
Life is a language in which certain truths are conveyed to us; if we could learn them in some other way, we should not live.
Arthur Schopenhauer

GEMINI
Happy the man who has learned the causes of things, and has put under his feet all fears and inexorable fate, and the noisy strife of the hell of greed.
Virgil

CANCER
Words are the only things that last forever.
William Hazlitt

LEO
I take refuge in the unity of Your Quality against all quality.
Niffari

VIRGO
You cannot lose what you never had.
Popular Mexican Saying

LIBRA
There might actually occur a case where we should say, "this man believes he is pretending."
Ludwig Wittgenstein

SCORPIO
The natural role of twentieth-century man is anxiety.
Norman Mailer

SAGITTARIUS
A person who knows the law but does not fulfill it reminds me of one who plows the land but does not put seed in it.
Eastern Wisdom

CAPRICORN
Success is easy to obtain; what is difficult is to deserve it.
Albert Camus

AQUARIUS
There are pioneer souls that mark, with flames, the way where roads were never built.
Sam Walter Foss

PISCES
If a man will begin with certainties, he shall end in doubts; but if he will be content to begin with doubts, he shall end in certainties.
Sir Francis Bacon

25
AUGUST

ARIES
There is always a risk, even in the safest of things.
Everardo Gout

TAURUS
The basic foundation of the understanding of God, any God, is inside of us.
William Ellery Channing

GEMINI
A dollar saved is a quarter earned.
John Ciardi

CANCER
We should therefore claim, in the name of tolerance, the right not to tolerate the intolerant.
Karl Popper

LEO
Fortune does not change men, it unmasks them.
M. M. Necker

VIRGO
The world is everything that is the case. The world is the totality of facts not of objects.
Ludwig Wittgenstein

LIBRA
Since the Holy Writ is true, and all truth agrees with truth, the truth of Holy Writ cannot be contrary to the truth obtained by reason and experiment.
Galileo Galilei

SCORPIO
Friendship is like money, it is easier to make than to save.
Samuel Butler

SAGITTARIUS
Whatever name you give to the origin of man, this spiritual quality of humans to understand, feel and exist, it is holy, it is divine, and therefore, it should be eternal.
Cicero

CAPRICORN
A habit is the fifth element in the whole universe.
Arabic Proverb

AQUARIUS
Having imagination, it takes you an hour to write a paragraph that, if you were unimaginative, would take only a minute. Or you might not write the paragraph at all.
Franklin P. Adams

PISCES
To dream is a divine state. He who sleeps is a God.
Amado Nervo

ARIES
The man who has never made a mistake will never make anything else.
George Bernard Shaw

TAURUS
I have lived long enough to look carefully the second time into things I am most certain of the first time.
Josh Billings

GEMINI
The whole world is a stage, but most of the actors do not know their lines.
Graffiti in Mexico City

CANCER
Don't wait for inspiration. Begin, and inspiration will come to you.
Latin Proverb

LEO
The whole universe is condensed in the body, and the whole body in the heart. Thus, the heart is the nucleus of the whole universe.
Sri Ramana Maharshi

VIRGO
We are all in the gutter, but some of us are looking at the stars.
Oscar Wilde

LIBRA
Don't be consistent, but be simply true.
Oliver Wendell Holmes

SCORPIO
Beware of telling an improbable truth.
Thomas Fuller

SAGITTARIUS
A good listener is not only popular, but after a while he knows something.
Anonymous

CAPRICORN
I like men to behave like men—strong and childish.
Françoise Sagan

AQUARIUS
Thoughts are exempt of taxes.
English Proverb

PISCES
When the rose blooms, the bees come from all over, without an invitation and without having been asked.
Sri Ramakrishna

27
AUGUST

Gaze and be dazzled.

ARIES
The most difficult thing to open is a closed mind.
Thomas Carlyle

TAURUS
Every man bears the whole stamp of human condition.
Michel de Montaigne

GEMINI
To "do" will always prevail over to "endure."
Norbert Guterman

CANCER
Yet to die, and to know a meaning in death, is a better destiny than to be saved from dying.
Rebecca West

LEO
He who wishes to see God should clean his mirrors and purify his heart.
Richard de Sainte-Victor

VIRGO
Before anything, there was chaos. And afterwards, the earth in all its glory. Everything is somewhere.
Aristotle

LIBRA
It's all the little things that add up to make an entire life.
Charles Dickens

SCORPIO
To approve is much more difficult than to admire.
Hugo Von Hofmannsthal

SAGITTARIUS
A glass of wine at the right moment can be worth more than all the riches in the world.
Gustav Mahler

CAPRICORN
The best of all possible negotiations is the one in which both sides are content.
Arabic Proverb

AQUARIUS
Success is a paradox; many men climb to the top by getting to the bottom of things.
Author Unknown/Attributed to Many People

PISCES
A doubt: the school of truth.
Sir Francis Bacon

An instance of hope is approaching.
Look around the bend.

28
AUGUST

ARIES
A prudent man will think more important what fate has conceded to him than what it has denied.
Baltasar Gracián

TAURUS
As soon you find self-confidence, you will know how to go about living.
Rumi

GEMINI
There is no need to worry about the outgoing tide; it always comes in again.
Fred Allen

CANCER
Man travels the world over in search of what he needs, and returns home to find it.
George Moore

LEO
There is an eye in the soul, which is worth more than ten thousand human eyes, because only with it, can one see the truth.
Plato

VIRGO
Who loves not wine, woman and song
Remains a fool his whole life long.
Martin Luther

LIBRA
The eyes are what we are, the mouth is what we become.
John Galsworthy

SCORPIO
Sometimes I think, and sometimes I am.
Paul Valéry

SAGITTARIUS
The spot where you sit is your own spot. Why? Because your spot gives you special access in your stillness. You hear what might be heard anywhere.
Thich Nhat Hanh

CAPRICORN
The wonderful thing about learning something is that nobody can take it away from you.
B. B. King

AQUARIUS
I much prefer to be a man of paradoxes than a man with prejudices.
Jean-Jacques Rousseau

PISCES
In every home in each household, there is always something beautiful, even though not everyone can see it.
Chang Po-Tuan

29
AUGUST

The end of any sequence will always bring a new order.

ARIES
Every great man first took the time to learn how to obey, whom to obey and when to obey.
General Omar Bradley

TAURUS
It is impossible to reign and be innocent.
Louis-Antoine de Saint-Just

GEMINI
I think that wherever your journey takes you, there are new golds waiting there, with divine patience—and laughter.
Susan Watkins

CANCER
Is it worth seeing? Yes, but it is not worth going to see.
Samuel Johnson

LEO
Who controls the past controls the future . . . who controls the present controls the past.
George Orwell

VIRGO
The anxiety of our times has fundamentally to do with space/place, without a doubt, much more so than with time.
Leon Foucault

LIBRA
Our author by experience finds it true,
'Tis much more hard to please himself than you.
John Dryden

SCORPIO
Skin is a damn thin shelter against the universe.
Ivan Doig

SAGITTARIUS
Time sparkles and the dream is knowledge.
Paul Valéry

CAPRICORN
Who dares not to ask is ashamed to learn.
Danish Proverb

AQUARIUS
Every dog has his day and every man his hour.
Anonymous

PISCES
What is amusing now had to be taken in desperate earnest once.
Virginia Woolf

ARIES
In-between the dreams of tomorrow and repentance for any yesterdays, lie today's opportunities.
Author Unknown

TAURUS
Hold Infinity in the palm of your hand / And Eternity in an hour.
William Blake

GEMINI
Half of the things that we worry about don't even happen and the other half will happen anyway, so why worry?
Popular Saying

CANCER
All of us must indulge in a few small follies if we are to make reality bearable.
Marcel Proust

LEO
Not to believe in force is like not believing in gravity.
Leon Trotsky

VIRGO
In all reality, only time will tell.
Erasmus of Rotterdam

LIBRA
I love metaphors. It provides two loaves where there seems to be only one. Sometimes it throws in a load of fish.
Bernard Malamud

SCORPIO
Our most important thoughts are those that contradict our emotions.
Paul Valéry

SAGITTARIUS
Each day is a room of time, in order to have room to understand that abandoning things is superior, pursuing things is inferior.
Yen-T'ou

CAPRICORN
Even though all experts agree, they could also be wrong.
Bertrand Russell

AQUARIUS
We only want that which is given naturally to all people of the world: to be masters of our own fate . . .
Golda Meir

PISCES
Without knowing the force of words, it is impossible to know men.
Confucius

31

AUGUST

Nothing should go unspoken for.

ARIES
Life is filled with golden opportunities to do things that we don't want to do.
Will Rogers

TAURUS
Zen teaches us that it is better to practice a little than to talk a lot.
Anonymous

GEMINI
If "its" and "buts" were candy and nuts, every day would be Christmas.
John Meredith

CANCER
We can believe what we choose. We are answerable for what we choose to believe.
John Henry Newman

LEO
The person who won't take advice is often less stubborn than the one who is giving it.
Anonymous

VIRGO
Emotions are caused by atoms impinging on the atoms of the soul.
Democritus (Marcelo Gleiser)

LIBRA
Wise men learn much from their enemies.
Aristophanes

SCORPIO
If you can speak what you will never hear, if you can write what you will never read, you have done rare things.
Henry David Thoreau

SAGITTARIUS
If I cannot do great things, I can do small things in a great way.
James Freeman Clarke

CAPRICORN
The second time around can be better than the first.
Lance Armstrong

AQUARIUS
He who is plenteously provided for from within, needs but little from without.
Goethe

PISCES
Think wrongly, if you please, but in all cases, think for yourself.
Doris Lessing

SEPTEMBER

SEPTEMBER

The reasonable man adapts himself to the world; the unreasonable one
persists in trying to adapt the world to himself. Therefore all progress depends
on the unreasonable man.
George Bernard Shaw

September could be called the "because" month. Kids go back to school
"because, we say so"; people come back from vacation right after Labor Day
"because it's time"; and summer is leaving "because the Earth keeps moving."
And *because* of all of this, if we are all lucky, at some point this September we'll
be able to tell the difference between a rule and what the rule applies to. So
stretch yourself—and your values. Pack away the suntan lotion and learn to
allow autumn to happen to *you*. Maybe it's time to get your house a bit more
in order. Just because.

ARIES
Gertrude Stein left this world, according to her companion, Alice B. Toklas, with a phrase that perfectly fits Aries in September. "What is the answer? I *was silent* says a voice. In that case, what is the question?" Aries, put two and two together—something you don't excel in at this time of year—and find out how things add up, and what you can do about them. Read everything twice, listen up, and watch for the little things, because as they say, little things mean a lot.
Keywords: Peewee challenges

TAURUS
Use all you've got this month, Taurus. Instead of being the lone Bull in the pasture, this is the time to lean on what your parents, grandparents, forefathers, and anyone in your family tree has taught or shown you. Find out some more about your personal DNA! Yes, yes, follow your own tracks, but gain fresh ground, too. Say what you feel, even if you don't really feel like it. Have a good time, because this month the grass is really greener in your own backyard.
Keyword: A priori

GEMINI
If you can remember to put yourself at ease once in a while by remembering the country proverb: "Better to be badly seated than to be standing only," and at the same time "show your true grit," each September for the next thousand years will be better and better. You may feel a bit roped in, but give others (and yourself) some slack. Loosen up and you'll see just how September can shine, right up until the next equinox at the end of this and every September.
Keywords: Cut yourself some slack

CANCER
For the ever-questful Cancer, September brings tides of sudden permanence. Sounds like a contradiction? Well, Cancer, this is a month of resolution. You decide when to park, when to pull out, and how many coins to put in the meter! Things are going to crop up for the better, as well as for the worst—be aware and make the changes you need to. Think of all of it as opportunity knocking instead of as doors slamming against you, and then, whatever the consequences, they won't be so hard on your sensitive souls.
Keywords: Get on your case

LEO

Things that you hold dear usually come your way, but this month, if you are not careful, they could fall out of your grasp! But hold that roar, curtail the cub in you a little, and instead, prepare for the unpredictable. Don't just pounce on any old solution. Take your time, try to figure out what and why you are doing too much for others—or, if others should be doing a bit more for you. It could get you purring!

Keywords: Figuring out

VIRGO

September is no time to be quiet, Virgo! As sure as the leaves are about to change and show their true colors, so can you—and just as beautifully. All you have to do is trust yourself and do your best to give those around you the opportunity to see your more valuable side. Virgo, you always search for perfection, but remember, perfection is within *you*!

Keywords: Carve out your own space and change for the better

LIBRA

You Librans are usually intuitive about yourselves. But those uncanny things that one cannot explain are about to rear their heads. The unconscious and the conscious; signs and symbols that you would prefer to neither see nor recognize; things you'd prefer that other people not know—all are things that can be tackled during these wonderfully arcane days. Your glass is either half-filled or half-empty just now. You decide.

Keywords: Uncanny intuition

SCORPIO

Don't resist temptation this month, Scorpio. Toss away your date book and simply take things as they come—full speed ahead with happiness! But even you can sometimes be overwhelmed, so listen with your "third ear" (something like your third eye) and prick up your ears to others' wisdom. Don't doubt yourself for a second, and if things don't turn out as you wish, remember the best is always yet to come. By the 30th of any September, any year, you should find yourself a bit older and surely wiser.

Keyword: Listen

SAGITTARIUS

Once in a while you need to repeat to yourself "Trust me, but look to thyself" in order to get perspective. Don't confuse what you'd like to happen with what is actually going on, and try to conciliate everyone and everything (never, ever, with nothing at all). Your high spirits will help you take this month at a gallop. Things can change—but watch out, it's all by chance.

Keywords: Changes by chance

CAPRICORN

"Every person has a poet inside who had an early death," said Stephan Kanfer, something that should get you Capricorns musing. You can be the most unyielding sign in the Zodiac, but put a little poetry in your staunch soul and magic can happen! So use your imagination. Take short-cuts, try for new insights by seeing every side of every story. September days will flip, fly, or drag by for you, but by the end of the month, when Libra appears, everything will again be under perfect Capricorn control.

Keywords: Do what you have to do

AQUARIUS

Fixing what's broken, eliminating encumbrances, putting things in their place, and happy endings are some of the September byways on your celestial highway, Aquarius! You need to make your impression on people—the same way you need to make up your own schedule—but better than making an impression is making *friends*. The next few years are filled with unexpected delights, so why not coast a bit this month?

Keywords: Take a break

PISCES

That grand statesman Marcus Aurelius was born a Pisces. He once said (could it have been in September?), "as the mill can grind all kinds of grain, healthy souls must always find themselves ready to face all kinds of situations." That's September for you, Pisces! Just remember that "nothing is either good or bad, but thinking makes it so." So think happy thoughts, don't take the bait, and, remember, calmer waters are just ahead.

Keyword: Stoicism

1

SEPTEMBER

Forget nothing, just let it pass.

ARIES
Examine well your own thoughts.
Chaucer

TAURUS
If happiness was in our state of being, we would not need to have fun to be happy.
Blaise Pascal

GEMINI
And so, good for you, you make mistakes trying.
Portuguese Proverb

CANCER
After you have learned to distinguish reality from the imaginary, dare.
Swedish Proverb

LEO
It can be better to quarrel than to be alone.
Irish Proverb

VIRGO
Space has been separated and has made "places."
Martin Heidegger

LIBRA
At any moment I open my eyes and exist. And, before this, during all eternity, what was there?
Ugo Betti

SCORPIO
I prefer to feel confused than to understand the definition of its meaning.
Thomas à Kempis

SAGITTARIUS
Never trust the teller. Trust the tale.
D. H. Lawrence

CAPRICORN
Although one does not always notice, modern man lives under the tyranny of numbers.
N. Eberstadt

AQUARIUS
I can resist everything, except temptation.
Oscar Wilde

PISCES
Evolution moves from unconsciousness to ecstasy through pain.
Amado Nervo

ARIES
If you want good advice, consult an old man.
Portuguese Proverb

TAURUS
To act mad once a year is something quite tolerable.
Saint Augustine

GEMINI
Each stubborn soul enjoys his moment of dumbness.
Mexican Quote

CANCER
Time passes, we say. Time doesn't exist; we are the ones that move on.
The Talmud

LEO
If misery enjoys company, it has company enough.
Henry David Thoreau

VIRGO
Spatial existence is the first condition of all perception.
M. Merleau Ponty

LIBRA
Push on, and faith will catch up with you.
Jean-le-Rond D'Alembert

SCORPIO
A definition is the solitude of an idea locked up inside a wall of words.
Samuel Butler

SAGITTARIUS
As a general rule, prosperity is what keeps us in debt.
Anonymous

CAPRICORN
It is much better to know where to ride than to be a good rider.
Montana Quote

AQUARIUS
Increased means and increased leisure are the two civilizers of man.
Benjamin Disraeli

PISCES
Two dangers constantly threaten the world: order and disorder.
Paul Valéry

3
SEPTEMBER

Do not lower your expectations.

ARIES
Answers are what we have for "others" problems.
Will Rogers

TAURUS
Freedom of speech has no value if you have nothing to say.
Joseph Joubert

GEMINI
I tell you, one must still have chaos in oneself, to give birth to a dancing star.
Nietzsche

CANCER
How many of our dreams would turn into nightmares if they came true!
Logan Smith

LEO
We consider too much the good luck of the early bird, and not enough the bad luck of the early worm.
Franklin D. Roosevelt

VIRGO
Times change and we with them.
Latin Proverb

LIBRA
I can never constitute myself as anything but object.
Jacques Lacan

SCORPIO
It is the end that crowns us, not the fight.
Robert Herrick

SAGITTARIUS
Too many wish to be happy before becoming wise.
S. Necker

CAPRICORN
In time, with patience, any and everybody comes on down . . .
Popular Spanish Saying

AQUARIUS
Perfect behavior is born of complete indifference.
Cesare Pavese

PISCES
Man is demolishing nature: we kill things that keep us alive.
Thor Heyerdahl

Your potential is neverending—
and always rejuvenating.

ARIES
There is no perfect solution for any problem, if it has something to do with human beings.
Leo Tolstoy

TAURUS
Have a good time today, and don't waste any time in a foolish yesterday.
Mae West

GEMINI
(Once a day) Stop, Look and Listen!
Anonymous

CANCER
One of these days is none of these days.
Anonymous

LEO
No man is destroyed as much as by himself.
T. Bentley

VIRGO
Look around. Let things happen and be. Rectify some.
Pope John XXIII

LIBRA
There is nothing more real than nothing.
Samuel Beckett

SCORPIO
Often we say something and only later do we see HOW much truth it holds.
Ludwig Wittgenstein

SAGITTARIUS
A good example is worth exactly twice some good advice.
Swiss Proverb

CAPRICORN
The worst of all questions is the one never posed.
Anonymous

AQUARIUS
All other great minds with their ideas are still to come.
Graffiti

PISCES
To be social is to be forgiving.
Robert Frost

5

Pick a tree and help it hold up the sky.

SEPTEMBER

ARIES
What is rational is actual and what is actual is rational.
Hegel

TAURUS
Enjoying means sharing.
Santayana

GEMINI
The worst danger for this generation is to take an example from the past one.
Anonymous

CANCER
There are times when what you imagine to be the worst possible thing turns out to be the best possible thing.
Zen Proverb

LEO
Courage comes and goes. Hold on for the next supply.
Thomas Merton

VIRGO
A modest man can be admired, if he is talked about.
Ed Howe

LIBRA
My body is that part of the world which can be altered by my thoughts.
Lichtenberg

SCORPIO
A conclusion is the place where you got tired of thinking.
Arthur Bloch

SAGITTARIUS
The enemy of man is his stubbornness; his friend is his acumen.
Muslim Proverb

CAPRICORN
Without a penny, there is no dollar.
Anonymous

AQUARIUS
A single prayer moves heaven.
Japanese Proverb

PISCES
Every meeting is the beginning of a goodbye.
Anonymous

Listen hard, listen soft—but listen.

6
SEPTEMBER

ARIES
Begin at the beginning and don't keep silent.
Anonymous

TAURUS
Bygone years wrinkle the face, but the lack of enthusiasm wrinkles the soul.
Lucille Ball

GEMINI
Each person's personal memory is his own literature.
Aldous Huxley

CANCER
Dive right into it, words will come later!
Mexican Proverb

LEO
We are all born mad. Some stay that way.
Samuel Beckett

VIRGO
The go-between always uses up thousands of clogs.
Japanese Quote

LIBRA
Names are not always what they seem. The common Welch name Bzjxxllwcp is pronounced "Jackson."
Mark Twain

SCORPIO
Once we have understood, we listen in retrospect.
Marcel Proust

SAGITTARIUS
A life is never worth little, it cannot be exchanged for anything.
Fanny Ardent

CAPRICORN
It wasn't raining when Noah built the ark.
Howard Ruff

AQUARIUS
To find a friend, close an eye. To keep a friend, close both.
George Norman Douglas

PISCES
There is nothing wrong in living, unless you live wrongly.
Diogenes

7

SEPTEMBER

There is always something you can excel in.

ARIES
An argument is a question with two sides and no end.
Jonathan Swift

TAURUS
Actually, to have a sense of humor is to be conscious of the relativity of things.
A. de Senillosa

GEMINI
Nobody knows what they have 'til they loose it.
Anonymous

CANCER
I need authority even if I don't believe in it!
Ernst Junger

LEO
Intuition tells me that man is inhabited by different wills, everyone is many.
Sergio Pitol

VIRGO
. . . to draw out strength from weakness.
Baltasar Gracián

LIBRA
Foolish things are useful only because common sense is so limited.
Santayana

SCORPIO
Such as we are made of, such we be.
William Shakespeare

SAGITTARIUS
He who knows the way of the arrow as it leaves the bow is the wisest.
Mayma-Al-Amtal

CAPRICORN
There is time for everything, if you know how to organize it!
Mexican Quote

AQUARIUS
There is more shame in accusing your friends than in being cheated by one.
La Rochefoucauld

PISCES
For I have already once been a boy and a girl, a bush and a bird, and a leaping journeying fish.
Empedocles

Change compels you because it
is the dawning of another chance.

ARIES
Modern youth is looking for new answers to old questions.
Socrates

TAURUS
Old expressions are the best, and short ones even better.
Sir Winston Churchill

GEMINI
God is not a cosmic bellboy.
Harry Fosdick

CANCER
Anything that anyone can imagine can be made into reality by others.
Jules Verne

LEO
All is not sex that appeals.
Hamilton Chaperon

VIRGO
Learn to be your own master, and then you can be the same of others.
Baltasar Gracián

LIBRA
What happens to the hole when the Swiss cheese is eaten?
Bertolt Brecht

SCORPIO
Everything good that life holds is found in young feelings and mature thoughts.
Joseph Joubert

SAGITTARIUS
Most of our happiness depends on our disposition, not on circumstances.
Martha Washington

CAPRICORN
Since man is his own history, be a good story for the ones who stay on.
Al-Saquindi

AQUARIUS
Life, we learn too late, is in the living, in the tissue of every day and hour.
Stephen Leacock

PISCES
To penetrate one's being, one must go armed to the teeth.
Paul Valéry

9

SEPTEMBER

There will always be a reaction to your actions.

ARIES
Life should be a challenge even if you live to be 100 or own zillions.
Beah Richards

TAURUS
One returns to the place one came from.
Jean de la Fontaine

GEMINI
Nobody likes to be put in his place, and nobody likes to feel out of place.
Anonymous

CANCER
Even without a breeze, the sail has character.
Stanislaw Lec

LEO
No man is better than another if he doesn't do more than another.
Cervantes

VIRGO
Whoever says "I" has already made a distinction.
Somali Proverb

LIBRA
In larger things we are convivial; what causes trouble is the trivial.
Richard Armour

SCORPIO
There is nothing more beautiful than happiness written on an old face.
Jean-Paul Richter

SAGITTARIUS
The only sin passion can commit is to be joyless.
Dorothy Sayers

CAPRICORN
He who resembles his father can do no wrong.
Muslim Quote

AQUARIUS
The proper study of man is mankind. (for all Aquarians, forever)
Alexander Pope

PISCES
Maturity consists of no longer being taken in by oneself.
Kajetan von Schlaggenberg

Do not play at settling your disagreements. Mend
each as you would a rare porcelain tea cup.

ARIES
We get ourselves into trouble when young; trouble gets into us when old!
Fernando Benitez

TAURUS
The most authentic things to me are my dreams.
Eugene Delacroix

GEMINI
Careful! What most men do not like about marriage is its permanence.
Anonymous

CANCER
All famous artists were once only beginners.
Greek Proverb

LEO
"Doing" is a tangible intangible.
Graffiti

VIRGO
It doesn't get better 'til the worst is over.
Swedish Proverb

LIBRA
It is by far better to have a firm anchor in foolishness, than to travel without direction in the agitated oceans of thought.
John Kenneth Galbraith

SCORPIO
Nature never breaks its own rules.
Leonardo da Vinci

SAGITTARIUS
Do not judge if you cannot do it with compassion.
A. McCaffrey

CAPRICORN
You are compared to the person you are seen with.
Egyptian Quote

AQUARIUS
And much it grieved my heart to think / What Man has made of Man.
William Wordsworth

PISCES
Freud is the father of psychoanalysis. It has no mother.
Germaine Greer

11
SEPTEMBER

Tamper the threshold of your consciousness.

ARIES
To be a wise man, one needs lightness and fluidity.
Yaqui Quote

TAURUS
To grow old is to pass from passion to compassion.
Albert Camus

GEMINI
To really feel at ease, you have to be able to yawn at ease.
Anonymous

CANCER
Winners are losers who keep trying.
Greek Proverb

LEO
You are a child, you will have a child. As you have done, you will do.
Spanish Quote

VIRGO
Everything comes to him who knows how to wait for it.
English Quote

LIBRA
No one is ever old enough to know better.
Holbrook Jackson

SCORPIO
Adversity shows our temper, and prosperity hides it.
Horace

SAGITTARIUS
Fiction reveals truths that reality obscures.
Jessamyn West

CAPRICORN
Whoever does not listen to his elders will have problems.
Anonymous

AQUARIUS
Man is the only animal that blushes, or that needs to.
Mark Twain

PISCES
Act as men of thought; think as men of action.
Henry Bergson

To develop you need a vehicle. Move. Exist.

12

SEPTEMBER

ARIES
A man really starts to get old when he doesn't care any more.
Alberto Moravia

TAURUS
An optimist looks at your eyes; a pessimist looks at your feet.
Madagascan Quote

GEMINI
All our friends should be immortal; all our enemies, mortal.
Anonymous

CANCER
Speak in a way that makes your words more eloquent than silence.
Jewish Proverb

LEO
A diamond on a dunghill is a precious diamond still.
Anonymous

VIRGO
If you can't catch the bull by the horn, catch him by his tail.
Arabic Quote

LIBRA
It's never to late to mend.
Anonymous

SCORPIO
Better be the head of a lizard than the tail of a dragon.
Anonymous

SAGITTARIUS
'Tis better to be corrected by wise men than to be blessed by fools.
Pindar

CAPRICORN
A favor thrown in your face is no favor at all.
Mexican Quote

AQUARIUS
Human beings cannot stand too much reality.
T. S. Eliot

PISCES
The best marksman may miss the mark.
Anonymous

13

SEPTEMBER

ARIES
The trouble with the rat race is that even if you win, you're still a rat.
Lily Tomlin

TAURUS
The moment of "change" is the only poem.
Adrienne Rich

GEMINI
No law is convenient enough to everyone.
Livy

CANCER
Whoso would be a man must be an nonconformist.
Ralph Waldo Emerson

LEO
An indecent mind is a perpetual saying.
English Quote

VIRGO
The universe is one of God's thoughts.
Friedrich Schiller

LIBRA
Flattery is like a cigarette—it's all right so long as you don't inhale.
Adlai Stevenson

SCORPIO
Pray to the dead and defend the living with all your might.
Mother Jones

SAGITTARIUS
Do not take strange roads: follow the footsteps of those who have already been right.
Joaquin Setanti

CAPRICORN
The trouble with our times is that the future is not what it used to be.
Paul Valéry

AQUARIUS
Human beings must invent themselves every day.
Jean-Paul Sartre

PISCES
Hands have no tears to flow.
Dylan Thomas

ARIES
Where there are great doubts, there will be great awakenings.
Zen Proverb

TAURUS
If something is worth doing, it is worth doing to the hilt.
G. K. Chesterton

GEMINI
The world would end if pity wouldn't do away with anger.
Seneca

CANCER
Without analysis, no synthesis.
Friedrich Engels

LEO
If you can't bite, don't show your teeth.
Yiddish Proverb

VIRGO
Facts do not cease to exist because they are ignored.
Aldous Huxley

LIBRA
Patience is a bitter plant but it has sweet fruit.
Old Proverb

SCORPIO
Acquire well earned fame, and take a break.
South African Quote

SAGITTARIUS
The riches that are not found in our soul do not belong to us.
Demetrius

CAPRICORN
There are too many people, and too few human beings.
Robert Zend

AQUARIUS
There is an exception to every rule.
English Quote

PISCES
There is always more time than life.
Ancient Greek Quote

15

There is a knight in shining armor inside of you.

SEPTEMBER

ARIES
If we wouldn't try so hard to be happy, we would have more fun.
Edith Wharton

TAURUS
The family is the nucleus of civilization.
Will and Ariel Durant

GEMINI
Are you here to see, or to be seen?
Ovid

CANCER
One's country is not a historic or political reality, it is intimacy.
Ramon Lopez Velarde

LEO
To most men, experience is like the stern lights of a ship, which illumine only the track it has passed.
Samuel Taylor Coleridge

VIRGO
If you want to get good service, serve yourself.
Italian Proverb

LIBRA
One may say, "the eternal mystery of the world is its comprehensibility."
Albert Einstein

SCORPIO
Words are the pedigrees of nations.
Samuel Johnson

SAGITTARIUS
It isn't that they can't see the solution. It is that they can't see the problem.
G. K. Chesterton

CAPRICORN
Doubt is not a pleasant state, but certainty is.
Voltaire

AQUARIUS
Where there is no perception, all is lost.
Anonymous

PISCES
A glance at myth and method will make us stronger owners of our future.
Leon Garcia Soler

Support a grass-root community.

ARIES
I sort of see it like this: if you want the rainbow, you have to take the rain.
Dolly Parton

TAURUS
Time is a tailor who specializes in alterations.
F. Baldwin

GEMINI
Luck is infatuated with the efficient.
Persian Quote

CANCER
All serious daring comes from within.
Eudora Welty

LEO
Levity is the soul of wit.
Eli Perkins

VIRGO
Progress is sometimes followed by a comma, never by a period.
Anonymous

LIBRA
In the fight between you and the world, back the world.
Franz Kafka

SCORPIO
I love my country too much to be a nationalist.
Albert Camus

SAGITTARIUS
What you see, yet cannot see over, is as good as infinite.
Thomas Carlyle

CAPRICORN
The world wants to be deceived.
Sebastian Brant

AQUARIUS
Wonders are willingly told and willingly heard.
Samuel Johnson

PISCES
To flee vice is a virtue, and the beginning of wisdom is to be done with folly.
Horace

There is a worldly consciousness within your grasp.

ARIES
Man's extremity is God's opportunity.
Zen Proverb

TAURUS
When it comes to choosing what to do with your life, don't forget to live it.
Samuel Johnson

GEMINI
Man is an ironic animal.
Amado Nervo

CANCER
A penny is something we see every day but never look at.
Stephen Potter

LEO
I dreamt thousands of new roads. I awoke and took the one I had already traveled.
Chinese Proverb

VIRGO
The day you decide to do it, is your lucky day.
Japanese Quote

LIBRA
It is your own conviction which compels you; that is, choice compels choice.
Epictetus

SCORPIO
Everything that can be said, can be said clearly. (see tomorrow's quote)
Ludwig Wittgenstein

SAGITTARIUS
It is always a mistake not to close one's eyes, whether to forgive or to look better into oneself.
Maurice Maeterlinck

CAPRICORN
No non-poetic account of reality can be complete.
John Myhill

AQUARIUS
I am an idealist. I do not know where I am going, but I am on my way.
Carl Sandburg

PISCES
Self-interest is the rule, self-sacrifice is the exception.
Vermont Proverb

Embark on a new adventure, a silent voyage.

ARIES
Events that happen during childhood are never over: they are repeated like the seasons . . .
Anonymous

TAURUS
Destiny shuffles the cards, and we play them.
Arthur Schopenhauer

GEMINI
Who listens and learns, does well to heed and hush.
Sor Juana Inés de la Cruz

CANCER
If you believe that you can, you can. . . .
Mary Kay Ash [See Tomorrow's Quote]

LEO
The miser piles up everything except friendship.
Irish Quote

VIRGO
He did each simple thing as if he was doing nothing else.
Charles Dickens

LIBRA
There is no better path than the one that doesn't stop.
Mexican Quote

SCORPIO
What cannot be said clearly should not be said. (see yesterday's quote)
Ludwig Wittgenstein

SAGITTARIUS
One must always ask, one should always doubt.
Latin Proverb

CAPRICORN
Where all men think alike, no one thinks very much.
Walter Lippman

AQUARIUS
I do not share anybody's ideas, I have my own.
Ivan Turgenev

PISCES
The way up and the way down are both the same way.
Heraclitus

ARIES
Sell your skill and buy wonder.
Rumi

TAURUS
Life needs illusions, that is, non-truths taken as truths.
Nietzsche

GEMINI
What came first, crisis or inefficient solutions?
Carlos Monsivais

CANCER
. . . If you believe that you cannot, you might be right.
Mary Kay Ash (See Yesterday's Quote)

LEO
The guest of the host soon learns to give lodging.
Arabic Quote

VIRGO
A dose of fantasy and misery should pervade any story of our daily lives.
Janet McNeil

LIBRA
True and definite redemption is found within knowledge.
Alfonso Reyes

SCORPIO
The greatest thing in the world is for man to know how to be his own.
Michel de Montaigne

SAGITTARIUS
There is no better heaven than the one you make for yourself on earth.
Greek Quote

CAPRICORN
The service we render others is really the rent we pay for our room on earth.
Sir Wilfred Grenfell

AQUARIUS
To dream the impossible dream . . . to reach the unreachable star.
Joe Darion

PISCES
Truth is too naked, she does not inflame men.
Jean Cocteau

*Inevitably, you can make something out
of what was not supposed to be.*

ARIES
One takes too long in not understanding anything.
Edward Dahlberg

TAURUS
The ideas of the things we are not thinking about are within our spirit . . .
Wilhelm Leibniz

GEMINI
When there is no freedom to make mistakes, there is no freedom.
Mikhail Gorbachev

CANCER
Yesterday I dared to fight. Today I dare to win.
Bernadette Devlin

LEO
A sage is he who can turn an enemy into a friend.
Irish Proverb

VIRGO
A tiny flame can consume a whole barn.
From the Alphabet of BenSira

LIBRA
To think is not enough; you must think of something.
Jules Renard

SCORPIO
Memory is a social reaction to the condition of absence.
Attributed to Janet McNeil

SAGITTARIUS
Today it is, tomorrow it is not.
Macedonian Quote

CAPRICORN
We must be conscious of where we are and what it is that worries us.
Abraham Lincoln

AQUARIUS
Indecision is fatal, so decide.
Mayan Proverb

PISCES
In Nature's infinite book of secrecy, a little can I read.
William Shakespeare

21
SEPTEMBER

Power should be encouraged and applauded if it helps to free.

ARIES
Nothing is too insignificant for whoever thinks things out with sensitivity.
Anonymous

TAURUS
Power is no more than effortlessness of expression.
Giulio Andreotti

GEMINI
Idiots are always sure of their truths.
Milan Kundera

CANCER
You may be disappointed if you make a mistake, but you're lost if you don't try.
Beverly Sills

LEO
A word is not a bird; when it takes flight, it cannot be caught.
Russian Proverb

VIRGO
What you find here, is also there, and what is not here, is nowhere.
Vishwasara Tantra

LIBRA
Any student who pays attention will be an expert some day.
Persian Quote

SCORPIO
The world is independent of my will.
Ludwig Wittgenstein

SAGITTARIUS
A normal day, let me find out the treasure that you are.
Greek Proverb

CAPRICORN
The wild places are where we began. Where they end, so do we.
David Brower

AQUARIUS
Instant gratification is not soon enough.
Carrie Fisher

PISCES
Everything in this life has an "upper" and a "downer."
Anonymous

ARIES
Astounding: everything has a grain of intelligence.
Graffiti in Cambridge

TAURUS
Power is the biggest aphrodisiac.
Henry Kissinger

GEMINI
Throw in your little grain of sand.
Anonymous

CANCER
Nothing can take the place of intelligence.
James B. Sumner

LEO
You cry about your sins, but you pay for your debts.
Armenian Quote

VIRGO
For whoever teaches from the heart, your throne is in heaven.
Saint Augustine

LIBRA
Seek and you will always find.
Greek Proverb

SCORPIO
A mirror doesn't have a heart, but it does have a lot of ideas.
Chazal

SAGITTARIUS
Do not ask of life what only eternity can bestow upon you.
Latin Proverb

CAPRICORN
"Mañana" does not mean tomorrow. It just means not today.
Mexican Saying

AQUARIUS
What goes around, comes around.
Anonymous

PISCES
I know how much I am worth because of the amount I disdain.
Graffiti

23
SEPTEMBER

There is an action needed, waiting to be done.

ARIES
If the horn cannot be twisted, the ear can.
Malay Proverb

TAURUS
Nobody should obey those who do not deserve to command.
Cicero

GEMINI
To please people is a great step towards persuading them.
Lord Chesterfield

CANCER
It is the eye which makes the horizon.
Emerson

LEO
Good is good, but better beats it.
Italian Quote

VIRGO
There's no glory without sacrifice.
Filipino Quote

LIBRA
We are all crazy, or I don't understand a thing.
José Saramago

SCORPIO
Whatever I do, I do it for myself, that is why I am here.
Anthony Hopkins

SAGITTARIUS
Happiness does not give, it only lends.
Anonymous

CAPRICORN
It is never too late to renounce all prejudice.
Henry David Thoreau

AQUARIUS
Simplify. Simplify. Our lives are spent on details.
Henry David Thoreau

PISCES
We're all of us sentenced to solitary confinement, inside our own skins, for life.
Tennessee Williams

The sea of potentiality is stirring. Be ready.

24
SEPTEMBER

ARIES
God is always on the other side of your prayers.
Christian Quote

TAURUS
The heart is half a prophet.
Yiddish Quote

GEMINI
Reason in my philosophy is only harmony among irrational impulses.
Santayana

CANCER
Pessimism does win us great happy moments.
Max Beerbohm

LEO
Nobody can count their money in the cemetery.
Richard Burton

VIRGO
Help yourself and God will help you.
Anonymous

LIBRA
Every bubble bursts.
Polish Quote

SCORPIO
To me, life is just a novitiate eternity.
Dame Felicitas Corrigan

SAGITTARIUS
Be not water taking the tint of all colors.
Syrian Quote

CAPRICORN
Each counts for one. That is why more count for more.
Derek Parfit

AQUARIUS
The voice is the second face.
Gerard Bauer

PISCES
Whoever starts out toward the unknown must consent to venture alone.
André Gide

25
SEPTEMBER

Swing and learn to enjoy the motion in swinging for it is a good way to keep time.

ARIES
What you do not do today, you probably won't do tomorrow either.
Oscar Wilde

TAURUS
Enthusiasm creates more action than precision, and it is contagious.
Anonymous

GEMINI
The universe does not jest with us, but is in earnest.
Ralph Waldo Emerson

CANCER
The most beautiful things are those that madness prompts, and reason writes.
André Gide

LEO
Gold and lovers are the most difficult things to hide.
Spanish Quote

VIRGO
Nobody listens to anybody, and if you try for a while, you will see why.
Mignon McLaughlin

LIBRA
Ideas, contrary to events, never happen without precedents.
Hannah Arendt

SCORPIO
The flower in the vase still smiles, but does not laugh.
Chazal

SAGITTARIUS
I wish that every human life could be pure and clear freedom.
Simone de Beauvoir

CAPRICORN
Will cannot be quenched against its will.
Dante Alighieri

AQUARIUS
Man is born to live, not to prepare himself for life.
Boris Pasternak

PISCES
Where I cannot satisfy my reason, I love to humour my fancy.
Sir Thomas Browne

Try to be awake so you can speak to the dawn.

ARIES
What a pity that to reach God we must pass through faith!
E. M. Cioran

TAURUS
Everyone is a hero to his imagination.
Anonymous

GEMINI
Neither the word nor the name is identical with the object of intention.
Walter Benjamin

CANCER
Its not what you are but what you don't become that hurts.
Clifford Odets

LEO
If woman didn't exist, all the money in the world would have no meaning.
Aristotle Onassis

VIRGO
It takes time to spoil the world, but time is all it takes.
Bernard de Fontenelle

LIBRA
We keep passing unseen through little moments of other people's lives.
Robert T. Pirsig

SCORPIO
Every social class has its own pathology.
Marcel Proust

SAGITTARIUS
The secret of power is in will.
Giuseppe Mazzini

CAPRICORN
Keep yourself useful, have a pastime, learn to be satisfied and enjoy people.
Schindler

AQUARIUS
If you want to make it, dress British and think Yiddish.
Charles Collingwood

PISCES
My soul does not search for immortality, but to exhaust a world of possibilities.
Pindar

27

SEPTEMBER

Look for and lean on a master.

ARIES
Words are but an imperfect tool, however we don't have a better one.
Anonymous Zen Master

TAURUS
Meditate, but without following a pattern; question, following your feelings.
Zen Quote

GEMINI
Nature has bestowed some vice on every creature.
Anonymous

CANCER
I will show you fear in a handful of dust.
T. S. Eliot

LEO
A diploma is a proof of knowledge that proves nothing.
Gustave Flaubert

VIRGO
The secret of happiness is to find a congenial monotony.
Sean O'Casey

LIBRA
Hurry brings no blessings.
Swahili Quote

SCORPIO
Crowds comfort those who are dissatisfied with themselves.
Chazal

SAGITTARIUS
Power is pleasure, and pleasure sweetens pain.
William Hazlitt

CAPRICORN
Very few succeed before making a mistake.
Mexican Quote

AQUARIUS
We are pieces of steel, and thy love is the magnet.
Divani Shamsi Tabriz

PISCES
The future is made of the same stuff as the present.
Simone Weil

ARIES
Duty should be a byproduct.
Brenda Ueland

TAURUS
All is not sex that appeals.
Anonymous

GEMINI
The art of knowing is the art of knowing what to ignore.
Rumi

CANCER
A rose, is a rose, is a rose.
Gertrude Stein

LEO
Fish bite best on a golden hook.
Norwegian Quote

VIRGO
Make good use of bad rubbish.
Elizabeth Beresford

LIBRA
There are plenty of ruined buildings in the world, but no ruined stones.
Hugh MacDiarmid

SCORPIO
If fame is to come only after death, I am in no hurry for it.
Marcus Valerius Martialis

SAGITTARIUS
In a crisis, frequently the most daring way is the safest.
Henry Kissinger

CAPRICORN
Your own secret is your slave, but if you tell it, you are its slave.
A. de Tortosa

AQUARIUS
Soar like an eagle!
Bantu Proverb

PISCES
There is no hope in joy except in human relations.
Antoine de Saint-Exupéry

29

SEPTEMBER

Be truthful to your teacher (once in a while).

ARIES
Sometimes, progress is going around the same circle, but faster.
Graffiti

TAURUS
Wrong reasoning sometimes lands poor mortals in right conclusions.
George Eliot

GEMINI
Nothing is really work unless you prefer to be doing something else.
Hindu Quote

CANCER
Ask for advice, then use your head.
Norwegian Proverb

LEO
Comfortable things are the best of all modern discoveries.
Gustave Flaubert

VIRGO
It's better to be a lion for a day than a sheep all your life.
Elizabeth Henry

LIBRA
To understand everything is to pardon everything.
Madame de Staël

SCORPIO
Displayed merits bring reputation; hidden merits, fortune.
Sir Francis Bacon

SAGITTARIUS
We seemed to think that because of power we were wise.
Stephen V. Benet

CAPRICORN
Only he who carries the bundle, knows what it weighs.
Anonymous

AQUARIUS
Be wisely worldly, be not worldly wise.
Francis Quarles

PISCES
There is always more to know, to tell, to suggest, to be told. Persist.
Joseph Campbell

ARIES
A good question to ask yourself is what would the world be like if everybody were like me?
Anonymous

TAURUS
Life is a succession of moments. To live each one is to succeed.
Corita Kent

GEMINI
A proverb put to good use can reap one hundred good deeds.
Ancient Greek Quote

CANCER
Inject a few raisins of conversation into the tasteless dough of existence.
O. Henry

LEO
We cannot escape destiny by running.
Ibo Proverb

VIRGO
The dust has its reasons, wherever it goes.
Nat Crane

LIBRA
To be somebody you must last.
Ruth Gordon

SCORPIO
I shall spend all of the sky, doing good on this earth.
Saint Teresa of Lisieux

SAGITTARIUS
Salt water cures anything: sweat, tears, or the ocean.
Isak Dinesen

CAPRICORN
The unknown always passes for the marvelous.
Tacitus

AQUARIUS
Very soon it is too late.
Anonymous

PISCES
Go speed the stars of Thought.
Ralph Waldo Emerson

OCTOBER

OCTOBER

Imagination is not the talent of some men, but the health of every man.
Ralph Waldo Emerson

Our Universe, at last count, is around 16 billion years old. That makes a lot of Octobers, and in each one, throughout any millennium, a great number of generous souls were born: Marsilio Ficino, Mahatma Gandhi, Saint Francis of Assisi, and John Lennon, to name a few. Is it any wonder why so many people call October the month of values and imagination, a month to think about what you stand for—and why? It's the perfect time to tune into your own personal ceremony or ritual, as the air nips, the leaves show off, and everything transforms—including you.

ARIES

Aries, up until the last seven days of October, the Sun is in your opposite sign of Libra. This might mean conflicts of interest for you in some way, but don't butt heads about it. Even if the path becomes a little outrageous along the way, this could be just what you need to keep you going, get you there, and find yourself. The month may have some "it's now or never" days, so hang in there—push on, and triumph!

Keyword: Relax

TAURUS

Taurus, to paraphrase the Robert Frost poem, you have "miles to go and promises to keep." Specifically, Taurus, it would do you enormous good to make a promise to yourself or someone else to give in to something at least once this month, if not every month. Learn from Libra, who shares your ruler, who to share. Time can be your best ally now, as can Venus, the grand ruler of Libra, and the heavenly guardian of your fortunes. Look, too, to your elders, who might prove wiser than you think. You may feel like a beast of burden, but have faith—things could just fall off your back and right into place.

Keyword: Trust

GEMINI

Though you are a summer child, Gemini, and it's well into autumn, you may be shielded by a feeling that this is a "golden age." The energy of the Sun in Libra makes a fine combination with your volatile ways, and you, Gemini, should try looking at things in a slightly artistic way. Put some color in your life, your abode, or even in your cheeks. Paint a portrait—or the town! And if you have the chance to choose, choose what's most pleasurable, each and every time.

Keyword: Notoriety

CANCER

The German phrase *Schaffe, schaffe, hause baue* means "work, work on building your life and/or home" but in your case this month, Moon children, it might be translated as "home sweat home." But this month, Cancer, don't sweat the details. Instead, find solace and comfort in what is already there and what has gone before. Search for a few father figures instead of waiting for Godot. Carry on tradition rather than just carrying on. All of which can show you what the Chinese like to call "the way." So go ahead, find yours.

Keywords: Collective unconscious

LEO

Just when you thought your kingdom was under your perfect rule, Leo, little insurrections pop up. Relationships and interactions change course. Your communication valves suddenly need servicing. But keep your claws sheathed, Leo. Learn not to pounce. Be more of a pussycat and learn to tell little white lies to help others on their way. Usually, Leo, more people listen to you than you know. So wait and with absolute leonine grace, listen to the replies.

Keywords: Noble decisions

VIRGO

Stop worrying so much about what others are thinking about you and tune in to what *you* think and feel, Virgo! First, just prepare—then dare! October offers and November delivers an autumnal cornucopia of delights. So go ahead and feast. Nourish your ego and take a little time to digest Winston Churchill's words: "Without victory there is no survival."

Keyword: Abundance

LIBRA

This is the month to have your birthday cake and eat it, too, Libra. Lighten up, yet with focus, "contemplate what you are as you become what you contemplate," something almost exactly as the medieval mystic Jan Van Ruysbroek advised more than one thousand years ago. October's sky makes your nights—that time of all things subconscious—long and full of possibility. Time is truly on your side, this month, so make every moment count.

Keyword: Aims

SCORPIO

There is a wonderful Arabian aphorism that describes the four types of men in the world. Perhaps it also describes the four kinds of Scorpios: "He who knows nothing, but knows not that he knows nothing; he who knows nothing and knows he knows nothing; he who knows but knows not that he knows; and he who knows and knows he knows." Why not see which one fits you by trying one—or all—on for size, for fun, for insight, and as preparation for your birthday.

Keyword: Reasoning

SAGITTARIUS

This month, if you're female, you're anything but the so-called weaker sex. Take aim and shoot for the stars, because this month you can turn your power to your advantage even more than usual, provided you keep your eye on the goal. If you are a male (and remember, in astrology, it's your sex, not your preference, that matters) cooperation is the objective, not attainment of your desires. Be wise, be wary, be wonderful.

Keywords: Make an effort

CAPRICORN

Remind yourself, high-climbing Goat, not to stumble over the rocks in your path, and you'll scale your heights with greater ease. Since you could be your own worst enemy just now, look to others in your flock instead to discover just how you can turn things around to your advantage by using some kind of family trait. Lucky you! You most probably will find you have a lot to count on *and* to be proud of.

Keyword: Affinities

AQUARIUS

This October, Aquarius, reflect on this Stephen Hawking (the scientist who was chosen to take Newton's chair of honor and the author of A Brief History of Time) quote: "If we could find the answer to why we exist (we and the universe), it would be the most wonderful triumph of human reason: we would know God's thoughts." So ponder your world, and everyone in it, and as you tune in to yourself, don't forget to fine-tune your antenna as well so that you listen to others better.

Keywords: Cross any bridge

PISCES

If you feel like fishing for a fight, October is the month to do it, Pisces. You are able to get very much in touch with what Horace, two thousand years ago, called "a brief madness." But ire (as long as it isn't exasperation) can be just the perfect good to get you going on a new journey. Let things out. Let things go. And remember, still waters run deep, so get in touch with all your feelings.

Keywords: Anything goes

1

OCTOBER

Let go. Put your trust in something
entirely new and untested.

ARIES
Vanity is as ridiculous as delirium is tragic.
Gregorio Marañón

TAURUS
I cannot tell you a secret, for you already hold the secret within.
Anonymous Zen Master

GEMINI
Art is, more than anything else, a direction of the soul.
Marc Chagall

CANCER
Man carries within himself truths that float out upon words.
Socrates

LEO
May justice be done, although the sky falls down.
Latin Quote

VIRGO
The darkest hour is today.
Adlai Stevenson

LIBRA
Time always walks at your side and resists passing you by.
C. Fry

SCORPIO
Stay away from the first person; show the second; wake up the third; and
follow the last one in the list. He can help you.
Arabic Quote

SAGITTARIUS
God give me hills to climb, and strength for climbing.
A. Guiterman

CAPRICORN
A man must ride alternately on the horses of his private and public nature.
Ralph Waldo Emerson

AQUARIUS
You shall know the truth and the truth shall be your liberation.
John 16:13

PISCES
If you deceive me once, the fault is yours. If you deceive me twice, it is mine.
Anaxagoras

Never allow your fire to burn too low.

ARIES
A real prophet will point out the wisdom from your own heart.
Persian Quote

TAURUS
Sometimes, talking is silver, and silence is gold.
German Quote

GEMINI
Wise men change their opinions.
Mexican Quote

CANCER
It is bestowed on men to know themselves and to be wise.
Heraclitus

LEO
Learning is its own exceedingly great reward.
William Hazlitt

VIRGO
From the sublime to the ridiculous is but a step.
Napoleon Bonaparte

LIBRA
Truth is not what makes a great man: it is man that can make truth great.
Confucius

SCORPIO
The afternoon always knows what the morning has been waiting for.
Swedish Quote

SAGITTARIUS
If good laws are not obeyed, there is not a good government.
Aristotle

CAPRICORN
Only a person who does absolutely nothing, never makes a mistake.
Mexican Proverb

AQUARIUS
Truth and lies belong to language, not to things . . .
Thomas Hobbes

PISCES
We may say that hysteria is a caricature of an artistic creation.
Sigmund Freud

3

OCTOBER

*Return to the beginning even if only
to see how far you've come.*

ARIES
Any kind of thought is an intellectual and vital part of life itself.
Meister Eckhart

TAURUS
With all thy getting get understanding.
Proverbs 4:7

GEMINI
A person should stay alive, if only out of curiosity.
Yiddish Proverb

CANCER
During one sole day, there are one thousand reasons for praying.
Persian Quote

LEO
The spiritual being that we all are, needs a body.
Saint Bernard

VIRGO
As the generation, so the leader.
The Talmud

LIBRA
Try to know everything of something, and something of everything.
Henry Peter, Lord Brougham

SCORPIO
Coitus is a slight attack of apoplexy.
Democrutus of Abdera

SAGITTARIUS
Sometimes it is preferred to abandon certain things than to pursue them.
Yen-Tou

CAPRICORN
Adversity makes us wise until the next misfortune comes.
Anonymous

AQUARIUS
Truth exists; it is lies that are inventions.
Georges Braque

PISCES
Love is the wind that blows and hides.
Anonymous

ARIES
Every man is a composite of the heavenly and the earthly.
Spinoza

TAURUS
Actuality has only three realities: to exist, to be, to value.
Lagneau

GEMINI
You're bored? Idler!
Wallace Stevens

CANCER
How beautiful it is to do nothing and then rest afterward.
Spanish Quote

LEO
By God, let it be, and let's have some more!
Anonymous

VIRGO
Man has an inner conversation with himself alone, and it is wise to regulate it well.
Blaise Pascal

LIBRA
Certainty is usually an illusion, and rest is not man's destiny.
Oliver Wendell Holmes

SCORPIO
If it can lick, it can bite.
French Proverb

SAGITTARIUS
Right view, right aim, right speech, right action, right living, right effort.
Buddha

CAPRICORN
Things resemble their owners.
Anonymous

AQUARIUS
Everybody has his own opinion . . . watch yours!
Graffiti

PISCES
Hell is filled with fathers and sons as well as grandchildren.
Russian Quote

5

OCTOBER

Do not only look straight ahead. There are wonders in the periphery.

ARIES
Approach the light you carry within and you will need no shelter.
Buddha

TAURUS
Reason is to stand up to life and its doings.
Ernst Toller

GEMINI
Art does not reproduce the visible, but makes visible what is not always so.
Paul Klee

CANCER
There is something wrong when you don't feel at home, at home.
Anonymous

LEO
I don't know what art is, but I know what I like.
Anonymous

VIRGO
An idea is not the responsibility of the people who believe in it.
Don Marquis

LIBRA
How many roads must a man walk down before you can call him a man?
Bob Dylan

SCORPIO
Love should not dominate, it should cultivate.
Goethe

SAGITTARIUS
Laws, just like houses, lean on each other.
Edmund Burke

CAPRICORN
All the while one is angry, one is lost from being content.
Benjamin Disraeli

AQUARIUS
Do I contradict myself? Very well then I contradict myself.
Walt Whitman

PISCES
Could eternity belong to me?
Edward Young

Let go, cut loose, and take your time. It will be wild.

6
OCTOBER

ARIES
Whosoever tries to force circumstances becomes a slave of circumstances.
The Talmud

TAURUS
One's country is the country in which one feels well.
John Milton

GEMINI
Literature is as life, it is lying well about the truth.
G. K. Chesterton

CANCER
Be it ever so humble there's no place like home to wear what you like.
George Ade

LEO
Important things should be said simply. Emphasis spoils it.
Jean de La Bruyère

VIRGO
My favorite subject—is myself.
James Boswell

LIBRA
Whatever God has written on your forehead is what you shall achieve.
The Koran

SCORPIO
He who is outside his door has the hard part of his journey behind him.
Dutch Proverb

SAGITTARIUS
Some circumstantial evidence is very strong, as when you find a trout in the milk.
Henry David Thoreau

CAPRICORN
One must like people as they are, for there is not a soul without a fault.
Anonymous

AQUARIUS
I am large, I contain multitudes.
Walt Whitman

PISCES
Most people forget everything, except to be ungrateful.
The Koran

7

OCTOBER

Night and day carry the same importance.

ARIES
Whosoever takes advantage of any circumstance becomes the master of circumstance.
The Talmud

TAURUS
Fame is proof that humans are too credulous.
Anonymous

GEMINI
Style is to a person what structure is to a work of art.
Luis Goytisolo

CANCER
A true home is built with bricks made of patience.
Anonymous

LEO
Spoken words perish; the written word lasts.
Latin Proverb

VIRGO
To be free is to have achieved your life.
Tennessee Williams

LIBRA
Fear, as love, has a certain smell.
Margaret Atwood

SCORPIO
Emotion has taught mankind to reason.
Marquis de Vauvenargues

SAGITTARIUS
After all, that is what laws are for, to make and break them.
Emma Goldman

CAPRICORN
Do not allow me to ask for protection in the wake of perils, but rather courage to face them.
Rabindranath Tagore

AQUARIUS
I must create a system or be enslaved by another man's.
William Blake

PISCES
There really is a silver lining behind every cloud!
Anonymous

Know that anything will return if you let it.

OCTOBER

ARIES
There is nothing softer or more flexible than water yet nothing can resist it.
Lao-Tzu

TAURUS
All man, all art, contain their own hypocrisy.
Romain Rolland

GEMINI
Beautiful things, once taste is formed, are obviously and unaccountably beautiful.
Santayana

CANCER
Tact consists in knowing how far to go in going too far.
Jean Cocteau

LEO
The vow that binds too strictly snaps itself.
Alfred Lord Tennyson

VIRGO
We will be damned, but it shall be theatrical.
Ralph Waldo Emerson

LIBRA
You can't use your friends and have them too.
Anonymous

SCORPIO
It does no harm to believe in fate if you act as if you did not.
Anonymous

SAGITTARIUS
Enlightening very well may be: do what you want and eat what is there.
Jack Kerouac

CAPRICORN
In life's daily battle, do not allow me to search for allies, if not my own strength.
Rabindranath Tagore

AQUARIUS
Love your enemy: you'll drive him crazy.
Eleanor Doan

PISCES
There is much pleasure to be gained from useless knowledge.
Bertrand Russell

9

OCTOBER

ARIES
If you want to understand function, study structure.
Francis Harry Compton Crick

TAURUS
Beauty is everlasting, and dust is for a time.
Marianne Moore

GEMINI
The brain is the organ of longevity.
George Alban Sacher

CANCER
Things are the way they are because they were the way they were.
Fred Hoyle

LEO
An individual is merely a component in a system called a species.
A. Sibatani

VIRGO
Too much truth / Is uncouth.
Franklin P. Adams

LIBRA
Winning is not everything, but to want to win is.
Vince Lombardi

SCORPIO
Better bent than broken.
Scottish Quote

SAGITTARIUS
Quick to believe is easy to deceive.
Serbian Quote

CAPRICORN
All lay load on the willing horse.
English Proverb

AQUARIUS
If not now, when?
Yiddish Quote

PISCES
All or nothing.
French Saying

Ask yourself: Is seeing believing?

10
OCTOBER

ARIES
My race being run, I love to watch the race.
John Masefield

TAURUS
You could not discover the limits of soul, not even if you travel down every road.
Heraclitus

GEMINI
There's no bad publicity, except an obituary notice.
Brendan Behan

CANCER
Charm is a way of getting the answer "yes" without having asked a clear question.
Albert Camus

LEO
The minority is sometimes right; the majority always wrong.
George Bernard Shaw

VIRGO
Do not get angry with me if I tell you the truth.
Socrates

LIBRA
It is no longer clear which way is up, even if one wants to rise.
David Riesman

SCORPIO
We do not know one millionth of one percent about anything.
Thomas Alva Edison

SAGITTARIUS
No man says all he means, and no woman means all she says.
Anonymous

CAPRICORN
First comes to be, and then comes the way of being.
Anonymous

AQUARIUS
Theory is a good thing, but a good experiment lasts forever.
Pyotr Leonidovich Kapitsa

PISCES
If thou follow thy star, thou canst not fail of glorious heaven.
Dante Alighieri

Calm someone, understand who they are and why.

ARIES
It is not what people don't know, it is what people pretend to know.
Jean-Jacques Rousseau

TAURUS
Does a cow see the stars? It is quite amazing to see something so usable and not to notice it.
Zen Quote

GEMINI
Parents are the last people on earth who ought to have children.
Samuel Butler

CANCER
A house is a machine for living in.
Le Corbusier

LEO
Writing, one learns to write.
Latin Quote

VIRGO
The beginning of knowledge is the definition of terms.
Socrates

LIBRA
At night, atheists almost believe in God.
Edward Young

SCORPIO
Never try to tell everything you know. It might take too short a time.
Norman Ford

SAGITTARIUS
I respect only those who resist me, but I cannot tolerate them.
Charles de Gaulle

CAPRICORN
You are as young as your faith, as old as your doubts.
Anonymous

AQUARIUS
Enjoy the honored vessel today: tomorrow it may be broken.
The Talmud

PISCES
Froth is not beer.
Dutch Quote

ARIES
Perfection of means and confusion of ends seem to characterize our age.
Albert Einstein

TAURUS
I go, you stay; two autumns.
Haiku Matsumura Goshun

GEMINI
Speech is civilization itself . . . It is silence which isolates.
Thomas Mann

CANCER
One of the pleasures of getting older is finding that one was right.
Ezra Pound

LEO
The virtue of the soul does not consist in flying high, but in walking orderly.
Michel de Montaigne

VIRGO
Money is always there. It's the pockets that change.
Gertrude Stein

LIBRA
Discoveries are made by men whose feelings surpass their ideas.
Edward Young

SCORPIO
Languages are the lights of the mind.
John Stuart Mill

SAGITTARIUS
There are no gains without pains.
Anonymous

CAPRICORN
There are spots even on the sun.
Anonymous

AQUARIUS
A family that prays together, stays together.
Al Scalpone

PISCES
Much always longs for more.
Icelandic Saying

13

Share an experience.

ARIES
. . . the doubter fights only with himself.
Graham Greene

TAURUS
Do not believe anything until you find how to guide your thoughts.
Buddha

GEMINI
A herd of deer led by a lion is much worse than a pride of lions led by a deer.
Plutarch

CANCER
Humanity does not carry civilization in its genes.
Margaret Mead

LEO
Every and each age has its own toys.
French Quote

VIRGO
They are not the same pockets after the change, and that is all one has to say about money.
Gertrude Stein

LIBRA
After all, to make a beautiful omelet, you have to break an egg.
Spanish Proverb

SCORPIO
I ask for forgiveness from the poor. . . .
Sub Commander Marcos (Zapatista)

SAGITTARIUS
Nobody can take away a good night of dancing already done!
Anonymous

CAPRICORN
Some people like to make a little garden out of life and walk down a path.
Jean Anouilh

AQUARIUS
We tend to forget that life can only be defined in the present tense.
Dennis Potter

PISCES
Those who only see with their eyes are blind in the dark.
Antonio Perez

ARIES
Certain laws have not been written but they are more fixed than all the written laws.
Seneca

TAURUS
Among the infinite stars as among grains of sand, one shines towards me.
Masaoka Shiki

GEMINI
. . . but today, Today we have naming of parts.
Henry Reed

CANCER
It is all as clear as mud.
Norbert Guterman

LEO
Any truth told intimately, is always a universal truth.
Cournos

VIRGO
A writer is someone who makes a riddle out of an answer.
Karl Kraus

LIBRA
Every element has a relationship that holds something of everything else.
Wilhelm Leibniz

SCORPIO
May you live for the rest of the days of your life.
Johnathan Swift

SAGITTARIUS
Every reasonable human being should be a moderate socialist.
Thomas Mann

CAPRICORN
To live is, in itself, a value judgment.
Albert Camus

AQUARIUS
Life . . . it is "is" and it is "now" only.
Dennis Potter

PISCES
A man is known by the company he organizes.
Ambrose Bierce

15

OCTOBER

A phrase from the poet Virgil can always help.

ARIES
Life has no sense without a purpose.
Giuseppe Mazzini

TAURUS
We all know what we are, but we know not what we will be.
William Shakespeare

GEMINI
We are ephemeral, but we are eternal.
Marcel Marceau

CANCER
Happiness is good for the body, but sadness develops the soul.
Marcel Proust

LEO
Truth is whatever we think it is at any given moment.
Luigi Pirandello

VIRGO
I give so that you give back, or I gave, so now you give.
Latin Quote

LIBRA
Every element is a living and perpetual mirror of the universe.
Wilhelm Leibniz

SCORPIO
The less the routine, the more the life.
A. B. Alcott

SAGITTARIUS
Whom knows not his worth, knows nothing at all.
Anonymous

CAPRICORN
Time wasted is existence, used is life.
Edward Young

AQUARIUS
The sun visits cesspools without being defiled.
Diogenes

PISCES
The bird thinks it is an act of kindness to give the fish a lift in the air.
Rabindranath Tagore

ARIES
Solvency is entirely a matter of temperament and not of income.
Logan Persall Smith

TAURUS
The future, actually, is made of the same things as the present.
Simone Weil

GEMINI
. . . I like a moral issue so much more than a real issue.
Elaine May

CANCER
God made the country, and human beings made the city.
William Cowper

LEO
A tyrant is only a slave turned inside out.
Herbert Spencer

VIRGO
Nothing links man to man like the frequent passage from hand to hand of cash.
Walter Sickert

LIBRA
Entity is a responsibility before being an intention.
Emmanuel Levinas

SCORPIO
Creative minds have been known to survive any kind of bad training.
Anna Freud

SAGITTARIUS
Error carries victory, but truth carries hope.
Alfonso Herrera

CAPRICORN
Riches without work, pleasure without conscience. Two of the seven sins.
Mahatma Gandhi

AQUARIUS
Nobility obligates.
French Quote

PISCES
Useless wisdom is double foolishness.
Icelandic Quote

17

OCTOBER

ARIES
Cliché is but pauperized Ecstasy.
Chinua Achebe

TAURUS
Soul has been laid in our bodies to grasp the notion of time and feeling.
Blaise Pascal

GEMINI
Life, which we find too short, is made of many days which we find too long.
Octave Feuillet

CANCER
I am always confused about which of my own stories I should believe.
Washington Irving

LEO
It is not wise to be wiser than necessary.
Philippe Quinault

VIRGO
Money can buy you whatever misery you wish for.
Hobart Brown

LIBRA
Soul, thou hast much goods laid up for many years.
Luke 12:19

SCORPIO
For the thoughtful, life is a comedy; for the sensitive, a tradgedy.
Hugh S. Walpole

SAGITTARIUS
Tis a lesson you should heed . . . if at first you don't succeed, try, try again.
William Hickson

CAPRICORN
Knowledge without character, business without morality; Two more of the seven sins.
Mahatma Gandhi

AQUARIUS
When things go wrong, don't go with them.
Anonymous

PISCES
As he brews, so shall he drink.
Ben Jonson

Take some time to educate yourself about
something you ignore.

ARIES
Tact is the art of treating everyone as if they know what they are talking about.
Samuel Johnson

TAURUS
It is easy to tempt a frog to the river.
Serbian Quote

GEMINI
Humankind must at last grow up!
E. P. Thompson

CANCER
If you can't take the heat, get out of the kitchen.
Harry S. Truman

LEO
Some people only worry about what will happen if they loose their wealth.
Count de Rivarol

VIRGO
Little friends might prove great friends.
Aesop

LIBRA
Who knows about names, also knows about what is named.
Catullus

SCORPIO
Youth has nothing to do with age, people are born young or old.
Natalie Barney

SAGITTARIUS
Wrong count is no payment.
Anonymous

CAPRICORN
Science without love for humanity, religiousness without sacrifice. Another two of the seven sins.
Mahatma Gandhi

AQUARIUS
Whatever is rational is actual, and what is actual is rational.
Georg Wilhelm Hegel

PISCES
There is something of all men in each man.
Lichtenberg

19

OCTOBER

Listen to your own advice.

ARIES
I have learned, in whatsoever state I am, therewith to be content.
Philippians 4:11

TAURUS
Check before you bite if it is bread or stone.
Croation Quote

GEMINI
All knowledge requires a concept.
Immanuel Kant

CANCER
All are not hunters who blow the horn.
Anonymous

LEO
A prudent question is half of any knowledge.
Sir Francis Bacon

VIRGO
Only the exceptionally equanimous person can allow himself to be absurd.
Allan Goldfein

LIBRA
Patience and tenderness are powers on their own.
Leigh Hunt

SCORPIO
The goal of all life is death.
Sigmund Freud

SAGITTARIUS
Cancel the false door of "I don't know" or "I can't."
Graffiti

CAPRICORN
Politics without principles.
The seventh of the seven capital sins.
Mahatma Gandhi

AQUARIUS
Love is blind; and friendship closes its eyes.
Nietzsche

PISCES
I squandered time, and now time squanders me.
William Shakespeare

Accept the conclusion of a phase. Then, go on.

20
OCTOBER

ARIES
If wishes were horses, beggars might ride.
Anonymous

TAURUS
Thunder clouds do not always give rain.
Armenian Quote

GEMINI
. . . All our words from loose using have lost their edge.
Ernest Hemingway

CANCER
Every man under his vine and under his fig tree.
1 Kings 4:25

LEO
Nobility of character manifests itself at loopholes when it is not provided
with large doors.
Mary Wilkins Freeman

VIRGO
'Tis a long road knows no turning.
Sophocles

LIBRA
Unworthy praises are disguised satires.
Broadhurst

SCORPIO
The whole world is in a state of chassis.
Sean O'Casey

SAGITTARIUS
Most comparisons usually offend someone.
Anonymous

CAPRICORN
Keep what you've got: the known evil is best!
Plautus

AQUARIUS
The blue-bird carries the sky on his back.
Henry David Thoreau

PISCES
Nothing in the world is single: all things by a law
divine / In one spirit meet and mingle.
Percy Bysshe Shelley

21
OCTOBER

Consider the trajectory of the path you are on.

ARIES
Learn calm to face what's pressing.
Horace

TAURUS
To marvel is a philosophical feeling, and philosophy begins with wonder.
Plato

GEMINI
No matter how skepticall one is, it's never enough.
Woody Allen

CANCER
The end justifies the means.
Machiavelli

LEO
Wonders will never cease.
Sir H. B. Dudley

VIRGO
Grab a chance and you won't be sorry for a might have been.
Arthur Mitchell Ransome

LIBRA
Flirting: attention without intention.
Max O'Neil

SCORPIO
Great spirits have always found violent opposition from mediocrities.
Albert Einstein

SAGITTARIUS
Reason of unreason makes reality open our eyes.
Anonymous

CAPRICORN
It is never, never too late.
Anonymous

AQUARIUS
There is no easy way out.
Anonymous

PISCES
Time is . . . time was . . . time past. . . .
R. Greene

Become aware of the larger picture or story.

22
OCTOBER

ARIES
Sits he on never so high a throne, a man still sits on his bottom.
Michel de Montaigne

TAURUS
Ask yourself each day philosophically: "what is all this about?"
Alfred North Whitehead

GEMINI
Man's mind, stretched to a new idea, never goes back to its original dimensions.
Oliver Wendell Holmes

CANCER
From a drop of water a logician could predict an Atlantic or a Niagara.
Arthur Conan Doyle

LEO
What we have to do is be what we are.
Thomas Merton

VIRGO
I couldn't wait for success, so I went ahead without it.
Jonathan Winters

LIBRA
There is no large nor small; infinity is found before my eyes.
Seng-T'san

SCORPIO
One must have old memories and new hopes.
Arsene Houssaye

SAGITTARIUS
The power of thought is huge.
Mahatma Gandhi

CAPRICORN
The only means of conservation is innovation.
Peter Drucker

AQUARIUS
Freedom is nothing else but a chance to be better.
Albert Camus

PISCES
Past badness and goodness there is an extension. See you there.
Rumi

23
OCTOBER

Others also have vast and enduring stories.
Learn them.

ARIES
Calumnies are answered best with silence.
Ben Jonson

TAURUS
For what is virtue, courage, wit / In all men, but a lucky hit?
William Somerville

GEMINI
The stories that some people tell are stranger than truth and fiction.
Anonymous

CANCER
Results are what you expect and consequences are what you get.
Anonymous

LEO
This generation of Americans has a rendezvous with destiny.
Franklin D. Roosevelt

VIRGO
I don't want to see the uncut version of anything.
Jean Kerr

LIBRA
Joy in the universe, and keen curiosity about it all—that has been my religion.
John Burroughs

SCORPIO
Only a mediocre person always behaves well.
W. Somerset Maugham

SAGITTARIUS
The natural state of man is to be healthy.
A. Newman

CAPRICORN
The way a person gives reveals more of the giver's character than anything.
Solomon the Wise

AQUARIUS
An undisturbed mind is the best sauce for adversity.
Plautus

PISCES
Eternity is in love with the productions of time.
William Blake

A calendar is not simply a chronology.

ARIES
A good means to discovery is to take away certain parts of a system and find out how the rest behaves.
Lichtenberg

TAURUS
A little sincerity is a dangerous thing, and a great deal of it is fatal.
Oscar Wilde

GEMINI
It is better to be an unsatisfied man than a satisfied pig.
John Stuart Mill

CANCER
In the battle between man and the world, it is not the world that starts.
Gaston Bachelard

LEO
I was old till you came . . .
Hilda Doolittle, a Well Known Poet Known as H.D.

VIRGO
There is no security on this earth; there is only opportunity.
Douglas MacArthur

LIBRA
What is pride? A rocket that emulates a star.
William Wordsworth

SCORPIO
Millions saw the apple fall, but only Newton asked himself why.
Bernard Baruch

SAGITTARIUS
Everybody uses the wood from a fallen tree.
Mexican Quote

CAPRICORN
Hope is the pillar that holds up the world: the dream of a waking man.
Pliny the Elder

AQUARIUS
It is much easier to measure than to know exactly what one is measuring.
J. W. N. Sullivan

PISCES
He said, "What is time? Leave Now for dogs and apes! / Man has Forever."
Robert Browning

25
OCTOBER

It is the last day of the hurricane season—
remind yourself to let go of something.

ARIES
Of course heaven forbids certain pleasures, but one finds compromise.
Molière

TAURUS
Destructiveness is the result of unclear lives.
Erich Fromm

GEMINI
Art is a lie that prepares us to see the truth.
Pablo Picasso

CANCER
If you haven't forgiven yourself something, how can you forgive others?
Dolores Huerta

LEO
Out of the strain of the doing, into the peace of the done.
Julia Louise Woodruff

VIRGO
Life loves the liver of it.
Maya Angelou

LIBRA
One hour of sleep before midnight, is well worth three after.
George Herbert

SCORPIO
Annihilating desires, annihilates the mind.
Claude-Adrien Helvetius

SAGITTARIUS
I haven't the humility to find anything beneath me.
Beryl Bainbridge

CAPRICORN
Travelling with hope is better than arriving.
Sir James Jeans

AQUARIUS
There is nothing evil in the atom; there only is evil in the human soul.
Adlai Stevenson

PISCES
Three o'clock in the afternoon is either too early or too late for what you want to do.
Jean-Paul Sartre

ARIES
The better part of valour is descretion.
William Shakespeare

TAURUS
It is the wisdom of crocodiles that shed tears when they would devour.
Sir Francis Bacon

GEMINI
Poets are people who despise money except what you need for today.
Sir James M. Barrie

CANCER
My thoughts do not impose any necessity whatsoever on things.
René Descartes

LEO
Put your heart, mind, intellect and spirit even into your smallest deeds.
Swami Sivananda

VIRGO
Every moment dies a man. Every moment one is born.
Alfred Lord Tennyson

LIBRA
Duties are ours, events belong to God.
William Cecil

SCORPIO
When you annihilate desire you destroy the spirit.
Claude Adrien Helvetius

SAGITTARIUS
If the drawer is open, even an honest man can be caught stealing.
Guatemalan Quote

CAPRICORN
Intermingle . . . jest with earnest.
Sir Francis Bacon

AQUARIUS
We live as we dream. Alone.
Joseph Conrad

PISCES
The difference between past, present and future is no more than an illusion, a persistent one.
Albert Einstein

27
OCTOBER

ARIES
Kindness enriches our lives: with kindness the mysterious is cleared.
Ralph Waldo Emerson

TAURUS
Each part of your nature carries its own angel.
B. Shahn

GEMINI
Only artists and children see life as it really is.
Hugo von Hofmannsthal

CANCER
Passion is all humanity.
Honoré de Balzac

LEO
A man can travel around the world in search of something that he finds at home.
Grace Moore

VIRGO
Enough is as good as a feast.
Anonymous (Roget's Thesaurus 1957)

LIBRA
A handful of sand is an anthology of the universe.
David McCord

SCORPIO
It is not the same thing to be naked as to have nothing on.
Josephine Baker

SAGITTARIUS
The degree and kind of a man's sexuality reach up into the ultimate pinnacle of his spirit.
Novalis

CAPRICORN
There can be little liking where there is no likeness.
Aesop

AQUARIUS
There is superstition in avoiding superstitions.
Sir Francis Bacon

PISCES
Great is this organism of mud and fire, terrible this vast, painful, glorious experiment.
Santayana

ARIES
I am more afraid of my own heart than of the pope. I have within me the great pope, Self.
Martin Luther

TAURUS
Take care in this world of shadows and echos.
Fang Li-zhi

GEMINI
It's a poor sort of memory that only works backwards.
Lewis Carroll

CANCER
The mystic sees the ineffable, and the psycho-pathologist the unspeakable.
W. Somerset Maugham

LEO
Home is the place where we come from.
T. S. Eliot

VIRGO
Elsewhere, the same story is being told by someone else.
Charles Wright

LIBRA
May a thought mature within you to become, as it was, a thought on its own.
Chu-Hi

SCORPIO
Thanks to differences of opinion, there are horse races.
Mark Twain

SAGITTARIUS
Today's witches are but the fairies of other times who aged badly.
Mada Carreño

CAPRICORN
A fellow feeling makes one wondrous kind.
David Garrick

AQUARIUS
We have been the recipients of the choicest bounties of Heaven.
Abraham Lincoln

PISCES
Science without conscience is but the ruin of the soul.
François Rabelais

29
OCTOBER

Time is the most personal possesion.

ARIES
Be closer to the friends who reproach you and stay away from those who flatter you.
Eric Hoffer

TAURUS
I am sure that a definite maybe will do you some good.
Samuel Goldwyn

GEMINI
Easy does it.
Anonymous

CANCER
All epochs represent a microcosm that calls for a new world.
Valeriu Marcu

LEO
A drop on the stone is always sending it a sign and a signal.
Chinese Saying

VIRGO
The best race hasn't been run.
Berton Braley

LIBRA
Never brag about what you know, rather ask the unlearned, who know a lot of many things.
Piahohtep (Egyptian from Sacred Texts, 2,500 Years Ago)

SCORPIO
Attack is the reaction. I never think I have hit hard unless it rebounds.
Ben Jonson

SAGITTARIUS
He who limps is still walking.
Stanslaw Lec

CAPRICORN
One must keep hope alive.
Jesse Jackson

AQUARIUS
Tears, actually, live inside onions.
English Proverb

PISCES
The scene changes but the aspirations of men of good will persists.
Vannevar Bush

ARIES
From the errors of others a wise man corrects his own.
Publilius Syrus

TAURUS
Life is a tragedy when seen in close-up, but a comedy in long-shot.
Charles Chaplin

GEMINI
Do not all you can; spend not all you have; believe not all you hear; and tell not all you know.
Bohn

CANCER
Think twice before repeating your story.
Christianne Grautoff

LEO
Who doesn't know how to enjoy luck when it comes, should not complain when it passes him by.
Cervantes

VIRGO
Back of the Job, the Dreamer who's making the dream come true!
Berton Braley

LIBRA
The true mystery of the world is the visible, not the invisible.
Oscar Wilde

SCORPIO
Funerals are a nice thing, compared to death.
Tennessee Williams

SAGITTARIUS
He that would have the fruit must climb the tree.
Thomas Fuller

CAPRICORN
The profoundest affinities are those most readily felt.
Santayana

AQUARIUS
Two heads are better than one.
Anonymous

PISCES
When mind is nowhere it is everywhere. When it occupies one tenth it is absent in the other nine tenths.
Takuan

31
OCTOBER

Nothing spent can be completely restored.

ARIES
There rises an unspeakable desire, after the knowledge of our buried life.
Matthew Arnold

TAURUS
Millions of spiritual creatures walk the earth, Unseen, both when we wake, and when we sleep.
John Milton

GEMINI
Who hath hardened himself against him, and hath prospered?
Job 9:4

CANCER
He who does not fill his world with phantoms remains alone.
Antonio Porchia

LEO
If one truly lost hope, one would not be at hand to say so.
Eric Bentley

VIRGO
No soul is rested til it is made naught as to all things that are made.
Julian of Norwich

LIBRA
Death can make even triviality momentous.
Edward Le Compte

SCORPIO
I am inclined to think that we are all ghosts, every one of us.
Henrik Ibsen

SAGITTARIUS
The grave is the first stage of the journey into eternity.
Muhammad

CAPRICORN
Ghost. The outward and visible sign of an inward fear.
Ambroise Bierce

AQUARIUS
A hunter of shadows, himself a shade.
Homer

PISCES
Ghosts were created when the first man woke in the night.
Sir James M. Barrie

NOVEMBER

NOVEMBER

We need a faculty that enables us to see our objectives from afar. That faculty is intuition.

Jules-Henri Poincaré

November is a good time to examine your needs and capabilities while expanding your intuition. Ancient sages and Buddhist philosophers and even modern references identify November as a month of great creative force, a time for making serious journeys of the soul in serious ways, of thinking more deeply about your own psyche. So give thanks for the turkey feast and for this opportunity. Because anything can happen this month, any soul's journey can head off in a new direction and triumph. This type of journey of the soul is recounted in many wonderful legends such as that of Gilgamish and in *The Odyssey*. Kabbalists have interpreted the Hebrew letter "Nun" as the battleground of the soul. In short, the Sun being in Scorpio for most of November, Scorpio adds extra power. If you are so lucky as to have a Scorpio nearby, ask him or her what they think about Douglas Adams's quote for Scorpio on the first day of November, please.

ARIES

Dig out of November's darkness, Aries, by digging deep into your psyche. Feel before you think. Act on instinct, don't dictate. Take new turns and then watch how things will turn around with you. And rather than let things take you by surprise, surprise "them" with your wit, daring, and innovation. And finally, keep in mind Nietzsche's words: "Existence begins in every instant," and let that instant begin even as you read this passage.
Keyword: Surprise!

TAURUS

Stimulation. Dialogues. Arguments. Unavoidable expenses. This month you have a choice: you can allow these things to get your back up or let them slide right off. The Sun is opposite your sign this month, but opposites can attract (especially in physics). If you keep a clear mind in a sound body, you can build up any castles in the air that you deem worthy of you! Just try to rein in your need to exaggerate—charming as it may be—and try to see things as they really are.
Keywords: Unlimited opportunities

GEMINI

The old proverb "Know thyself" has special meaning for you, Gemini, because you can be so many different people all at once! However, this is the perfect month to concentrate on learning all you can about your one true self. Fill your head with facts, figures, and contemplation. Focus on the words of poetry master Nemesianus, who won one of the very first poetry competitions on record, more than 1,000 years ago: "Time feeds all things, time takes away all things; enjoyment only lasts for a brief space of time." Things change as quickly as you do, Gemini, so savor every second.
Keywords: Watch your back

CANCER

In November, Cancer has much to be thankful for. Scorpio is in your sign, lightening your mood and your spirits. You should take the whole month off (yes, every year) and read poetry. (Yeats would be wonderful for starters, but take your pick of poets, Cancer.) Let it induce you to keep moving forward in your dreamy way, energized by the idea that the Earth keeps hurtling through space, quickening time—and all your chances.
Keywords: Great days ahead

LEO

Though dares, formidable tasks, and provocations could spice up the month and even ruffle your fur a bit, November is actually quite run-of-the-mill for you, Leo. Still, your need to be the King Cat of all the Zodiac signs will get you to go on the prowl looking for ways to prove your greatness to everyone, or at least to give it your best try.

Keywords: Forza (push) destiny

VIRGO

This November, stretch! Pull and push yourself in all directions, as long as they are new ones. Invoke your love of planning by participating in a party, a scheme, or simply some all-out fun. Dante ends his *Inferno* with the lines, "We emerge so as to see, once again, the stars," and with this in mind, shrug off any little mishaps and think about tackling anything, agelessly, continuously, pleasantly. There is a light at the end of any tunnel, and it shines for you.

Keywords: Reach, and exceed your grasp

LIBRA

This is the month to kiss without commitment, move the furniture without worrying about Feng Shui, and ride the waves without thought of an undertow! Although you like to ponder causes and effects, now, a month after your birthday, is not the time to try for perfect balance in life. Instead, loveable Libra, take things easy, sort things out, and take anything that upsets your equilibrium with a grain of salt (but just one!).

Keywords: Making things easy for yourself

SCORPIO

Your month, your time, your space, your way, and your definitions. Have tolerance, not only for the things and people around you, but for yourself. Respond to what you encounter as positively as possible and with your whole being. As a Scorpio in the month of your own sign, this birthday reflect on the fact that on the first day of this new millennium the Moon was in Scorpio. I wonder, as we all should, just what this will mean for us.

Keyword: Self-assurance

SAGITTARIUS
During leap years, Sagittarius begins on November 22, a day earlier than usual. This is a good thing, because you make everyone feel good, offering support and sustenance, especially during the Scorpio phase of this month, just before the Sun lands with a joyful whoop in your sign. Have no fear, it seems that during the whole millennium, leap years will always give us that special feeling: "Hooray! An extra day with a Sagittarius!"
Keywords: Support systems

CAPRICORN
Variety can be the spice of your life this November, Capricorn. Sample new ways and means, develop some different social graces, fall into a new step with those around you, and treat yourself to any and all opportunities that help you expand your horizons. "Tasting makes for knowing what to put on a plate" is a quote by an anonymous gifted scribe. It is provided for you here to enlighten the winter days ahead.
Keywords: Trying things out

AQUARIUS
Aquarians, each and every one of you, usually map out your own cycles in the most delightfully unique way. This book is all about cycles, so whatever overwhelms you this month will probably overwhelm you sometime, maybe even the same time, next year. The main thing is for you to take a stand. Find things out, ask yourself what you can do to make things better—or at least *seem* better.
Keywords: Working things out

PISCES
Melancholy makes up about one fourth of your psyche, Pisces. And there's no better time than the present to begin to understand it. So listen to your inner calling. School yourself in yourself. You can even speed up the process with a little help from some inspiring poetry or music. And remember, you're not just any fish in the sea, Pisces. You are a prize catch!
Keyword: Amelioration

1

Intensify your focus; strive for a moment of calm.

NOVEMBER

ARIES
Surprise is the greatest gift which life can grant us.
Boris Pasternak

TAURUS
People say that good-byes are not sad . . . so have those people say good-bye.
Mexican Quote

GEMINI
The worst thing that could happen to me would be to find myself alone in paradise.
Goethe

CANCER
Life is painting a picture, not doing a sum.
Oliver Wendell Holmes

LEO
Soul receives from soul the knowledge thereof
Rumi

VIRGO
Let us retire, in all honor.
William Shakespeare

LIBRA
If you scatter thorns, don't go barefoot.
Italian Proverb

SCORPIO
We are all intimately connected with all the versions of ourselves.
Douglas Adams

SAGITTARIUS
It is a necessary provision to understand that it is impossible to prevent everything.
Jean-Jacques Rousseau

CAPRICORN
The secret of success in life is known only to those who have not succeeded.
John Churton Collins

AQUARIUS
Let him that thinketh he standeth take heed lest he fall.
1 Corinthians 10:12

PISCES
Ah, but a man's reach should exceed his grasp, or what's a heaven for?
Robert Browning

Repair an object if not your ego.

ARIES
Let it be your own personal intention that your own absence amazes you and that this should not amaze you.
Lao-Tzu

TAURUS
You can get lonesome being that busy.
Isabel Lennart

GEMINI
Life, well lived, is long enough.
Seneca

CANCER
Death is an illness of the imagination.
Henri Fournier Alain

LEO
Between sadness and nothing, I prefer sadness.
William Faulkner

VIRGO
There should always be enough to go around.
Anonymous

LIBRA
The new space has a kind of invisibility to those who have not entered it.
Mary Daly

SCORPIO
Give me what I have.
Horace

SAGITTARIUS
The unknown is an ocean. What is conscience? The compass of the unknown.
Richard Burton

CAPRICORN
With me, a change of trouble is as good as a vacation.
Lloyd George

AQUARIUS
The wise man lives on after death; the ignorant is already dead, though alive.
'Ali

PISCES
Through "you," a person becomes "me."
Martin Buber

3

Learn the language of your senses.

NOVEMBER

ARIES
There is no game of return between a man and his stars.
Samuel Beckett

TAURUS
There are two sides to every story.
Anonymous

GEMINI
There are two main things one needs to be happy: good health and a short memory.
Albert Schweitzer

CANCER
Birth, living and passing by, is changing forms.
Denis Diderot

LEO
A man's dying is more the survivors' affair than his own.
Thomas Mann

VIRGO
Taste is made of thousands of distastes.
Paul Valéry

LIBRA
Above all, devote yourself to the study of beginnings.
Epicurus

SCORPIO
Imagination is more important than knowledge.
Albert Einstein

SAGITTARIUS
Industry is a better horse to ride than genius.
Walter Lippmann

CAPRICORN
An ounce of loyalty is worth a pound of knowledge.
Elbert Hubbard

AQUARIUS
Be nice to the people on your way up, because you'll meet them on your way down.
Wilson Mizner

PISCES
Take rest; a field that has rested gives a beautiful crop.
Ovid

Everything, even love, is a chemical reaction.

4
NOVEMBER

ARIES

No one can avoid what is to come.
Baltasar Gracián

TAURUS

And yet, the true creator is necessity, who is mother of our own invention.
Plato

GEMINI

I often read the Bible, but the original text is inaccessible to me. . . .
Albert Einstein

CANCER

Never underestimate the power of passion.
Eve Sawyer

LEO

Criticism is a great bite out of someones back.
Elia Kazan

VIRGO

To turn around is not running away.
Cervantes

LIBRA

I have developed a new philosophy: I am only terrified one day at a time.
Charles M. Shultz

SCORPIO

Happiness is a mystery like religion, and it should never be rationalized.
G. K. Chesterton

SAGITTARIUS

Within the subject of conscience, the law of the majority has no place.
Mahatma Gandhi

CAPRICORN

Whoever is in charge must think about the hunger and thirst of those who obey.
Gengis Khan

AQUARIUS

Damn those who have said what we wanted to say!
Aelius Donatus

PISCES

Take nothing but photographs. Leave nothing but footprints.
David Bellamy

5
NOVEMBER

ARIES
The path never shows the traveller what the end of the day has to offer.
Bantu Quote

TAURUS
Before enlightenment, chop wood, carry water; after enlightenment, chop wood, carry water.
American Proverb

GEMINI
Science without religion limps, religion without science is blind.
Albert Einstein

CANCER
It is not the sex that gives the pleasure, it is the lover.
Marge Piercy

LEO
Some guys are wise, and some are wise guys.
Anonymous

VIRGO
Each snowflake in an avalanche pleads not guilty.
Stanislaw Lec

LIBRA
There are some people who lie just for the pleasure of lying.
Blaise Pascal

SCORPIO
A thing of beauty is a joy forever: its loveliness increases.
John Keats

SAGITTARIUS
Valour is recognizing that you are the only one who is afraid.
F. P. Jones

CAPRICORN
There is great strength in a kind command.
George Herbert

AQUARIUS
The unexpected always happens, and the extraordinary will never stop happening.
Anonymous

PISCES
A good friend is one who used to be better.
Cleveland Amory

A good day to reorganize your own time,
or retune your timing.

6

NOVEMBER

ARIES
I sharpened my knife. I returned without cutting. You have won, rose.
Sampu

TAURUS
Life ought to be a struggle of desire toward adventures whose nobility will fertilize the soul.
Rebecca West

GEMINI
Who hears but me hears all.
Paul Eluard and Benjamin Peret

CANCER
He who has no poetry in himself will find poetry in nothing.
Joseph Joubert

LEO
Blessed are the merciful: for they shall obtain mercy.
Matthew 5:7

VIRGO
Search, searcher. The future is made of searchers.
Anonymous

LIBRA
What you are given, is a way; what you give is a life.
Lillian Gish

SCORPIO
Better one safe way than a hundred on which you cannot reckon.
Aesop

SAGITTARIUS
An insignificant man can tire just as much as a great one.
Arthur Miller

CAPRICORN
A hero is anyone who does all he can.
Romain Rolland

AQUARIUS
Lead us not into temptation, but deliver us from evil.
Matthew 6:13

PISCES
In nothing do men approach so nearly the gods as doing good to men.
Cicero

7

Help something bloom.

ARIES
One arrow does not bring down two birds!
Turkish Quote

TAURUS
From now on, it's all clear profit, every sky.
Issa Haiku

GEMINI
We are not human beings trying to be spiritual. We are spiritual beings trying to be human.
Jacqueline Small

CANCER
Find out why a cat has nine lives!
Graffiti

LEO
No notice is taken of a little evil, but when it increases it strikes the eye.
Aristotle

VIRGO
Trifles make perfection, but perfection is no trifle.
Italian Proverb

LIBRA
I am not afraid of death, because she is a woman.
Emilio (El Indio) Fernandez

SCORPIO
Lavishness is not generosity.
Thomas Fuller

SAGITTARIUS
There are those who feel with their heads and think with their hearts.
Lichtenberg

CAPRICORN
Dreams have no logic. Let us wait 'til we awaken.
Amado Nervo

AQUARIUS
Knowledge comes but wisdom lingers.
Alfred Lord Tennyson

PISCES
Every sound shall end in silence, but the silence never dies.
Samuel Miller Hageman

We are always en route to the stars.

ARIES
A woman can change the vital trajectory of a man.
Severo Ochoa

TAURUS
It is said that logic is the science that teaches the spirit what it owes itself.
Henri Fournier Alain

GEMINI
Notion without intuition is empty; intuition without notion, blind.
Immanuel Kant

CANCER
Sex rarely has to do only with sex.
Shirley MacLaine

LEO
You want to be a little bit out of control of being in control.
Warren Beatty

VIRGO
Once in a while, a fool will say a wise thing.
Latin Proverb

LIBRA
It is great and noble to transform imperfections into virtues.
J. E. Hartzenbuch

SCORPIO
Every work of art generates light.
Carlos Pellicer

SAGITTARIUS
I would rather be a philosopher and a coward, than a hero and a fool.
Ambrose Pratt

CAPRICORN
Money is power, and you should be reasonably ambitious to get it.
R. H. Conwell

AQUARIUS
What has already been thought cannot be unthought.
Friedrich Durrenmatt

PISCES
No matter how much the ant toils, she cannot produce honey.
English Proverb

9

Walk tall and leave firm footprints behind.

NOVEMBER

ARIES
Hope is generally a wrong guide, though it is very good company.
Halifax

TAURUS
All men are ordinary men. The extraordinary men are those who know it.
G. K. Chesterton

GEMINI
Victory has a hundred memories but defeat has amnesia.
Bill Gates

CANCER
Arrange whatever pieces come your way.
Virginia Woolf

LEO
Nobody pretends to be someone worse than themselves.
Salvador Elizondo

VIRGO
Watch the pennies, and the dollars will take care of themselves.
Anonymous

LIBRA
Never run after a woman who leaves, nor a letter that doesn't arrive.
José Vasconcelos

SCORPIO
The only abnormality is the incapacity to love.
Anaïs Nin

SAGITTARIUS
In about the same degree that you are helpful, you will be happy.
Karl Reiland

CAPRICORN
No one is powerful in another's free will.
Calderon de la Barca

AQUARIUS
Nothing ventured, nothing gained.
Anonymous

PISCES
He measures others by measuring himself.
French Proverb

ARIES
What is of interest is life, and the direction of that life.
Guy Fregault

TAURUS
It is as hard to see one's self as to look backwards without turning round.
Henry David Thoreau

GEMINI
It would be terrible if you actually could convince your PC to do as you say.
Andrea Valeria

CANCER
If you see a saintly man, think: how could I be like him . . . ?
Chinese Quote

LEO
If the spirit is not released first, we will never catch the tangible.
José Vasconcelos

VIRGO
Love is . . . to realize something extremely difficult to accept, that something besides oneself is real.
Iris Murdoch

LIBRA
Try anything once.
Anonymous

SCORPIO
My richness is mostly in terms of lucky breaks.
Mario Cuomo

SAGITTARIUS
True eloquence consists in saying all that should be said, and that only.
La Rochefoucauld

CAPRICORN
Carry only what you enjoy, and it will never be to heavy.
Anonymous

AQUARIUS
I don't mind what you say to me, I mind how you say it to me.
Anonymous

PISCES
Men ought to be more conscious of their bodies as an object of delight.
Germaine Greer

11
NOVEMBER

Address an ultimate cause.

ARIES
Taking good advice requires more wisdom than giving any advice.
Churton Collins

TAURUS
Dreams have as much influence as actions.
Mallarmé

GEMINI
We live and learn, we learn and live.
Anonymous

CANCER
If you see a wasted man, think: could I have the same vices?
Chinese Quote

LEO
We believe what we wish and wish what we believe is good for us.
Anonymous

VIRGO
The exception proves the rule.
Anonymous

LIBRA
If you keep your face towards the sun, you don't see the shade.
Helen Keller

SCORPIO
Cruelty is a mystery and a waste of pain.
Anne Dillard

SAGITTARIUS
My understanding is my kingdom.
Thomas Campbell

CAPRICORN
The soul is a chord; untuning is its illness.
Pythagoras

AQUARIUS
Would there be this eternal seeking if the found existed?
Antonio Porchia

PISCES
I celebrate myself, and sing myself.
Walt Whitman

12
NOVEMBER

ARIES
Everything can be expected and feared from time as well as from man. . . .
Marquis de Vauvenargues

TAURUS
Mistakes are part of the debts that one pays for living fully.
Sophia Loren

GEMINI
Oh! let us never, never doubt, What nobody is sure about!
Hilaire Belloc

CANCER
The scholar who thinks but does not create is like a cloud that does not spill drops.
Tibetan Quote

LEO
Each man is Adam. Each man had the world for himself.
José Emilio Pacheco

VIRGO
Success is like total liberation or the first phase of a love story.
Jean Moreau

LIBRA
Love is not a feeling worthy of respect.
Colette

SCORPIO
We can be absolutely certain only about things we do not understand.
Eric Hoffer

SAGITTARIUS
Man is an animal of reason.
Seneca

CAPRICORN
The world grows old, and with age saddens.
Torcuato Tasso

AQUARIUS
Do not torment yourself. Ever.
Aelius Donatus

PISCES
We forget because we must. And not because we will.
Matthew Arnold

13
NOVEMBER

ARIES
Either here or there, everyone will get their due.
Anonymous

TAURUS
It is never, never too late, in a story or in real life, to correct.
Nancy Thayer

GEMINI
College is a refuge from hasty judgment.
Robert Frost

CANCER
There are too many people trying to own something so as to call it "mine."
Anonymous

LEO
We're swallowed up only when we are willing for it to happen.
Nathalie Serraute

VIRGO
I can take anything, if I know what it is. What anguishes me is the unknown.
Frances Newton

LIBRA
Sign and purpose leads to meditation.
José Bergamin

SCORPIO
Better to die of love than to love without regret.
Paul Eluard and Benjamin Peret

SAGITTARIUS
For those whose vigorous and expansive thoughts follow the path of the sun, day is an everlasting morning.
Attributed to Henry David Thoreau

CAPRICORN
Only balance can annihilate force.
Simone Weil

AQUARIUS
An ass is beautiful to an ass, and a pig is beautiful to a pig.
John Ray

PISCES
You don't have to look for distress; it is screaming at you!
Samuel Beckett

ARIES
Often we find our own destiny on the same roads that we have been avoiding.
Jean de la Fontaine

TAURUS
This is learning. Suddenly you understand something you have understood all your life, but in a new way.
Doris Lessing

GEMINI
We are all amateurs, in our short lives we have no time for anything else.
Charles Chaplin

CANCER
Those who ignore their own intellect, throw away a part of their lives.
Amiel

LEO
A tree has its roots; a brook, its source.
Chinese Proverb

VIRGO
Language makes culture, and we make a rotten culture when we abuse words.
Cynthia Ozick

LIBRA
To none will we sell, to none deny or delay, right or justice.
Magna Carta

SCORPIO
If you want sex during your travels, travel with your own woman.
Mali Quote

SAGITTARIUS
One thing asks the help of another.
Horace

CAPRICORN
To be a banker is a career from which one never really recovers.
John Kenneth Galbraith

AQUARIUS
To each his own!
Anonymous

PISCES
Every man is the creature of the age in which he lives.
Voltaire

15
NOVEMBER

Welcome a day into the world.

ARIES
A fool will tell you what he will do; a boaster, what he has done. A wise man does things and says nothing.
Chinese Quote

TAURUS
Everything in life that we really accept undergoes a change.
Katherine Mansfield

GEMINI
Whoever understands the truth of the human body can then know the truth of the universe.
Hindu Quote

CANCER
I think that the best lesson I have ever learned is that there is no substitute for paying attention.
Diane Sawyer

LEO
Art has passed away. Its ghost is more alive than ever!
José Emilio Pacheco

VIRGO
The only thing I had to offer was my own confusion.
Jack Kerouac

LIBRA
I don't know everything, I just do everything.
Toni Morrison

SCORPIO
The meaning of a word to me is not as exact as the meaning of a color.
Georgia O'Keeffe

SAGITTARIUS
Profit is profit, even in Mecca.
Hausa Quote (West Africa)

CAPRICORN
It is always absolutely indispensable to be able to distinguish between what is and what is not.
André Maurois

AQUARIUS
Art, as morality, consists in drawing a line somewhere.
G. K. Chesterton

PISCES
Very few are able to raise themselves above the ideas of the times.
Voltaire

ARIES
Prevention equals conservation.
Lawyer's Maxim

TAURUS
So suffering must become Love. That is the mystery.
Katherine Mansfield

GEMINI
Life is like coffee, or chestnuts in autumn. Always smelling better than it tastes.
Maruja Torres

CANCER
. . . while I'm upon this earth, I want to be what I am.
Epictetus

LEO
Adversity reveals a general's genius: good luck hides it.
Horace

VIRGO
Don't confuse being stimulating with being relentless.
Barbara Walters

LIBRA
What does one woman see in another that a man cannot see? Tenderness.
Sylvia Plath

SCORPIO
Each word is a prejudice.
Nietzsche

SAGITTARIUS
When someone thinks well of you, care about them being right.
Mahoma

CAPRICORN
If you frequently add little to little, it will become a lot.
Hesiod

AQUARIUS
I said that you had a good voice, not that I wanted to hear you sing.
Anonymous

PISCES
I like what one finds in work: the opportunity to find oneself.
Joseph Conrad

17
NOVEMBER

Build around an inspiring experience.

ARIES
I am the owner of my shoulders, the tenant of my hips.
Chazal

TAURUS
I take advantage of all that comes, and let go of whatever leaves.
Sara Teasdale

GEMINI
Let not they will roar, when thy power can but whisper.
Thomas Fuller

CANCER
There can be no worse way to guide your life than to follow others' advice.
Anselm Feuerbach

LEO
The test of a vocation is the love of the drudgery it involves.
L. P. Smith

VIRGO
I took a deep breath and listened to the old brag of my heart. I am, I am, I am.
Sylvia Plath

LIBRA
Destiny is something men choose: women attain it by omission or wondrous suffering.
Helen Rosenstein

SCORPIO
The supreme finality of living is love in all its forms.
Diego Rivera

SAGITTARIUS
He who has begun has half done. Dare to be wise; begin!
Horace

CAPRICORN
Sense is the soul of writing; words are but the attire.
Anonymous

AQUARIUS
Our humanity were a poor thing but for divinity that stirs within us.
Anonymous

PISCES
The soul is the mirror of an indestructible universe.
Wilhelm Leibniz

ARIES
A man cannot be comfortable without his own approval.
Mark Twain

TAURUS
Truths are illusions that we forget as such.
Nietzsche

GEMINI
Those splendid fortunes, as happens with impetuous winds, produce great shipwrecks.
Plutarch

CANCER
One hour of honest and serious thoughts is worth more than weeks of empty talks.
Anonymous

LEO
Words are like money, there is nothing as useless if put to the wrong use.
Jules Renard

VIRGO
The no that was hanging over the buildings / Faded like the moon at dawn.
Yoko Ono

LIBRA
Not all songs are religious, but there is scarcely a task, light or grave, scarcely an event, great or small, but it has its fitting song.
Natalie Curtis

SCORPIO
All kinds of joy are similar, but every misfortune has its own peculiar trait.
Tolstoy

SAGITTARIUS
Learning is the agriculture of intelligence, but not all earth produces foliage.
Ben Saraf

CAPRICORN
Old age lives minutes slowly, hours quickly; childhood chews hours and swallows minutes.
Chazal

AQUARIUS
Every why hath a wherefore.
William Shakespeare

PISCES
If you can see, observe.
José Saramago

19

NOVEMBER

Give yourself some room to wiggle.

ARIES
The power of perception is what we call understanding.
Dhammapada

TAURUS
Two unpardonable excesses: exclusion of reason and admitting only reason.
Blaise Pascal

GEMINI
Investment in knowledge produces the best interests.
Benjamin Franklin

CANCER
He suffers more than necessary, who suffers before it is necessary.
Seneca

LEO
Truth is the surest lie.
Hebrew Quote

VIRGO
Nonsense is often the wisest form of allegory.
Leftwich

LIBRA
The effects of men vary according to circumstances.
Lucas Alaman

SCORPIO
We are never as happy or as sad as we think.
La Rochefoucauld

SAGITTARIUS
Waste not, want not.
Anonymous

CAPRICORN
Where there is presumption, there is ignorance; where there is humility, there is wisdom.
Wisdom of Solomon, Apocrypha

AQUARIUS
It is better to light a candle than to curse the darkness.
Chinese Quote

PISCES
Wise is he who is happy with the spectacle of the world.
Richard Reis

ARIES
You start on a voyage; you know where you will end up, but not what will occur along the way. You want to be surprised.
Federico Fellini

TAURUS
I am just too much!
Bette Davis

GEMINI
When Pleasure is at the bar the jury is not impartial.
Aristotle

CANCER
I am but an individual on a small planet in a solar system inside one of the galaxies.
Roberto Assagioli

LEO
How awful to reflect that what people say of us is true!
L. P. Smith

VIRGO
The road of excess leads to the palace of wisdom.
William Blake

LIBRA
Winning can be defined as the science of being totally prepared.
Allen Ginsberg

SCORPIO
We become what we are only by refusing profoundly and radically what others have turned us into.
Jean-Paul Sartre

SAGITTARIUS
Give me the ready hand rather than the ready tongue.
Garibaldi

CAPRICORN
Only the wearer knows where the shoe pinches.
English Quote

AQUARIUS
Experience is not what happens to you, it is what you do with what happens to you.
Aldous Huxley

PISCES
When people leave, they always seem to scoop themselves out of you.
Jane Smiley

You can revive yourself each day by simply listening.

ARIES
We do what we must, and call it by the best names.
Ralph Waldo Emerson

TAURUS
Invest in the soul. Who knows, it might turn to be a diamond in the rough.
Bethune

GEMINI
Whatever a wise man needs to know he will find within himself; a common man will find it in others.
Confucius

CANCER
There is no easy way towards the stars from the earth.
Seneca

LEO
I am not an optimist, I am a possibilist.
Julian Huxley

VIRGO
Ambition, if it feeds anything, does so on top of other's ambition.
Susan Sontag

LIBRA
Always put off till tomorrow what you shouldn't do at all.
Anonymous

SCORPIO
For souls in growth, great quarrels are great emancipations.
L. P. Smith

SAGITTARIUS
Depression is a light and extensive coat of anger.
Graffiti

CAPRICORN
Modest in prosperity and sane under adversity.
Spanish Quote

AQUARIUS
Nothing nowadays is impossible, except some people.
Anonymous

PISCES
You cannot create experience. You must undergo it.
Albert Camus

Do you know how well equipped you are
for the struggle to survive?

22
NOVEMBER

ARIES
Love is a spirit within two forms.
Percy Bysshe Shelley

TAURUS
Neurosis is always a substitute for some kind of legitimate suffering.
Carl Jung

GEMINI
Reason speaks and feeling bites.
Petrarch

CANCER
There is no escape from necessities, but they can be overcome.
Seneca

LEO
I just want a little more than I am supposed to get.
Ashleigh Brilliant

VIRGO
That man must be quite ignorant, for he answers every question posed him.
Voltaire

LIBRA
Intelligent men are inconsistent, but intelligent: fools are also inconsistent, and also foolish.
Felix Palavicini

SCORPIO
When everyone is somebody, then no one's anybody.
Anonymous

SAGITTARIUS
The truth is neither one nor two.
Sri Ramana Maharashi

CAPRICORN
People define situations, but do not define them as they please.
Arthur L. Stinchcombe

AQUARIUS
It's not what you say, but how you say it.
Anonymous

PISCES
A neurosis is a secret that you don't know you are keeping.
Kenneth Tynan

23
NOVEMBER

Today is Kinrokansha no Hi—Japanese labor and thanksgiving day. Energy abounds.

ARIES
If a thing is worth doing, it's worth doing twice.
Anonymous

TAURUS
Saying and doing do not eat at the same table.
Antonio Perez

GEMINI
While the stubborn decide, the smart deliberate.
Plutarch

CANCER
Excessive riches interfere with the movements of our soul.
Demosthenes

LEO
After a chess game, the king and the queen are put back into the same box.
Italian Quote

VIRGO
Difficulties can fade away with good judgement.
Tancredo

LIBRA
Only the dreamer shall understand realities.
Margaret Fuller

SCORPIO
Great happiness and great sadness are both silent.
Shakerley Marmion

SAGITTARIUS
The peaceful state of one's soul is the most precious possession.
Swami Sivananada

CAPRICORN
Economy is the mother of liberality.
Seneca

AQUARIUS
A tree is known by its fruit.
Anonymous

PISCES
The world is an oyster, but don't open it on a mattress.
Arthur Miller

ARIES
Every medal has its reverse.
Spanish Quote

TAURUS
Work and love are the basics. Without them, there is neurosis.
Theodor Reik

GEMINI
A wise man will make more opportunities than he finds.
Sir Francis Bacon

CANCER
The soul does not live in the body as in a home, rather as in a tent, temporarily.
Hindu Quote

LEO
Man arrives as an apprentice at all the times of his life.
Chamfort

VIRGO
There is much more learning than knowing in the world.
Thomas Fuller

LIBRA
Every life is a poem, as is every death.
Daie-Soko

SCORPIO
Every day carries some sorrow.
Seneca

SAGITTARIUS
When you talk or think superficially, do not fall into emptiness.
Hui-Neng

CAPRICORN
Whoever tries to reach the unreachable is stronger than fate.
Stephan Zweig

AQUARIUS
Toot your own horn, lest the same be never tooted.
Anonymous

PISCES
Various excuses are always less convincing than one.
Aldous Huxley

25

NOVEMBER

Open your mind to wider possibilities.

ARIES
Loving is the strongest bewitchment for being loved.
Baltasar Gracián

TAURUS
New York City is the thyroid gland of the nation.
Christopher Morley

GEMINI
In uplifting, get underneath.
George Ade

CANCER
Question: Could the facade of flowers intimidate the delicate Moon? Answer: Yes.
Daito

LEO
Life is ours to spend, not to store.
D. H. Lawrence

VIRGO
Every human creature is constituted to be that profound secret and mystery to every other.
Charles Dickens

LIBRA
Practice makes perfect.
Anonymous

SCORPIO
Man must learn patiently to carry on what he cannot deliberately avoid.
Michel de Montaigne

SAGITTARIUS
You can't do without philosophy, since everything has its hidden meaning, which we must know.
Maxim Gorky

CAPRICORN
The sun shines down on a humble blade of grass as it does on a cedar tree.
Persian Quote

AQUARIUS
As you make your bed, so you must lie in it.
Anonymous

PISCES
Philosophy begins in wonder. And, at the end, when philosophic thought has done its best, the wonder remains.
Alfred North Whitehead

ARIES
Do not take a bite from pleasure's bait until you have found out if a hook doesn't follow.
Hindu Quote

TAURUS
Paris is the great café of Europe.
Ferdinand Galiani

GEMINI
A liar is always prodigious at making an oath.
Corneille

CANCER
Don't be a fool and don't believe in fools.
Anonymous

LEO
Never, never doubt, what others cannot assure us of.
Hilaire Belluc

VIRGO
There is no meaning to life except the meaning given by the unfolding of powers, by living productively.
Erich Fromm

LIBRA
Time and I against any other.
Cervantes

SCORPIO
Posterity for the philosopher is what the other world is for the religious man.
Denis Diderot

SAGITTARIUS
The more we know about our ignorance, the more we can learn.
Nicholas of Cusa

CAPRICORN
Whoever expects wool from a ass, is as asinine as an ass.
Celsus

AQUARIUS
To find out what is coming your way, ask those who are going back.
Chinese Quote

PISCES
All good things come to an end.
Anonymous

27
NOVEMBER

ARIES
A man has only one way of being immortal on this earth: he has to forget he is a mortal.
Jean Giraudoux

TAURUS
There are two kinds of people in the world: those who enter a room and say, "there you are," and those who say, "here I am."
Abigail Van Buren

GEMINI
Without pity, justice becomes cruel. And pity, without justice, is weakness.
Pietro Metastasio

CANCER
Every man contemplates an angel in his future.
Ralph Waldo Emerson

LEO
Men are cruel, but man is kind.
Rabindranath Tagore

VIRGO
Do not defy the diagnosis, try to defy the verdict.
Norman Cousins

LIBRA
I love you because it is you, because it is myself.
Attributed to Montaigne

SCORPIO
Lies are only useful for men as medicine. The use of such medicine should only be practiced by doctors.
Plato

SAGITTARIUS
To know and not to do is, as a fact, not to comprehend.
Wing Yang-Ming

CAPRICORN
It's now or never.
Anonymous

AQUARIUS
Flowers grow out of dark moments.
Corita Kent

PISCES
Ten thousand difficulties are not worth one single doubt.
John Newman

ARIES
It has been my experience, that the people who have no vices have few virtues.
Abraham Lincoln

TAURUS
If you take large steps leave enough space in between.
Burmese Proverb

GEMINI
Impatience is the mark of independence, not of bondage.
Marianne Moore

CANCER
There is one spectacle grander than the sea, that is the sky.
Victor Hugo

LEO
This world cannot explain its own difficulties without the assistance of another.
Charles Caleb Colton

VIRGO
It is healthy to be ill once in a while.
Henry David Thoreau

LIBRA
Why is thought being a secretion of the brain more wonderful than gravity a property of matter?
Charles Darwin

SCORPIO
There is something about humility that produces a strange exaltation of the heart.
Saint Augustine

SAGITTARIUS
God is intelligence occupied in knowing himself.
Meister Eckhart

CAPRICORN
What could be unexpected for he who expects nothing?
Paul Valéry

AQUARIUS
Life, within doors, has few pleasanter prospects than a neatly arranged and well-provisioned breakfast-table.
Hawthorne

PISCES
Care and diligence bring luck.
Thomas Fuller

29
NOVEMBER

It is not terrible to be proud of yourself.

ARIES
Temptation to behave is terrible.
Bertolt Brecht

TAURUS
We do not become older with the passing of years, but newer with each day.
Emily Dickinson

GEMINI
God in his wisdom made the fly and forgot to tell us why.
Ogden Nash

CANCER
. . . there is one spectacle grander than the sky, that is the interior of the soul.
Victor Hugo

LEO
Taste is made of thousands of distastes.
Paul Valéry

VIRGO
We say good-bye only to meet again.
John Gay

LIBRA
Remorse is the echo of a lost virtue.
Bulwer-Lytton

SCORPIO
A brother may not be a friend, but a friend will always be a brother.
Benjamin Franklin

SAGITTARIUS
If you find them worshiping a donkey, bring him grass.
Morrocan Quote

CAPRICORN
Understanding is the beginning of approval.
Spinoza

AQUARIUS
The use of fantasy allows me to go further, it gives me a larger spectrum of possibilities.
Toni Morrison

PISCES
The "I" is the cause of misfortunes and displeasures.
Honoré de Balzac

ARIES
The only effort worth making is the one it takes to learn the geography of one's own nature.
Paul Bowles

TAURUS
Beauty without expression tires.
Ralph Waldo Emerson

GEMINI
Pleasure is frail like a dewdrop, while it laughs it dies.
Rabindranath Tagore

CANCER
A crab by any other name, would not forget the sea.
Paul Eluard and Benjamin Peret

LEO
Every man in this world is better than some other, and not as virtuous as some other.
William Saroyan

VIRGO
Whoever would like to live without any inconvenience in this life should not be born into it.
Anonymous

LIBRA
Words are the daughters of men, but men's sons are things.
Samuel Madden

SCORPIO
And who knows as you do the voluptuosity of the future?
Attributed to Nietzsche

SAGITTARIUS
Deficit omne quod nascitur (everything that is born, comes to an end).
Quintillian

CAPRICORN
Row your own boat.
Euripides

AQUARIUS
Passion is only what is to come, not what has been.
Thomas Bernhard

PISCES
If you cry because you have lost the Sun, your tears will not allow you to see the stars.
Rabindranath Tagore

DECEMBER

DECEMBER

Ad astra per aspera. *(To the stars through hardships.)*
Latin Quote

It is a good thing that December has thirty-one days. That gives us twenty-four more hours to do some thinking as the year unfolds and a new one begins. Soul searching is what December can be all about, so do try to look for, and hopefully find, some sort of agent of salvation. Be it metaphysical, religious, agnostic, atheistic, or whatever. You might connect to the medieval Persian belief that each planet rules over one 7,000-year cycle of time (does time ever fly!), or that the various celebrations that occur during this month cradle some kind of need that we all must connect. There have been endless types of rituals in human history, all stored in our collective souls over the millenniums. Now is the time to find out what to do with this patterning, how to use these rites, and with whom—in short how to be a better person—if only once in a while, but especially during the month of holidays, December.

ARIES

This is the month where race-ahead Aries is more race ahead than usual. During the first three weeks of December, life seems to dance to whatever tune you're playing, so why not try out some new melodies? Then, as December rolls to its close, slow all your notes down a bit. Reflect. And let your spirit—and your spirituality—shine.

Keywords: Connect to high-rolling energy

TAURUS

"There's nothing new under the sun," is definitely *not* true for Taurus, especially during December. Life gives you something beautiful at least once a day, at the beginning of the month, and then many more times a day by month's end. Pamper your body, and don't forget your soul, because any kind of mystical lore is great for your persona.

Keyword: Shine

GEMINI

This is the month when most Geminis will be saying, thinking, or feeling, "Time flies." During December, the only thing that Gemini should not do is complain. You can do anything, even if the Sun is rolling along in your opposite sign Sagittarius and you might feel slightly "bullied" by emotions floating around you from your celestial peers. Now is the perfect time to indulge your Geminian tendency to joust and jostle others. So shake things up, and try not to let yourself be shook up too much, yourself!

Keywords: Align yourself

CANCER

Your extremely personal way of seeing things, and how you maneuver to put people as well as situations and things into place, colors this month. Work is the focus here, and it is where you must find your solace and figure out how to work things out, even if you approach it in your usual sensitivity. Whether you are selling tamales on a street corner or are the leader of a country is not as important as the way you relate to those around you to get things done.

Keywords: Mull over

LEO

Forget the dreams of sun screen, this month, Leo, and try to really warm things up. Take a few minutes a day to bask in the Sun. Can't find any? Then generate your own heat. Hug someone. Make connections. The warmth and responsiveness that you can hew from or to others is truly your cat's meow just now. Just give it a try.

Keyword: Include

VIRGO

Each time the first of December falls, there will be 31 days to the new year, 334 days passed since the last new year (unless it is leap year), and 13 billion years gone by since the Big Bang—and it all has an imprint on some of the atoms in your body, Virgo! So focus. December will end in fine finish for you if you just hang on a little and trust others as well as trust yourself.

Keywords: Get on the ball

LIBRA

Yes can be no. No can be yes. This month you can convince anyone that the Moon is green cheese if you need to, Mr., Mrs., or Ms. Libra. Think of the first three weeks of December as your annual meeting with yourself. The Sun in Sagittarius gives you a boost this month, but only you can—and should—put yourself on the fast track. So, taking a few big and hurried steps on your own behalf will result in even greater strides. But do it before the last days of the month when efficiency will slip a bit for you, but you'll be ready to stop and regain some balance.

Keywords: Cover and recover

SCORPIO

You brain-powered Scorpios can understand physics' new string theory of the Universe at a glance, so it's no surprise that you, better than any other sign, can also understand how breaking taboos can save you time and energy in the long run. This should be your "gathering month," Scorpio. Gather your resources, and your fun, as December continues into January.

Keywords: Engage yourself

SAGITTARIUS

Don't take on too many new responsibilities just now. Instead, remember the ancient wise words—*nadie es profeta en su propia tieria*—"no one is a prophet in his own land" and relate to that idea during December. You have been called since about forever the "philosopher/prophet" of the Zodiac, so get comfortable with that outfit and get others used to your certainties, uncertainties, and critiques (which usually are dosed with pure reason).
Keywords: Good thinking

CAPRICORN

It's a good month for goods, Capricorn. Money matters, stocks, and bonds take on extra interest points as the winter solstice appears. Our best bet is to ask *you*, Capricorn, how to go about our business just now, for you are there to point out how we can get what we want—all things considered.
Keywords: Inquire, resolve, replenish

AQUARIUS

Clearly, Aquarius, you can prove yourself invaluable to someone at sometime during this month. At least one day this month, you will feel very special. Secure friendships, ask for favors, have fun, but try not to do too much. A quality person like you doesn't need so much quantity just now!
Keywords: Juggle and catch

PISCES

Relax and go with the flow this month, Pisces—even when things get a bit sticky—and things will turn out just fine. Don't try to do too many things in too many ways during too few days. After all, what are days for? "Days are where we come from," says Philip Larkin, and that is the way you should tackle and hold this time of year. Attune yourself to your best side, and give your own tenure a chance.
Keywords: Lighten up

1

DECEMBER

ARIES
You are never wasting time while you prepare tomorrow's tools.
French Quote

TAURUS
Take care of the senses and the sounds will take care of themselves.
Lewis Carroll

GEMINI
Fate is moving you toward your destiny.
Anonymous

CANCER
Things that happen to you often make sense later.
De La Vega

LEO
Deep in their roots, All flowers keep the light.
Theodore Roethke

VIRGO
Unreality is an accepted part of reality.
Anonymous

LIBRA
The truth is that each leaf of white paper, due to its emptiness, proves that there is nothing as beautiful as that which does not exist.
Paul Valéry

SCORPIO
The bluebird carries the sky on his back.
Henry David Thoreau

SAGITTARIUS
Unity can be found within multiplicity, and multiplicity within unity.
Sufi Quote

CAPRICORN
Take good care of what is yours, and do not wish for what is not yours; so, nothing can prevent you from being happy.
Epictetus

AQUARIUS
All are but parts of one stupendous whole, Whose body Nature is, and God the soul.
Alexander Pope

PISCES
The most practical and important thing about a man is his concept of the universe.
G. K. Chesterton

ARIES
They would glimpse the splendor of eternity, which is forever still.
Augustine of Hippo

TAURUS
Where there was an "I," there will be an ego.
Sigmund Freud

GEMINI
From the moment of time's first-drawn breath, Love resides in us.
Bibi Hayati

CANCER
Most of the grounds of the world's troubles are matters of grammar.
Michel de Montaigne

LEO
Be aware enough to notice some moment of perfection during this day.
William Law

VIRGO
And remember, expect nothing and life will be velvet.
Lisa Gardiner

LIBRA
O what a reward after a thought is a long glance at the calm of the gods.
Paul Valéry

SCORPIO
Distance is the proof of resistance for a horse as time reveals the character of man.
Chinese Quote

SAGITTARIUS
The color of water is the color of the jug that holds it.
Junayd

CAPRICORN
Construct yourself.
Rumi

AQUARIUS
There are also others who know something.
Severys Sebokt

PISCES
One may understand the cosmos, but never the ego; the self is more distant than any star.
G. K. Chesterton

3

DECEMBER

Read a lore or a legend. Find yourself a hero.

ARIES
All lazy people are great projectors.
Blaise Pascal

TAURUS
The least of anything that makes sense is worth more than the most of anything without sense.
Carl Jung

GEMINI
Keep cool and collect.
Mae West

CANCER
Jump, and you will find out how to unfold your wings as you fall.
Ray Bradbury

LEO
A good traveler has no fixed plans and is not intent upon arriving.
Lao-Tzu

VIRGO
The only time you can't miss, is the last time you try.
Anonymous

LIBRA
A man of honor should never forge what he is because he sees what others are.
Baltasar Gracián

SCORPIO
Kindness is simple, evil is multiple.
Aristotle

SAGITTARIUS
The egg is in the hen, the chicken is in the egg. Two in One, and also One in the two.
Angelius Silesius

CAPRICORN
The best way to make your dreams come true is waking up.
Paul Valéry

AQUARIUS
The golden key opens every door.
Anonymous

PISCES
What is a fool? Perhaps simply an undemanding mind, which is satisfied with little. Could it be that a fool is really wise?
Paul Valéry

ARIES
It's better to die on your feet than live on your knees.
Dolores Ibarruri

TAURUS
The means and the methods cannot be separated from the goal.
Emma Goldman

GEMINI
If your body is undeviating, it matters not that your shadow is crooked.
Chinese Quote

CANCER
Sometimes, what is really hurting you is your own perception of things.
Isaac Asimov

LEO
You can see a lot, just by simply watching.
Yogi Berra

VIRGO
Help yourself, for just now nobody else will.
Felix F. Palavicini

LIBRA
Your own path is the best one.
Mexican Quote

SCORPIO
Anger is a slight madness.
Horace

SAGITTARIUS
Nothing is enough for whomever enough seems insufficient.
Epicurus

CAPRICORN
Knock on the door of reality, ruffle your thinking feathers, loosen your
shoulders and open up.
Jelalludin Rumi

AQUARIUS
Begin constructing your spider web, and you will achieve something.
Mexican Quote

PISCES
If freedom means anything, it is mostly the right to tell someone exactly what
he doesn't want to hear.
George Orwell

5

DECEMBER

Happy and cheerful are not the same thing,
but it's time to take either head on.

ARIES
There are those who have a desire to love, but do not have the capacity to love.
Giovanni Papini

TAURUS
The bigger, the better!
Anonymous

GEMINI
For each person who cannot do one thing, there is someone else who cannot do another.
Anonymous

CANCER
Time dissipates to shining ether the solid angularity of facts.
Ralph Waldo Emerson

LEO
The eyes indicate the antiquity of the soul.
Ralph Waldo Emerson

VIRGO
A man should have the fine point of his soul taken off to become fit for this world.
John Keats

LIBRA
I am certain of nothing but the holiness of the heart's afflictions and the truth of the imagination.
John Keats

SCORPIO
To see what is in front of one's nose needs a constant struggle.
George Orwell

SAGITTARIUS
Perfection in life consists in faith, hope and charity.
Saint Thomas Aquinus

CAPRICORN
A true leader does not need to lead; showing the way is enough.
Henry Miller

AQUARIUS
Death destroys man, but the idea of dying saves him.
E. M. Forster

PISCES
Eternity could be your personal equation.
Graffiti

Be inventive. Dazzle yourself.

6
DECEMBER

ARIES
Facts are all accidents. They might have all been different.
Santayana

TAURUS
Among all the written or spoken words, the saddest are, "we should have made that date."
Tallulah Bankhead

GEMINI
Life is short, art long, opportunity fleeting, experience treacherous, judgment difficult.
Hippocrates

CANCER
Each individual has his own measurement of time, which depends on the place he is in and how he is moving.
Stephen Hawking

LEO
In full winter I finally learned that there was an invincible summer in my sinews.
Albert Camus

VIRGO
The ultimate faculty of man is not reason, but imagination.
Edmundo O'Gorman

LIBRA
If you need something and you can't find it, come with me and I will show you how to be happy without it.
Quaker Quote

SCORPIO
The happy man is not he who seems thus to others, but who seems thus to himself.
Publilius Syrus

SAGITTARIUS
Arguments are to be avoided: they are always vulgar and often convincing.
Oscar Wilde

CAPRICORN
Difficulties are excuses that history never accepts.
Edward R. Murrow

AQUARIUS
He who asks questions cannot avoid the answers.
Camaroonian Quote

PISCES
Outside, among your fellows, among strangers, you must preserve apperances, 100 things you cannot do; but inside, the terrible freedom!
Ralph Waldo Emerson

7

DECEMBER

ARIES

A sonnet is a moment's monument, memorial from the soul's eternity . . .
Dante Gabriel Ronetti

TAURUS

It is better to be unfaithful than to be faithful without wanting to be.
Brigitte Bardot

GEMINI

Oh God, if there is a God: save my soul, if I have a soul. Amen.
Prayer of a Skeptic

CANCER

Behold! I do not give lectures on a little charity. When I give, I give of myself.
Walt Whitman

LEO

To have is to fear.
Spanish Quote

VIRGO

I came, I meditated, and I got filled with enthusiasm!
Albert Einstein

LIBRA

The significance of a man is not in what he attains but rather in what he longs to attain.
Kahlil Gibran

SCORPIO

Time takes care of what reason cannot.
Seneca

SAGITTARIUS

A people without history is like wind on the buffalo grass.
Sioux Proverb

CAPRICORN

The longer we live, the more do we realize that everything depends on coincidences.
Sir Winston Churchill

AQUARIUS

I am what I am and that's what I am!
Popeye

PISCES

For who gives in and turns his eye, back to the darkness from the sky, Loses while he looks below, All that up with him may go.
Attributed to Boethius

Comfort yourself with joy and there
will always be something else.

8

DECEMBER

ARIES
We learn by doing. There is no other way.
Joseph Holt

TAURUS
At the same time that you have protected someone, you have done the same thing for society.
Kenneth Kaunda

GEMINI
I wasted time and now time wastes me.
William Shakespeare

CANCER
I prefer something that says: entrance forbidden, to something that says, "no way out."
Stanislaw Lec

LEO
The greatest art of life is feeling; to feel that we exist, even in pain.
Lord Byron

VIRGO
Genius is an African who dreams up snow.
Vladimir Nabokov

LIBRA
All rising to a great place is by a winding stair.
Sir Francis Bacon

SCORPIO
We cry when born for we come to this huge scenery of madness.
William Shakespeare

SAGITTARIUS
The world is used only by consideration of advantages.
Friedrich Schiller

CAPRICORN
There are formalities between the closest of friends.
Japanese Quote

AQUARIUS
If we attain something, it was there from the beginning of time.
Ryokan

PISCES
The world is filled with small happinesses, the trick is to know how to find them.
Li Tai-Po

9

Energize your mind as you restore your body.

DECEMBER

ARIES

He who has a why to live can bear with almost any how.
Nietzsche

TAURUS

To live is like to love: all reason is against it, and all healthy instinct for it.
Samuel Butler

GEMINI

All religions must be tolerated, for every man must go to heaven in his own way.
Frederick the Great

CANCER

What is time but the stuff delay is made of.
Henry David Thoreau

LEO

Kick up your heels!
Anonymous

VIRGO

Woman's virtue is man's greatest invention.
Cornelia Otis Skinner

LIBRA

If youth knew, if age could only . . .
Henri Estienne

SCORPIO

Never trust the morning's splendor nor your mother-in-law's smile.
Japanese Quote

SAGITTARIUS

Human beings are not superior to animals because they can torture them without pity, but because they can feel compassion for them.
Buddhist Quote

CAPRICORN

Numbers constitute the only universal language.
Nathanael West

AQUARIUS

Dullness is a misdemeanour.
Ethel Wilson

PISCES

Some conform with understanding what they believe in. Others enjoy believing what they like.
Stanislaw Lec

ARIES
Each "something" is a celebration of the nothing that sustains it.
John Cage

TAURUS
Conformity is an imitation of harmony.
Ralph Waldo Emerson

GEMINI
Many men and women lived happily ever after, after one said no to the other.
Anonymous

CANCER
Lessons are not given, they are taken.
Cesare Pavese

LEO
The wish to pray is a prayer in itself.
George Bernanos

VIRGO
Nothing is too small to know, and nothing is too big to attempt.
William Van Horne

LIBRA
The best use you can make of life is to spend your time in something that outlives it.
William James

SCORPIO
Every man is a history of the world to himself.
Max Steiner

SAGITTARIUS
An atheist is a man who has no invisible means of support.
Harry Fosdick

CAPRICORN
Education begins at home.
Anonymous

AQUARIUS
If we lose something, it is hiding somewhere near us.
Ryokan

PISCES
Let me make the superstitions of a nation and I care not who makes its laws or its songs either.
Mark Twain

Interview yourself and find your own charisma.

ARIES

Renounce the "why" and look for the "how."
Richard Burton

TAURUS

Confusion is a word we have invented for an order which is not understood.
Henry Miller

GEMINI

The man who fears no truths has nothing to fear from lies.
Thomas Jefferson

CANCER

God made everything out of nothing. But the nothingness shows through.
Paul Valéry

LEO

Eyes that meet form a relationship.
Zimbabwean Quote

VIRGO

Our place is found somewhere in the middle of to be and not to be: between two fictions.
E. M. Cioran

LIBRA

Give a man a fish, and you feed him for a day. Show a man how to fish and you feed him for a lifetime.
Chinese Quote

SCORPIO

We are dust and shadow.
Horace

SAGITTARIUS

Our desires, once realized, haunt us again less readily.
Margaret Fuller

CAPRICORN

The experience that I really have at hand is my own.
Miguel de Unamuno

AQUARIUS

Greater dooms win greater destinies.
Heraclitus

PISCES

Never befriend the oppressed unless you are prepared to take on the oppressor.
Ogden Nash

Faith in the Lady of Guadalupe can always help,
for "now" has its own power.

ARIES
Feed your faith, and your doubts will starve to death.
Hindu Quote

TAURUS
All I have seen teaches me to trust in the creator for all I have not seen.
Ralph Waldo Emerson

GEMINI
The course of the true anything never runs smooth.
Samuel Butler

CANCER
Heaven always favors a good wish.
Cervantes

LEO
I have come to thank God for not answering all my prayers.
Jean Ingelow

VIRGO
Great men can't be ruled.
Ayn Rand

LIBRA
Two men look out through the same bars: One sees the mud, and one the stars.
Frederick Langbridge

SCORPIO
Christianity could be an excellent thing if people really practiced it.
George Bernard Shaw

SAGITTARIUS
Ask, and it shall be given you; seek, and ye shall find; knock, and it shall be opened unto you.
Matthew 7:7

CAPRICORN
Faith is one of the most efficient instruments of all the human tools.
Henry Ford

AQUARIUS
What the world needs is a Declaration of Interdependence.
Anonymous

PISCES
Women take on the form of the dream that they are contained in.
Juan José Arreola

13
DECEMBER

Throw something out, bring something in.
Get rid of a bad idea. Spark a bright one.

ARIES
To ask the hard question is simple.
W. H. Auden

TAURUS
Even sleepers are workers and collaborators in what goes on in the universe.
Heraclitus

GEMINI
If it happens to one of us, it can happen to all of us.
William Clinton

CANCER
Raindrops kiss the earth, murmuring: "we are your children who miss you mother, and we are returning from the sky."
Rabindranath Tagore

LEO
A dog's smile and God's prowesses are not understood by anyone.
Oromos of Ethiopia

VIRGO
Opposition brings concord. Out of discord comes the fairest harmony.
Heraclitus

LIBRA
After the storm comes the calm.
Anonymous

SCORPIO
God gave us memory to be able to have roses in December.
Sir James M. Barrie

SAGITTARIUS
I can accept what I don't understand.
The Sister Circle

CAPRICORN
To be able to triumph, it has always been indispensable to pass through the path of sacrifice.
Simon Bolivar

AQUARIUS
One must fight against nostalgia.
Chilean Quote

PISCES
The friend of all is the friend of none.
Arthur Schopenhauer

Find the survivor in your family tree. Relate.

14

DECEMBER

ARIES
We should take men as they are, not as they should be.
Franz Schubert

TAURUS
Assume a virtue if you have none.
William Shakespeare

GEMINI
Moral indignity is the typical strategy that gives an idiot dignity.
Marshall McLuhan

CANCER
Time is the only essential mystery.
Jorge Luis Borges

LEO
Do not take the wind out of your sails.
Anonymous

VIRGO
If today there is no longer any one clear figure of the sacred man, it is perhaps because we are all virtually *homines sacri*.
Georgio Agamben

LIBRA
It is much wiser to start a family than to end one.
English Quote

SCORPIO
Both the word and the silence transgress.
Zen Proverb

SAGITTARIUS
A good edge is good for nothing if it has nothing to cut.
Thomas Fuller

CAPRICORN
A cloak is not made for a single shower of rain.
Irish Quote

AQUARIUS
Faith and Zen are like looking for the glasses that are posed on the top of your head.
Zen Quote

PISCES
Man is lyrical; woman is epical; marriage, dramatical.
Novalis

15

DECEMBER

You are your own ride, your own special attraction.

ARIES
There is great enlightening where there has been curiosity.
Kokushi

TAURUS
In sandalwood lies the soul's ease; its odour doth the spirit please.
Nizami

GEMINI
Morality is what permits us to be faithful to ourselves.
Jeanne Moreau

CANCER
The anguish of a wise man is an opportunity to strengthen his wisdom.
Boethius

LEO
Long before I in my mother's womb was born, a god preparing did this glorious store, the world for me to adorn.
Thomas Traherne

VIRGO
The perfect definition of a gentleman is to say that he has never inflicted pain.
Cardinal John H. Newman

LIBRA
Words should be an intense pleasure just as leather should be to a shoemaker.
Evelyn Waugh

SCORPIO
A man who does not lose his reason over certain things has none to lose.
G. E. Lessing

SAGITTARIUS
The present is so short that it is past upon being named.
Luis Vives

CAPRICORN
How do I work? I grope.
Albert Einstein

AQUARIUS
From good earth comes debris, and from rubbish comes good earth.
Kurd Quote

PISCES
To love human beings in so far as they are nothing. That is to love them as God does.
Simone Weil

ARIES
If a tree falls in the forest and nobody has heard it, does it make a sound?
The Koran

TAURUS
All men desire to know.
Aristotle

GEMINI
Everything is everything.
Anaxagoras

CANCER
If the eye were a living being, sight would be its soul.
Aristotle

LEO
You are all you will ever have, for sure.
June Havoc

VIRGO
A fact, in science, is not a mere fact, but an instance.
Bertrand Russell

LIBRA
When you've got it, flaunt it.
George Lois

SCORPIO
Man is a fallen god who remembers heaven.
Alphonse de Lamartine

SAGITTARIUS
A fool that confesses is a fool that progresses.
Anonymous

CAPRICORN
The word impossible is put to best use by dropping the first two letters.
Adolfo Llanos

AQUARIUS
As for the Future, your task is not to foresee, but to enable it.
Antoine de Saint-Exupéry

PISCES
Painting is silent poetry; and poetry is painting with the gift of speech.
Simonides

Make sure you can get where you are going.

ARIES
Faith takes care of the person who has faith.
Chinese Quote

TAURUS
Between living and dreaming there is a third thing. Guess it.
Antonio Machado

GEMINI
Hope is such a bait, it covers any hook.
Ben Jonson

CANCER
There is reason in all things, but not in all people.
Anonymous

LEO
Make light of your troubles; if not, keep them dark.
Anonymous

VIRGO
One man's gravy is another man's poison.
Anonymous

LIBRA
A man's reach should exceed his grasp, or what's a metaphor.
Marshall McLuhan

SCORPIO
Everything intercepts us from ourselves.
Ralph Waldo Emerson

SAGITTARIUS
The two of us already are a crowd!
German Proverb

CAPRICORN
Passions make men live, knowledge simply makes them last.
Chamfort

AQUARIUS
When God expedites the arrangement of something, everything works out fine.
Muslim Quote

PISCES
Look out for the path that your feet must take, and your ways will be secure.
Proverbs 4:20-7 (The New English Bible)

Today, you lead the way. Others can falter or follow. **18**

DECEMBER

ARIES
It's perfect if you let yourself go, as long as you come back.
Max Jacob

TAURUS
If you kiss a scoundrel, count your teeth.
Hebrew Quote

GEMINI
I can find my biography in every fable that I read.
Ralph Waldo Emerson

CANCER
Most things get better by themselves. Most things, in fact, are better by morning.
Lewis Thomas

LEO
We carry within us the wonders we seek without us.
Sir Thomas Browne

VIRGO
Criticism is easy and art is difficult.
Destouches

LIBRA
The man who lets himself go should remember to come back.
Graffiti

SCORPIO
There are two evils in love: war and peace.
Horace

SAGITTARIUS
What is universal is eternal, because it does not exist as an individual. This is the condition of eternity.
Lao-Tzu

CAPRICORN
I am, I know and I want. I am knowledgeable and I am ready. I know myself to be and to love. I want to be and to know.
Saint Augustine

AQUARIUS
A weed is no more than a flower in disguise.
James Russell Lowell

PISCES
I never worry about the future. It comes soon enough.
Albert Einstein

19
DECEMBER

Stars twinkle and planets shine, and you are their wandering soul.

ARIES
One doesn't discover new lands without consenting to lose sight of the shore for a very long time.
André Gide

TAURUS
Innocence also weighs.
Racine

GEMINI
Modesty is a vastly overrated virtue.
John Kenneth Galbraith

CANCER
Music is a part of us and either enobles or degrades our behavior.
Boethius

LEO
Let us not be judges of peace, rather angels of peace.
Saint Theresa of Lisieux

VIRGO
Sadness dulls the heart more than the grossest sin.
Aaron of Karlin

LIBRA
Never reproach providence.
The Talmud

SCORPIO
Chaos is the score upon which reality is written.
Henry Miller

SAGITTARIUS
I am I: I cannot be thought, only knowledge.
D. H. Lawrence

CAPRICORN
The three most important things that any human being has are, briefly, their private parts, their money and their religious opinions.
Samuel Butler

AQUARIUS
There is a pleasure sure, In being mad, which none but madmen know!
John Dryden

PISCES
Happiness has no recipe: each person must cook it with the flavor of their own meditations.
Anonymous

You might be the only one with a difference of imagination. Lucky you!

20

DECEMBER

ARIES
The trouble is that the "key to success" doesn't always turn the motor on.
Anonymous

TAURUS
There is more pride than love in jealousy.
La Rochefoucauld

GEMINI
One always has a better opinion about things one doesn't know.
Wilhelm Liebniz

CANCER
History is the biography of great men.
Thomas Carlyle

LEO
Learn who you are and act accordingly.
Pindar

VIRGO
Nobody can use another person's teeth to smile.
Kalenjin of Kenya

LIBRA
Effort is only effort when it begins to hurt.
José Ortega y Gasset

SCORPIO
The tip of a finger cannot touch itself.
Sanskrit Proverb

SAGITTARIUS
Life just is. You have to flow with it. Give yourself to the moment. Let it happen.
Jerry Brown

CAPRICORN
The worst difficulties begin when one can do exactly as one pleases.
Thomas Henry Huxley

AQUARIUS
There is no such thing as pure pleasure; some anxiety always goes with it.
Ovid

PISCES
Give way to the Better, if way to the Better there be. It exacts a full look at the worst.
Thomas Hardy

21
DECEMBER

Dream on, wake up, guess, and suppose.

ARIES
Your body is the baggage that you will be taking with you on all your journeys.
Anonymous

TAURUS
It takes two to tango.
Anonymous

GEMINI
Elegant words are not sincere; words that are sincere are not elegant.
Lao-Tzu

CANCER
Do not envy the riches of your fellow being.
Homer

LEO
Every animal is sad after intercourse.
Latin Proverb

VIRGO
Praise the day at night and life at the end.
Anonymous

LIBRA
A swallow does not make a summer.
Anonymous

SCORPIO
Mouths do not sweeten when they talk about honey.
Turkish Quote

SAGITTARIUS
A soft hand can guide an elephant tied to a horse.
Indian Quote

CAPRICORN
Never call a man a fool, borrow from him instead.
Anonymous

AQUARIUS
A powerful idea communicates some of its power to the man who contradicts it.
Marcel Proust

PISCES
To love nothing is not to live; to love but feebly is to languish rather than live.
Françoise Fénelon

If you can measure you can manage.
Your best place is at the top.

ARIES
Rare luck it is indeed To be born in human form.
Issa Haiku

TAURUS
You are required to be yourself.
Graffiti

GEMINI
Do not allow your tongue to be a flag that blows in the breeze of any smell.
Imenhotep

CANCER
The point in life is to know what's enough.
Gensei

LEO
If you want to gain much you must lose much.
De La Vega

VIRGO
Today, for me; tomorrow for you.
Spanish Quote

LIBRA
I like life. It's something to do.
Sam Levinson

SCORPIO
Money seen in a dream cannot be spent.
Hindu Quote

SAGITTARIUS
When left to herself, nature is in no particular hurry.
Van Loon

CAPRICORN
To thy speed add wings.
John Milton

AQUARIUS
A shared joy is a double joy.
John Ray

PISCES
A world of thought in one translucent phrase.
H. B. Carpenter

23
DECEMBER

ARIES
God does not believe in our God.
Jules Renard

TAURUS
Do not mistake the moon for the finger pointing at it.
Buddhist Scripture

GEMINI
When necessity tears sincere words from us, the mask falls and men appear.
Lucretius

CANCER
God, whose love and joy are present everywhere, can't come to visit you unless you aren't there.
Angelus Silesius

LEO
I fought and prevailed.
Latin Quote

VIRGO
Nature is a catching of sorrows.
Maxine Kumin

LIBRA
Compete, don't envy.
Arabic Quote

SCORPIO
The powers that are in all things sing within me also.
Hermes

SAGITTARIUS
Opinions cannot survive if one has no chance to fight for them.
Thomas Mann

CAPRICORN
Some people count time, others make time count.
Anonymous

AQUARIUS
Don't say "one" until it's in the bag.
Muslim Quote

PISCES
Non, je ne regrette rien (No, I regret nothing).
Edith Piaf

ARIES
We have hearts within, Warm, live, improvident, indecent hearts.
Elizabeth Barrett Browning

TAURUS
Inspiration could be called inhaling the memory of an act never experienced.
Ned Rorem

GEMINI
There is no road towards peace; peace is the road.
Mahatma Gandhi

CANCER
Happiness depends, as Nature shows, Less on exterior things than most suppose.
William Cowper

LEO
He who kisses the Joy as it flies, Lives in Eternity's sunrise.
William Blake

VIRGO
Soul, thou hast much goods laid up for many years.
Luke 12:19

LIBRA
I believe heretically, that God suffers and enjoys with us.
Juan José Arreola

SCORPIO
A good laugh and a good night's sleep cures all evils.
Irish Proverb

SAGITTARIUS
The Infinite Goodness has such wide arms that it takes whatever turns to it.
Dante Alighieri

CAPRICORN
To the poet, to the philosopher, to the saint, all things are friendly and sacred, all events profitable, all days holy, all men divine.
Ralph Waldo Emerson

AQUARIUS
No pleasure lasts long enough.
Propertius

PISCES
Peace is when time doesn't matter as it passes by.
Maria Schell

25
DECEMBER

Celebrate kindness; indulge in forgiveness.
Life is too short to go sour.

ARIES
Express yourself naturally and let somebody else take care of the calm.
F. Colby

TAURUS
Divine fires do not blaze each day, but an artist functions in their afterglow hoping for their recurrence.
Ned Rorem

GEMINI
All places are distant from heaven alike.
Robert Burton

CANCER
. . . Feeling that under this dream one will never awaken from the dream itself.
José Bergamin

LEO
I want nothing, for I want it all.
Antonia Rivas Mercado

VIRGO
What a wonderful life I've had! I only wish I'd realized it sooner.
Colette

LIBRA
Many eyes go through the meadow, but few see the flowers in it.
Ralph Waldo Emerson

SCORPIO
The nicest thing about Christmas is that it is communatory, like thunder, and we all walk through it together.
Garrison Keillor

SAGITTARIUS
Engrave this within your heart: every day is the best of the year.
Ralph Waldo Emerson

CAPRICORN
Something divine within my spirit, had its being, That stirs and spurs me.
Catharina Regina von Greiffenberg

AQUARIUS
Everything that we see or seem is no more than a dream within a dream.
Edgar Allan Poe

PISCES
Intelligence is characterized by a natural incomprehension of life.
Henri Bergson

ARIES
Faith is blind because it shouldn't, nor can it, have a doctrine.
Kabbala

TAURUS
My arms grow beautiful in the coupling and grow lean as they come away.
Venmanipputi

GEMINI
Our heads are round so that our thoughts can change direction.
Francis Picabia

CANCER
It delights our bodies and yet more our souls.
Paul Scarron

LEO
Butterflies do not count months, but moments, and has time enough.
Rabindranath Tagore

VIRGO
Meanwhile, time flies, never to return.
Virgil

LIBRA
Everything carries within itself its own and intimate innovation.
Tetzusan Shinagawa

SCORPIO
Glittering generalities! They are blazing ubiquities.
Ralph Waldo Emerson

SAGITTARIUS
The opportunity for doing mischief is found a hundred times a day, and of doing good once in a year.
Voltaire

CAPRICORN
Love is not consolation, it is light.
Simone Weil

AQUARIUS
Honor lies in honest toil.
Grover Cleveland

PISCES
There is an hour in each man's life appointed, To make his happiness, if then he seize it.
Beaumont and Fletcher

27
DECEMBER

Go with your gut.

ARIES
Trust the instinct to the end, though you can render no reason.
Ralph Waldo Emerson

TAURUS
Happiness consists in the multiplicity of agreeable consciousness.
Samuel Johnson

GEMINI
When I play, I make love; it is the same thing.
Arthur Rubinstein

CANCER
The mind is its own place, and in itself can make a heaven of hell, a hell of heaven.
John Milton

LEO
In everything the middle course is best: all things in excess bring trouble to men.
Plautus

VIRGO
Let us be of good cheer, however, remembering that the misfortunes hardest to bear are those which never come.
Robert Lowell

LIBRA
Every day cannot be a feast of lanterns.
Chinese Quote

SCORPIO
Even genius is tied to profit.
Pindar

SAGITTARIUS
The reason why the universe is eternal is that it does not live for itself; it gives life to others as it transforms.
Lao-Tzu

CAPRICORN
Age is the acceptance of a term of years. But maturity is the glory of years.
Martha Graham

AQUARIUS
Unrest of spirit is a mark of life.
Karl Menninger

PISCES
Propensity comes from the heavens; the "yes" or "no" are mine; as the genie of free will has no jurisdiction over my personal time.
Juan Ruiz de Alarcón

Find a mystical or magical meaning to something.

ARIES
Welcome is the best cheer.
Thomas Fuller

TAURUS
It is essential to keep in mind, that by natural events Buddhism includes many phenomena, including consciousness.
The Dalai Lama

GEMINI
Eat little and sup less, for the body's health is forged in the office called the stomach.
Cervantes

CANCER
Believe that you have it, and you will have it.
Erasmus of Rotterdam

LEO
God cannot be everywhere, and that is why he invented mothers.
Hebrew Quote

VIRGO
Prudence gives us tranquility, but with frequency it does not produce happiness.
Samuel Johnson

LIBRA
A borrowed cloak does not keep one warm.
Arabic Quote

SCORPIO
Who does what he can, does more than he should.
Anonymous

SAGITTARIUS
Educate children and it will not be necessary to punish men.
Pythagoras

CAPRICORN
He who inherits a penny is expected to spend a dollar.
German Quote

AQUARIUS
When a man's willing and eager, God joins in.
Aeschylus

PISCES
It is difficult for a mother to give birth, but more difficult still to give her children their freedom.
A. Guzman

29
DECEMBER

An oracle, a seer, a psychic, a tarot card, reader; believe in something quite out of the ordinary.

ARIES
Trifles make perfection, but perfection is no trifle.
German Quote

TAURUS
Welcome life! I go to encounter for the millionth time the reality of experience.
James Joyce

GEMINI
I am my own ancestor.
General Junot

CANCER
Where thou art, that is Home.
Emily Dickinson

LEO
Time gives good advice.
Maltese Quote

VIRGO
There are so many things that I do not want.
Socrates

LIBRA
The world must be coming to an end. Children no longer obey their parents and every man wants to write a book.
Babylonian Tablet, 2800 B.C.

SCORPIO
For men may come and men may go, But I go on forever.
Alfred Lord Tennyson

SAGITTARIUS
It is this moment, that is always eternal, where the real life of a person exists.
Tsesze

CAPRICORN
To forget is a way of freedom.
Solomon the Wise

AQUARIUS
Each situation has its own language.
Ibn Hisam al-Lami

PISCES
There are always two reasons to do what we are doing: a good one and the real one.
John Pierpont Morgan

Give yourself the time to plan a new ritual.

30

DECEMBER

ARIES
Wine is the perfect proof that God loves us and wants us to be happy.
Benjamin Franklin

TAURUS
Gourmandism is an act of judgment.
Graffiti

GEMINI
He who lives by the sword shall perish by the champagne cocktail.
Saul Alinsky

CANCER
The environment is everything that isn't me.
Albert Einstein

LEO
The world is nothing without life, and all that lives takes nourishment.
Brillat-Savarin

VIRGO
Time for a little something.
A. A. Milne

LIBRA
Eat, drink and be merry, for tomorrow ye diet.
Lewis C. Henry

SCORPIO
Food is an important part of a balanced diet!
Fran Lebowitz

SAGITTARIUS
The holes in your Swiss cheese are somebody else's Swill cheese.
Melvin Fishman

CAPRICORN
This is the month, and this the happy morn.
John Milton

AQUARIUS
I enjoyed the mealtimes more than the meals.
Muriel Spark

PISCES
Appetite comes with eating.
Rabelais

31
DECEMBER

ARIES
Life must never cease; life must be sustained and must create.
Turgenev

TAURUS
Point me out the way, To any one particular beauteous star.
John Keats

GEMINI
The character of each man is the arbitrator of his own fortune.
Publilius Syrus

CANCER
There is a tide in the affairs of men, Which, taken at the flood, leads on to fortune.
William Shakespeare

LEO
We are wiser than we know.
Ralph Waldo Emerson

VIRGO
Good luck is your friend, my son, for at the time of your birth the good fairies danced around that event.
John Milton

LIBRA
Eternity, then, is a full and perfect possession of the whole of everlasting life at once and altogether.
Boethius

SCORPIO
The world goes on because a few men in every generation believe in it utterly, accept it unquestioningly; they underwrite it with their lives.
Henry Miller

SAGITTARIUS
Knowledge is the treasure, but judgment the treasurer of a wise man.
William Penn

CAPRICORN
Love is space and time made directly perceptible to the heart.
Marcel Proust

AQUARIUS
All things shall return to their original chaos.
Lucan

PISCES
It is the stars as not known to science that I would know; the stars which the lonely traveler knows.
Henry David Thoreau

Things are as they are
because they were as they were

Thomas Gold

Perpetual Calendar

The perpetual calendar, based on the Julian and Georgian calendars, which have been used by Western civilization to "keep" time for centuries, enables us to find the exact day of the week upon which any particular date falls—whether it is two thousand years ago or two hundred years into the future.

To use the perpetual calendar, find the century (500–2300) in which the year falls along the horizontal axis of the first chart below. Then along the vertical axis, locate the exact year (0–99). Where the two intersect on the grid, there will be a letter (A–G), which is called the dominical letter. (If you get two letters combined you'll find that only one of those letters will appear in the second chart for any given month. Just use whichever one appears.)

Year / Century

Year				Julian calendar							Gregorian calendar				
				0 700 1400	100 800 1500*	200 900	300 1000	400 1100	500 1200	600 1300	1500†2000	1600 2100	1700 2200	1800 2300	1900
0				DC	ED	FE	GF	AG	BA	CB	...	BA	C	E	G
1	29	57	85	B	C	D	E	F	G	A	F	G	B	D	F
2	30	58	86	A	B	C	D	E	F	G	E	F	A	C	E
3	31	59	87	G	A	B	C	D	E	F	D	E	G	B	D
4	32	60	88	FE	GF	AG	BA	CB	DC	ED	CB	DC	FE	AG	CB
5	33	61	89	D	E	F	G	A	B	C	A	B	D	E	A
6	34	62	90	C	D	E	F	G	A	B	G	A	C	F	G
7	35	63	91	B	C	D	E	F	G	A	F	G	B	D	F
8	36	64	92	AG	BA	CB	DC	ED	FE	GF	ED	FE	AG	CB	ED
9	37	65	93	F	G	A	B	C	D	E	C	D	F	A	C
10	38	66	94	E	F	G	A	B	C	D	B	C	E	G	B
11	39	67	95	D	E	F	G	A	B	C	A	B	D	F	A
12	40	68	96	CB	DC	ED	FE	GF	AG	BA	GF	AG	CB	ED	GF
13	41	69	97	A	B	C	D	E	F	G	E	F	A	C	E
14	42	70	98	G	A	B	C	D	E	F	D	E	G	B·	D
15	43	71	99	F	G	A	B	C	D	E	C	D	F	A	C
16	44	72		ED	FE	GF	AG	BA	CB	DC	...	CB	ED	GF	BA
17	45	73		C	D	E	F	G	A	B	...	A	C	E	G
18	46	74		B	C	D	E	F	G	A	...	G	B	D	F
19	47	75		A	B	C	D	E	F	G	...	F	A	C	E
20	48	76		GF	AG	BA	CB	DC	ED	FE	...	ED	GF	BA	DC
21	49	77		E	F	G	A	B	C	D	...	C	E	G	B
22	50	78		D	E	F	G	A	B	C	...	B	D	F	A
23	51	79		C	D	E	F	G	A	B	..	A	C	E	G
24	52	80		BA	CB	DC	ED	FE	GF	AG	...	GF	BA	DC	FE
25	53	81		G	A	B	C	D	E	F	...	E	G	B	D
26	54	82		F	G	A	B	C	D	E	C	D	F	A	C
27	55	83		E	F	G	A	B	C	D	B	C	E	G	B
28	56	84		DC	ED	FE	GF	AG	BA	CB	AG	BA	DC	FE	AG

*On and before October 14, 1582.   †On and after October 15, 1582.

Keeping this letter in mind, look at the second chart below and find the
month in which your date appears along the top vertical axis; then move right
along the row until you find your dominical letter. Once you've found it,
follow the column down until you are in line with the date (1–31) on the
lower vertical axis. Wherever you stop is the day of the week on which
your date falls in a particular year.

Example: July 4, 1975.

Line up where 1900 and 75 intersect on chart one, and you'll see that the dominical letter is E. Then
find July in the third row of the month column and move across the row until you find E, then move
down the column until you are aligned with the 4 and you'll see that that day was a Friday.

Month — Dominical Letter

Month						
January, October	A	B	C	D	E	F	G
February, March, November	D	E	F	G	A	B	C
April, July	G	A	B	C	D	E	F
May	B	C	D	E	F	G	A
June	E	F	G	A	B	C	D
August	C	D	E	F	G	A	B
September, December	F	G	A	B	C	D	E

1 8 15 22 29	Sunday	Saturday	Friday	Thursday	Wednesday	Tuesday	Monday
2 9 16 23 30	Monday	Sunday	Saturday	Friday	Thursday	Wednesday	Tuesday
3 10 17 24 31	Tuesday	Monday	Sunday	Saturday	Friday	Thursday	Wednesday
4 11 18 25	Wednesday	Tuesday	Monday	Sunday	Saturday	Friday	Thursday
5 12 19 26	Thursday	Wednesday	Tuesday	Monday	Sunday	Saturday	Friday
6 13 20 27	Friday	Thursday	Wednesday	Tuesday	Monday	Sunday	Saturday
7 14 21 28	Saturday	Friday	Thursday	Wednesday	Tuesday	Monday	Sunday